MW00782466

Unlearning Shame

How We Can Reject Self-Blame
Culture and Reclaim Our Power

Devon Price, PhD

HARMONY

NEW YORK

Copyright © 2024 by Devon Price

All rights reserved.
Published in the United States by Harmony Books, an imprint of
Random House, a division of Penguin Random House LLC, New York.
HarmonyBooks.com | RandomHouseBooks.com

Harmony Books is a registered trademark, and the Circle colophon is a
trademark of Penguin Random House LLC.

Library of Congress Cataloging-in-Publication Data
Names: Price, Devon, author.
Title: Unlearning shame / by Devon Price, PhD.
Identifiers: LCCN 2023026530 | ISBN 9780593581216 (hardcover) |
ISBN 9780593581230 (paperback) | ISBN 9780593581223 (ebook)
Subjects: LCSH: Shame. | Self-hate (Psychology) | Resilience (Personality trait)
Classification: LCC BF575.S45 P75 2024 | DDC 152.4—dc23/eng/20230928
LC record available at https://lccn.loc.gov/2023026530

ISBN 978-0-593-58121-6

Ebook ISBN 978-0-593-58122-3

Printed in the United States of America

Book design by Andrea Lau
Jacket design and art by David Drummond

10 9 8 7 6 5 4 3 2 1

First Edition

*For Heather—thank you for demanding to know the real me
when I was still dedicated to pretending to be fine.
Your vulnerability and loving friendship taught me to
tear down the barricades that closed me off from the world—
and exchanging letters with you made me a writer.*

Contents

Introduction:
My Shame-Based Personality

Every single time something good happens to me, or I ask for something I need, I'm immediately consumed with panic and shame.

The weekend after I completed my PhD in 2014, I traveled to Austin, Texas, with my boyfriend at the time, Nick. It was supposed to be a celebration, full of drinking, sightseeing, and music. Nick had even gotten us a reservation at a fancy restaurant with a prix fixe menu that I knew he couldn't normally afford. But I didn't enjoy a single second. Whenever he proudly told someone about me being a doctor, I tried to minimize the accomplishment. I did all that I could to direct attention away from me and end every conversation about my achievement. At dinner, I cried all the way through every course, horrified at the three-figure price tag, and choking down drinks, hoping that would soothe me. Later when I was drunk and still consumed with guilt, I roamed the city's downtown sobbing violently while Nick followed me, completely stunned. I was unable to explain myself, or even speak. All I wanted was to curl up somewhere and die.

What happened? What was wrong with me? Why wasn't I proud of what I'd just achieved? I didn't feel I deserved any of the good things that had happened to me. I'd wanted a PhD since I was a teenager. I'd believed success in academia would promise me safety and social acceptance. I'd spent most of my graduate-school years toiling in isolation, longing to find a place in the world where I'd be loved and accepted, yet doubting I'd ever get it. Despite completing my degree, securing a job, and finding a supportive relationship that had lasted many years, I found that deep down, I was still me—awkward, unhappy me, still miserable and unable to imagine a comfortable place for myself in the world. I'd chased after achievements and approval all of my life, believing it would grant me self-love. Now that all my external goals had been met, I felt even more empty.

I still hated myself. In fact, now that I lacked some promising, life-changing goal to aspire to, existence felt even more meaningless. I could not envision a long-term career for myself or imagine what growing old with Nick might look like. The future before me was a long, blank expanse. It felt like nothing I did ever mattered, and never could—because none of it would ever help me stop being me.

This consuming self-hatred and hopelessness emerged again two years later, as I finally admitted to myself that I was transgender. When I confessed my identity to a trans woman friend, Sarah, I initially felt bathed in warm, happy self-acceptance. I felt excited to move forward and could at last imagine who I wanted to be. But those positive emotions disappeared the second I contemplated what would happen next. I would have to start asking people to use a new name and new pronouns. When they got it wrong, I'd have to commit the unforgivable social sin of making things *awkward* by standing up for myself. I wanted to change my hair and my entire wardrobe, maybe pursue surgery—but it all struck me as an unforgivable extravagance. On masculinizing hormones, which I desperately longed to take, my body would get hairier, bulkier, acne-ridden, and confusing to others. The professional persona I'd cultivated over the years would fall apart, and the terrible me-ness of myself would unquestionably stand out.

Worst of all, there was no way my straight male partner would continue to be interested in me if I were a guy. I would no longer be the intelligent yet chill, pretty girlfriend that partners' families always found easy to like. My identity would become an uncomfortable distraction. My changing body would stand out even to complete strangers. Even my loved ones might be embarrassed to be seen around me. The respectable life I'd built would crumble apart.

I felt like I'd killed the person my boyfriend and family loved, all because I had some sick delusion about who I was. I hated myself for needing something so strange and inconvenient as a gender transition. So I went about meeting my needs as secretively as possible. I went to the courthouse and changed my name and gender marker without telling a single soul for months. I knew that I had to force myself to make the change before I sought approval from anyone else, or it would never happen. I began taking testosterone in private, literally ducking into the closet of the bedroom Nick and I shared each morning to slather my body with AndroGel. On Wednesday evenings, I slunk off to a genderqueer support group at the local LGBT center, shuddering every time I entered, fearing someone I knew would see me. When I finally tried to come out to my partner and family, I could not stop hedging, apologizing, and crying. I had to text them the words. I couldn't say them out loud. I longed to be rid of the *weird, perverted* desires that were making me do these things.

A few years into my transition, I even tried detransitioning for a while, in the hopes I could become the cute, easy-to-be-around straight girl people used to think I was.[1] It was the emotional low point of the pandemic, and I was locked away from all my trans friends, and any sense of community I'd been able to build. All that was left was Nick, my partner of nearly ten years, who'd become increasingly cold and aloof the more my transition had progressed.

I hoped that by making my body more feminine again, Nick might love me. I thought my conservative mother might stop treating me with wariness. I told myself that all my problems were my fault and that I had to give up trying to be something I was not.

But it didn't work. Because no matter how powerfully I felt it, my shame was a liar. My self-loathing and secrecy only locked my potential for growth and happiness away. And as much as it felt like my suffering as a transgender person was caused by my actions, it was all rooted in the work of powerful systems—such as cissexism, capitalism, and heteronormativity—that I was a victim of, but which I felt powerless to resist.

I have always believed that my desires and feelings are too much, and that I have to make up for who I am by being as diligent, virtuous, and as unobtrusive as possible. Whenever I succeed at something or receive positive attention, I can't help but think of all the people I know and love who deserve it more than I do. So many of my friends suffer from post-traumatic stress disorder, poverty, racism, homophobia, sexism, and so much more. All around me I see social problems I'm not doing enough to help solve. And no matter how much I strive to take care of others and put good things out into the world, or to make myself into a better or more lovable person, I feel like I'm forever throwing meager payments toward a debt that only continues to compound.

There are a lot of reasons why I feel this way. As a closeted queer child in the 1990s, I witnessed how AIDS patients were branded as disgusting and debauched and blamed for their illness. In the Drug Abuse Resistance Education (D.A.R.E.) program, I learned that addicts and incarcerated people deserved their fates because they didn't have the willpower to "just say no." Public service announcements and schoolbooks taught me that environmental destruction had been caused by people choosing to litter and waste water. When gay marriage bans swept through the country during my teen years, and my own high school tried to prevent me from protesting, I learned I could not count on any public institutions to protect me. When my conservative family seemed unmoved by my concern for queer rights, I was crestfallen. I knew that I couldn't count on anyone. I would always have to look after myself.

Over and over again, I had been taught that the only way to lead a worthwhile and meaningful life was through tons of willpower, perfection, and personal responsibility. Of course, no amount of effort or virtuousness was going to be enough to make me feel worthy. The ledger would never add up in my favor, because personal responsibility couldn't undo destructive systems.

Like so many other people, I suffer from Systemic Shame, the powerful self-loathing belief that says I am to blame for the circumstances I'm living in, and that the only way my problems can be overcome is through individual goodness and grit. Shame itself is a perfectly normal, if highly unpleasant emotion; philosophers seem to have always been interested in analyzing how it works, and we can find detailed descriptions of how shame feels and the postures and poses that ashamed people take across a wide array of cultures and points in history. At its most simple, shame is the feeling that not only have we done something wrong, but that we are bad, and that some core part of us is so horrible that it must be hidden away. Ashamed people typically feel demotivated, withdrawn from others, and powerless. They're usually low in energy and focus, much like we would expect a depressed or severely burnt-out person to be, and may require increased rest and social support in order to slowly rebuild a sense of themselves as worthwhile and lovable.

Shame itself can be quite damaging, but Systemic Shame runs even deeper than the remorse we might feel when we remember something cruel or harmful that we've done. That's because Systemic

Shame is not only an emotion—it's also a belief system about who is deserving of aid and who ought to be held responsible for any harm they incur. Shame tells us that we are bad, which itself is an incredibly terrible feeling. But Systemic Shame teaches that entire groups of people are bad, and that through our choices and our identities, we constantly signal to other people whether we belong to a redeemable group or to an innately wicked one. When we experience regular shame, we can begin to repair it by reexamining our actions, making amends, or committing to growth in some tangible way. But Systemic Shame is a wound that continues to be reopened in us day after day, no matter what we do or don't do, and no matter how desperately we wish we could love who we are. No matter how hard we work or how ardently we strive to be moral, Systemic Shame looms all around us in our culture, telling us that we are lazy, selfish, disgusting, and untrustworthy, and that all the problems we're facing in life are completely our fault.

When a marginalized person holds themselves personally responsible for solving the problem of their own oppression, Systemic Shame is the overwhelmed, hopeless feeling that results. When we blame ourselves as individuals for failing to do "enough" to combat injustices like transphobia, racism, labor exploitation, global climate change, or health epidemics, Systemic Shame extracts a heavy emotional toll from us as well. When we believe that we must remedy historic inequalities on our own, signaling our virtue with what we buy and consume and never accepting any help, we're suffering from Systemic Shame, too. It's just about everywhere. It pollutes so many conversations about what we owe to one another, and what it might look like to genuinely create a better, more socially just world.

Systemic Shame is a lingering emotional wound. But it's also an ideology about how the world works—a deeply damaging one that keeps us distracted and unhappy. It is closely linked to the Puritanical belief that morality is simple and absolute, and to long-standing American ideals that claim every person should be ruggedly independent. Because it is so deeply embedded in our culture and history, Systemic Shame appears in our political debates, our public service announcements and advertisements, our textbooks, the workshops and trainings we are asked to attend, the movies we enjoy and the conversations that we have about them, and even in how we judge our own actions and those of our friends.

Systemic Shame claims that the only way meaningful change can ever occur is if individual people put in a ton of effort and always make the "right" decisions. It tells us that disabled people must never let their conditions be an "excuse" for falling behind, and that poverty is remedied by hardworking people pulling themselves up by their bootstraps. Systemic Shame tells women that they can overcome sexism in the workplace if they learn to speak more confidently and commit to "leaning in," and it tells Black people that they can overcome racism in their professional lives by watching their tone.[2] When a Black woman struggles to follow these two contradictory pieces of advice simultaneously, Systemic Shame says it's her fault for not being strong enough or, paradoxically, for being too "angry."

Systemic Shame convinces us that global pandemics are caused by selfish people rather than corporate cruelty and government negligence. It preaches that acts of mass gun violence are random acts caused by evil and mentally ill people, rather than by the rise of white supremacist and other hate movements. Systemic Shame also tells us that we must obsess over our personal habits, choices, and purchases, because every action we take carries intense moral weight with it. According to Systemic Shame, the fate of the world rests upon every single decision we make. No matter how much we care about injustice and other people, Systemic Shame will always be

there to convince us that we are failing to live up to those values—
that we aren't committing adequate resources, doing enough for
other people, or working sufficiently hard.

Systemic Shame keeps so many of us trapped, as I have often
been trapped, hating myself for who I am, working desperately to
earn the right to be alive, and never believing that anyone could ever
really support or care for me. And I know I'm not the only one. This
line of thinking has absolutely ravaged our political discourse and
blocks us from having productive conversations about what real
change might look like on a systematic level—and what is needed
for us to fight for such change together.

Here are a few signs that you might be suffering from Systemic
Shame:

1. You are constantly looking at yourself through the eyes
   of people who disapprove of you.
2. You spend a lot of time ruminating over past decisions,
   even relatively small ones, worrying that things would
   have gone differently if you'd gotten it "right."
3. You only feel that you can relax and truly be yourself
   when you're alone—yet even when you are in private,
   there are thoughts and feelings you won't allow yourself
   to have.
4. You are hyperaware of the negative stereotypes people
   might apply to you, based on your identity, your appearance, or even your past experiences, and carefully monitor your behavior so as not to confirm those stereotypes
   as true.
5. You compulsively take in news of upsetting events
   throughout the world, but instead of feeling empowered
   by knowledge, you are left feeling guilty and panicked.

6. You have a difficult time imagining a future where you might feel content, or that your life is worthwhile.

7. You feel like you are carrying a heavy load of obligations, but that nothing you do in life seems to matter.

8. You find it hard to believe that anyone might really appreciate and care for the "real" you.

9. Your default attitude toward yourself is mistrust and disgust.

10. You try to do everything on your own—and you see slowing down or needing help as a failure.

By every measure, Systemic Shame is a problem that's incredibly widespread. And there is almost no social issue—from climate change to sexism, from medical fatphobia to global pandemics—that Systemic Shame hasn't touched. The more a person suffers, the more our economic system and public institutions are primed to convince us it's all their fault. But I can pretty much guarantee this ideology touches your life even if you don't tend to think of yourself as particularly oppressed, because all our lives are vulnerable to the damage wrought by forces like capitalism and environmental degradation. It's Systemic Shame that prevents us from recognizing we share these struggles with the majority of other beings living on this planet. Rather than coming together to demand better of our existing systems or to work on building alternative ones together, Systemic Shame consumes us with fear and self-loathing, and pushes us apart.

<hr>

A few years ago, I went on a grocery-shopping trip with my friend Gary, a deeply conscientious and anxiety-ridden soul. We were gathering supplies for a party at Gary's house, and he was a mess of apologies and preemptive explanations for his actions the entire time. We went to Whole Foods, Gary told me, because it was the closest grocery store, and it was better for the environment for us to walk there than to drive to the Aldi two miles down the street. Still, he told me he felt guilty shopping at a grocery chain so strongly associated with gentrification in the city—especially since Whole Foods was also owned by Amazon, a company infamous for mistreating its workers.

Gary brought a backpack filled with reusable tote bags with him to the store. But he fretted that we might need to buy a few disposable plastic ones, too. In the produce section, Gary reached for a container of pre-cut watermelon and explained to me that he couldn't carry a whole watermelon home, let alone cut it, because of his arthritis. Then he grabbed a package of biodegradable disposable forks, explaining that he needed them when his symptoms flared up and made scrubbing dishes painful. I wanted to offer to help Gary with household tasks that were painful to him—but I knew I couldn't really commit to traveling to an apartment three miles from my own to do that with any regularity. I didn't have a car, and public transit made me motion sick. Plus, my weekly schedule always left me feeling impossibly strapped. It seemed there was nothing either of us could do. A heaviness followed us from aisle to aisle.

I hated that my presence seemed to leave Gary feeling surveilled, like I was judging him for his choices. And part of me was also frustrated at Gary for his whole hand-wringing, shame-filled performance, too. It made me feel bad about my own decisions and limitations. Was Gary judging *me* for arriving to his house with a large Starbucks coffee in a disposable cup? Did he think I was a failure as a friend because I couldn't help him? As he quietly contemplated two bottles of basically identical seltzer, trying to figure out which ones weren't bottled by Coca-Cola, I wanted to shout at him, "There is no winning this game, Gary! None of our choices matter!" I felt defensive in the face of his moral meticulousness and thought forcefully declaring my apathy might spare us both all the unnecessary trouble.

Gary was trying to cope with the looming threat of climate change by fixating on the impact of his every decision. Like the character Chidi Anagonye, the neurotic, morally conflicted philosopher on the NBC sitcom *The Good Place*, Gary tried to consider the far-reaching social implications of his every purchase and move. But when a careful and well-read person like Gary tries to express his convictions at the grocery store, he often finds that *none* of the options available are particularly moral. On *The Good Place*, Chidi is an indecisive wreck who can never arrive at a decision he feels is ethically sound. He can't even select which kind of milk he wants to drink without descending into a panic. Almond milk might be superior to cow's milk from an animal rights perspective, yet it still damages the environment because of how much water almond plants require in order to grow. Rice milk consumes less water than almond milk, but it generates far more greenhouse gas emissions. There is no coherent answer to the question of what is "right" to buy—every single option is damaging because they're all produced by amoral corporations that do not care about the environment.

In a show filled with fictional "sinners" dwelling in hell, Chidi learns that he's been damned because his indecisiveness tormented everyone around him and served no purpose. He even fails to visit his mother in the hospital because he cannot decide between showing up for her on the day of surgery or honoring an earlier commitment he'd made to help his landlord's nephew program his phone. He feels anguish about all manner of issues, with no clear conception of scale—and so he misdirects his energy toward trivial efforts.

The fictional Chidi and my real-life friend Gary both cope with Systemic Shame by carefully evaluating the ethical weight of their every decision. On the flip side, I tend to protect myself by checking out and feeling jaded. Over a decade ago, I encountered the sentence "There is no ethical consumption under capitalism" on the blogging platform Tumblr, where it quickly became a rallying cry for the guilty and despondent. At times, I have used that saying—and the hopelessness it expresses—to try to protect myself from shame about the waste I produce, or from having to worry about how I spend my money. *Sure, Whole Foods creates a ton of waste and exploits its employees*, I tell myself, *but the manager at the bodega on the corner is abusive to his employees, too. There is no ethical consumption under capitalism. There are no good options, so I might as well give up.* But it wasn't really a solution. It just meant I never even listened to the discomfort roiling inside me.

Gary's inner conflict at the grocery store forced me back into reality. He helped me remember that every object laid before us had been grown, harvested, packaged, shipped, and stocked on the shelves by dozens of real human beings, all of whom were stuck within systems they also had nearly zero influence over. I'd already known that, of course, but clichés like "There is no ethical consumption under capitalism" seemed poised to make me forget. All around us there were shoppers who were just trying to live a life that mattered and was a net good on the world. And the consumption of all those shoppers was made possible through the efforts of the workers, who also had no control over their employer's actions and environmental practices. Everywhere I looked, there were people toiling as hard as possible and finding that no amount of effort changed the systems they were stuck in. It was almost too much collected human suffering for my mind to take in.

Not long before my shopping trip with Gary, a tweet criticizing

Whole Foods for selling pre-peeled oranges in plastic containers went hyperviral.[3] Why remove a fruit's natural, biodegradable wrapper, people wondered, and then cover it up in disposable plastic? How could someone be so *lazy* and *wasteful* as to buy a thing like that? Entitled customers like that were the reason the Pacific Ocean was filled with islands of trash.

Companies like Whole Foods and Amazon do waste huge quantities of paper and plastic on excessive packaging,[4] and criticizing that has value.[5] But to blame individual consumers for buying these wasteful products is to miss who is really at fault. Unfortunately, that's too often where Systemic Shame takes us—it confronts us with small-scale evidence of a widespread problem, provoking us to blame the horrible, lazy individuals who represent that problem to us.

There are a lot of reasons why a person might buy a pre-peeled orange in a heavy plastic container. People with physical disabilities (like Gary) often rely on prepared, individually packaged foods, because they don't have anyone around to assist with meal preparation. Busy parents without childcare support often need quick, easy ways to transport food that won't cause a mess or contamination in their diaper bags. Pre-packing food also can streamline the process of making food in bulk for large families.

In a better world, Gary could trust that people would be around to help him cut watermelon or wash dishes, and parents wouldn't have to do all their meal prep alone. But usually, that kind of aid just is not available. Everyone is so busy and isolated, and most of us are broke. No one has enough energy or resources to show up for the people we love at the level they deserve. Because of all this, many of us are forced to choose between putting lots of effort into doing the most righteous-seeming thing, or simply getting through a challenging day.

Whole Foods only stands to profit from this predicament. Products that make life more convenient and accessible for disabled people tend to come with extreme markups, which disability activists sometimes call the "crip tax."[6] Products marketed as ethically and sustainably sourced are often far more expensive too, and rarely live up to their branding. It's us individual consumers who have to pay for the lack of community support with our own consumption—and in the end, we're also the ones left feeling ashamed for needing to consume so much.

Everywhere we turn, there are messages encouraging us as individuals to behave responsibly, and to address systemic issues by making the right personal choices. Advertisements tell us to shop sustainably, while hocking poorly made products we don't need. Rideshare apps ask us to spend a few extra dollars to take rides in energy efficient vehicles, obscuring the massive damage to the environment their companies cause.[7] Cities like San Francisco, Chicago, and Los Angeles tax individuals for using plastic shopping bags, then turn around and offer up massive tax cuts to super-polluters like Amazon.[8]

When we consider our impact on the world as individuals, many of us feel immense shame. And it's not just about the environment. When I fail to donate what feels like "enough" money to my local mutual aid fund, I feel stingy and selfish, forgetting that government funding toward community resources has been going down massively for decades.[9] When my hairy, wide-hipped body gets odd looks on the street, I feel shame that I've transitioned into a form that's so "freakish," even though my real issue is centuries of cissexist gender norms. When I hear tales of my friends being discriminated against at work, or losing jobs because they were a little awkward or visibly neurodivergent, I feel ashamed I can't do enough to defend them. Despite myself, I keep wanting to believe that by behaving in the "right" ways, I could correct injustice, escape my own oppression, and even save the world. But of course, inequality and injustice don't work that way.

Thanks to Systemic Shame, I fixate far too much on the small failures of the people around me instead of keeping my focus on the laws and economic incentives that actually create injustice. My Jesuit employer refuses to pay for transition-related healthcare, and hormone replacement therapy is being banned for trans people all across the country—yet I spend more time resenting the one exhausted colleague who can't ever seem to get my pronouns right. I live in a neighborhood where there are no public trash cans for several blocks, yet it's my neighbor that I sneer at for tossing his beer cans on the ground. When my rumination is at its worst, I find it hard to feel much hope or compassion for humanity at all.

Systemic Shame touches the life of every marginalized and vulnerable person. And when I use the phrase "marginalized or vulnerable person," I have a very wide umbrella in mind. If you are reading this book, you almost certainly are vulnerable to economic and environmental factors outside your control. Forces like labor exploitation, rising costs of living, global pandemics, and the consequences of climate change touch your life, and you probably feel there is little you can do to forestall these threats. When you're struggling to pay your bills yet find yourself ordering Postmates most nights because you don't have the energy to cook, you might hear a guilty voice in the back of your head, saying that you're only broke and hungry because you're so irresponsible. You might get to thinking that the challenges you're facing are not as legitimate as other people's. But it's this very feeling of isolated helplessness that actually binds you to the majority of humans living on this planet.

Though many of us dream of living in a just world, where thriving communities care for one another and the planet, Systemic Shame makes it easy for us to lose the plot. We fixate so much on the morality of momentary choices, small purchases, and daily habits. *Is watching this movie feminist? Is buying this free-range beef good for the environment? Should I list my pronouns in my bio? Am I doing enough? Are my friends?* Systemic Shame convinces us we need to stay this anxious. And while we are stuck feeling this way, the powerful institutions that are actually responsible for our issues get off nearly scot-free.

America's laws and national myths are built upon the idea that individuals can and must choose their own fates. When vulnerable groups of people suffer, or have freedom and resources stolen from them, we hear time and time again that they are responsible for what's happened—and that they could have prevented it if they'd only tried harder.

In the years immediately after slavery was abolished, for example, political cartoons portrayed newly freed Black Americans as "lazy" grifters who only wanted reparations because they were looking for a handout.[10] It didn't matter that enslaved Africans had been ripped from their homelands, robbed of their autonomy, their names, and their family histories, or that their children were forced to toil in the fields with no pay for centuries. To the opponents of reparations, all that mattered was that recently freed Black people were not working hard "enough" to establish themselves as financially and educationally equal to white people.

Over a century later, single mothers who relied on welfare or food stamps in order to survive were depicted by the Reagan administration as irresponsible "welfare queens"—yet again deeming people in need as opportunists looking for a handout. These impoverished women supposedly did not deserve support, because some of them might have had unprotected sex, used drugs, or not tried hard "enough" find high-earning work.[11]

To this day, anyone who relies on disability benefits runs the risk of being accused of faking their condition to take advantage of the system. Videos of wheelchair users even slightly moving their legs or adjusting their postures get plastered all over social media, where thousands of people shame them for not really "needing" a mobility aid, or not suffering badly enough.[12] The myth of the fake disabled person is an incredibly well-worn media trope: It has appeared in *hundreds* of TV shows and movies, from *Law & Order* to *Detective Pikachu*.[13] When a disabled character appears on screen, it is more likely they'll be revealed to have been faking their condition all along than to actually be portrayed as a genuine disabled person with any human complexity.

Marginalized people learn quite early on that our every action will be scrutinized for proof we aren't trying hard "enough" or cannot be trusted. Research shows that many disabled people absorb the idea that no matter how debilitating their illness is (or how socially excluded they are), they somehow aren't trying hard enough to manage their health or put a positive spin on their illness. We also know empirically that when disabled people blame ourselves for our struggles, we are also less likely to take an interest in meeting other disabled people or forming a community with them.[14] Our socially imposed self-hatred breeds isolation, which only deepens our shame.

What solutions does our culture offer to people who are suffering from Systemic Shame? Hard work, self-sacrifice, and individual accomplishment. That's pretty much it. News articles claim it's "inspiring" when a man who can't afford a car exhibits the amazing discipline to walk twenty-one miles to work every day,[15] or when a paralyzed athlete "overcomes" their disability by winning a challenging race.[16] Celebrating these rare, extreme achievements just serves to raise the bar for everyone else who's suffering.[17] Instead of asking why a poor or disabled person has to be exceptional in order to simply survive, these stories preach that anything is possible if an individual tries hard enough. The fact is, not everyone can try that hard.

It isn't just disabled people who internalize the shame that society has tied to our identities, of course. Hundreds of empirical studies conducted over the last several decades have shown that Black Americans suffer from internalized racism in high numbers.[18] For centuries, Black people have been bombarded with messages painting them as lazy and at fault for the inequities they face, and unfortunately it's nearly impossible for someone to endure that level of external hatred without taking some of it in. When Black people begin to believe the negative images they have seen of themselves in media, they are at a heightened risk of depression, anxiety, problematic alcohol and drug use, social isolation, low self-esteem, hypertension, cardiovascular disease, and even insulin resistance. Absorbing the shame of racism is more than just painful—it can erode a person's quality of life, or even make their life far shorter.

A recent study on the attitudes of incarcerated Black youth found that while most teens recognized white supremacy had strongly influenced their lives in negative ways, acknowledging racism did nothing to curb their profound feelings of what researchers called "self-condemnation."[19] Black incarcerated teens felt powerless in the face of structural racism, but at the same time, they blamed *themselves* for how they coped with it. This is what Systemic Shame does to people. It overwhelms them and robs them of empowerment, while simultaneously convincing them they're only in this position because they haven't tried hard enough to make the right choices.

Research shows that when a negative stereotype is applied to a person or to a group that they belong to, it takes a heavy psychological toll even when the person recognizes the stereotype is unfair.[20] The HIV stigma researchers Phil Hutchinson and Rageshri Dhairyawan observe that even when an HIV-positive person *knows* that HIV stigma is inaccurate, the prejudices of others still diminish how they feel about themselves. If people refuse to shake your hand and few people in your community want to date you, it scarcely matters that you know that your serostatus can't be passed through skin or saliva or that your viral load is undetectable. You've still been marked in other's eyes as tainted, as defective—as having failed to protect yourself and therefore deserving of blame. Hutchinson and Dhairyawan describe shame as "a taking-on-board of the judgments (or morally-loaded perceptions) of others about oneself."[21] The immense pain of being seen by others as "dirty" or "dangerous" still lingers, even when a person knows that they do not deserve it.

When we discuss the weight that stereotyping and Systemic Shame carry, it's hard not to contrast the lives of marginalized people, who are under nearly constant attack, and the lives of the comparatively more privileged, who carry the mark of Systemic Shame far less visibly. For the groups directly targeted by systems of oppression such as anti-Blackness or homophobia, the strength and stakes of Systemic Shame are undeniably more extreme. Yet it is also true that the varying degrees of isolation, self-blame, and societal condemnation that we all experience under Systemic Shame are of the same piece—and that this massive social sickness of Systemic Shame will get better only once we begin to realize that we're all affected by it.

A suburban white woman who cannot manage work and child-care expectations and feels a lot of shame about that fact is operating with the very same systems as the far less privileged woman she employs for help around the house. Both women's lives are shaped by sexist expectations regarding parenting and house-cleaning duties; both are exhausted, overworked, and likely being underpaid (though to very different degrees); both women are forced to grapple with how isolating and inaccessible suburban life can be, and how difficult it is to exist in the public realm when you are caring for a kid.[22] This is true while the two women's lives and levels of social power are dramatically different, and in fact one woman holds power over the other. If we were to write off the wealthier white mom's hand-wringing as entirely privileged and pointless, we'd miss key pieces of the larger social puzzle laid before us. We'd also be declaring that her suffering is somehow not "bad enough" to deserve any critique—and under Systemic Shame, no person is ever a deserving enough victim. True solidarity building requires that we acknowledge people's struggles as legitimate—even while upholding that some people's struggles intersect in far more ways, and some who suffer hold the power to make others' suffering worse.

Because of Systemic Shame, no matter how much privilege or marginalization that a person holds (and every single one of us holds a combination of both), we are viewed as not trying hard enough to overcome our circumstances or to behave responsibly. Disabled people's complaints of inaccessibility, for example, are frequently written off by abled people as needless complaining or demands for coddling. Trans people's demands for healthcare are written off by "gender critical" people as a frivolous extravagance that we don't really need. In conversations about Systemic Shame, the needs of multiple marginalized people absolutely have to be centered—and such centering can help us better understand our shared vulnerability. This also does not mean that the struggles of others do not rank. It is only by recognizing that the root causes of our suffering are the same that we can share in building solutions to our shared problems.

If the suburban white woman in this example comes to realize that her life is difficult not because she is a "bad mom" or a "bad worker," but rather because of a historic legacy of overwork and sexism, she might begin to see a connection between what she needs and the well-being of the caregiver she employs. She might begin to question the pace at which she lives her life, and might recognize how racing to always be both the perfect parent and the endlessly reliable professional harms both her child and the woman she hires, whom she has economic power over.

Of course, this moment of realization doesn't always happen. Being compassionate toward the wealthiest, most powerful person in the room can't be where our conversations begin or where they stop. But understanding that both women are members of an oppressed class with shared concerns is important. As Jessica Friedman, author of the book *Things That Helped: On Postpartum Depression,* writes, "Motherhood is a political category."[23] And vulnerable and oppressed groups of people only begin to make steps toward justice once they realize they're in a political category.

When oppressed people fail to recognize that we are targeted on a systematic level, and instead only understand our lives and the choices we make through a personal lens, finding belonging and demanding better for our communities becomes impossible. In most elections in the United States, after all, white, well-off women vote in large numbers for conservative politicians—many of whom go on to enact social policies that hurt all women (as well as all other gender minorities). The women who vote this way often think about their decisions as protecting their own individual wealth and privilege—just as early white Suffragettes cared more about their

own individual right to vote and own property than about the liberation of Black and brown women and women in poverty. Matters
might be dramatically different if these women viewed sexism as a
force not to be escaped through personal responsibility and money,
but by creating a world where all gender minorities enjoy body autonomy, political representation, and fair access to resources.

I decided to write this book because I was desperate to figure out
what the solution to living with Systemic Shame is—since endlessly
chasing after perfection never helped me, and viewing my problems
as personal failures only left me miserably alone. Every desperate
attempt at earning my right to be alive made me feel emptier, because it separated me from other people and the rich web of life that
surrounded me. Even though I've made a lot of progress in accepting
myself, it seems I'm always uncovering sources of shame that I've
overlooked and noticing how much my behavior is still limited by
negative beliefs about who I "should" be and fears of how I come
across to others. I want out of this cycle. I want to stop staring inward with obsession and hatred and begin looking outward with
interest and trust.

To help better understand Systemic Shame and how we all
might heal from it, I have reviewed the psychological literature, ex-
amined shame's cultural history, and spoken to an array of therapists,
coaches, and labor organizers. I've interviewed marginalized people
who are working on healing their own Systemic Shame and read up
on activist movements that grappled with these issues and found
productive solutions. From all this data, I've developed a framework
for understanding how Systemic Shame works, where it comes from,
and why so many of us find blaming ourselves and others so damn

compelling. Despite how much shame entices us, the evidence is abundant that it does not work. Shame is *never* an effective motivator for inspiring behavior change, for a variety of psychological, cultural, and even physiological reasons. Despite this, societies keep reaching for shame and using it as a tool of social separation and control. But it doesn't have to be this way.

It turns out that while Systemic Shame is incredibly common, blaming yourself for structural issues is not inevitable. We do not have to feel frozen and despondent in the face of climate change, income inequality, systemic racism, violent transphobia, and global pandemics. It's possible to believe our lives have meaning, and to build richly interconnected communities that will care for us and aid us in carrying out our values and improving the world. Based on my research and interviews, I've developed a variety of tools designed to help people figure out what a connected and meaningful place the world can look like. In the second half of the book, we'll focus entirely on that process of healing from Systemic Shame on a personal, interpersonal, and even global level.

But before we dive into how we might overcome Systemic Shame, we first need to understand how it functions, and how our culture came to be so obsessed with it in the first place. Why are we so insistent on holding individuals responsible for structural injustice? Why do so many of us feel so guilty and helpless nearly all the time? Let's begin by taking a look at how Systemic Shame manages to get so many of us in its thrall.

Part One

Suffering Under Systemic Shame

CHAPTER 1

Understanding Systemic Shame

Ellen is a single mom living with a teen daughter, Jenna, just outside of Boston. For the past five years, Ellen has worked in grant writing, helping to raise funds for an organization that serves teenagers with mental health issues. In her free time, which she doesn't have a lot of, Ellen also volunteers as a content writer for the organization's blog and social media pages. On a typical evening she's up late into the night, double-checking grant applications for formatting errors, taking breaks to edit the organization's latest Instagram posts. Then she rolls over in bed with an alarm set for six in the morning, so she can take meetings with foundations and get her daughter off to school.

"I do all of this because I don't ever want to fail another kid," she says to me tearfully. She's referring to her daughter Jenna's experience with self-harm.

About a year and a half after Ellen got divorced, she found out her daughter had started cutting and burning herself. Ellen's still not sure how long it went on before she found out. It was a neighbor who first noticed injuries on Jenna's body. In the ensuing years—filled with therapeutic appointments, psychological assessments, mental health retreats, family meetings, and doctor visits—Ellen felt ashamed for not noticing more quickly. And she's coped with that shame by throwing herself into nonprofit work.

"I have to do all that I can to save other children from depression and pain," Ellen says to me. "In every client [the organization] served, I saw Jenna, but with even less support than Jenna has."

The long hours and volunteer gigs didn't bring Ellen and Jenna any closer. In fact, Ellen's work stress only made it easier for Jenna to pull away. Ellen says that she spiraled into self-recrimination every single time she caught Jenna self-harming again, which didn't make Jenna feel any better either. Ellen could only escape her worst feelings by burying herself in her work. But it turned out trying to save all other children from self-harm was impossible and did not "make up" for the harm Ellen felt responsible for.

"It has been an endless cycle," Ellen says. "Trying to escape how awful I feel about what's happened, but only making it worse." But finally, she tells me, she's ready for this cycle to stop. She wants to stop acting like Jenna's scars are too painful to look at. She wants to stop wrecking her own life with dreams of undoing the past. And most of all, she wants herself and her daughter to both be able to put down their shame, if only for one moment, so that they can be close again.

Shame and the Search for a Symbol

In early 2022, TikTok was overrun with videos about a man users called "West Elm Caleb." Several New York–based women had posted videos to the platform talking about disappointing dates they'd had with a charming, super affectionate guy who'd make them personalized playlists, shower them in compliments and attention, and then ghost them after having sex. Comparing details in the comments, these women quickly realized they'd all been played by the same guy—a man named Caleb who worked at West Elm.

A social media takedown campaign unfolded. Random users

attempted to track down Caleb's address and contact his employer to get him fired. Images of his face and his LinkedIn profile were broadcast across social media for anyone to view. Thousands of videos were posted under the #WestElmCaleb hashtag, fantasizing about him receiving retribution for his shady behavior, analyzing his actions and messages for signs of emotional abuse, and providing women with tips for how to identify "love-bombing" manipulators like him.[1] Within a month, the #WestElmCaleb hashtag accrued more than 85 million views.

By most standards, the worst thing West Elm Caleb was accused of doing was sending one woman an unsolicited nude photograph. The rest of his actions, as his former dates describe them, sound like pretty typical albeit douchey dating app behavior. Caleb sent multiple women the exact same Spotify playlist, telling each one he'd made it just for them. He told women he wasn't on the dating apps that much, though it's clear he was matching and hooking up with people all over town. He presented as affectionate and genuinely interested in his targets—but after having sex, he'd never message again. These are all actions well-deserving of an eye roll from across the bar or a roasting at a party. Yet Caleb morphed from an ordinary asshole into a gaslighting, love-bombing abuser in TikTok's eyes.[2]

In a video essay analyzing the saga, the internet culture YouTuber Sarah Z speculated about why TikTok users went after Caleb with such fervor:[3] She says he became the symbolic face of larger social problems like sexism, objectification, and dishonesty on dating apps.

"He's made into this icon," Sarah says, "a sort of representation of every other guy like him. You might not have been able to personally get any kind of remorse out of the [word censored in video] who ghosted you after weeks of seeing each other, but you *can* humiliate this Caleb guy."

Caleb at West Elm is by all accounts a tall, conventionally

attractive white guy with a cushy job in furniture design. Given all the privileges he holds in society, he's hardly the poster boy for what experiencing Systemic Shame typically looks like. Yet he is an individual who has been personally and publicly held responsible for a societal issue that's far larger than him. And in the reactions of his former sexual partners and the internet sleuths who hate him, we see the far-reaching effects of lives lived under sexism and shame.

West Elm Caleb played with the expectations and romantic hopes of numerous young women, some of them women of color. The first social media user to publicly put him on blast, Mimi Shou, specifically set out to warn other Asian women about him.[4] The majority of social media observers who participated in the West Elm Caleb saga online were women who mentioned past experiences with their own "Calebs" or who said the desire to "protect" other women from men was the motive behind their actions.

When you have repeatedly experienced a pattern of mistreatment, or you've been victimized by systems of oppression like sexism, it feels really good to find a suitable symbol of all that to attack. It makes your suffering, however large and amorphous, suddenly seem tangible. And psychological research shows that most humans have a powerful desire to take abstract concepts (like objectification, or sexism) and transform them into terms that are more manageable and concrete.[5]

Construal Level Theory is a theory in social psychology, which states that there is a massive psychological difference between thinking about our values in distant or big-picture terms (sometimes called abstract construal) and thinking about those same values in a short-term, practical way (often called concrete construal). Research into Construal Level Theory has found that when you translate a scarily vague, abstract goal (like "fighting sexism") into a far more concrete, small-scale solution (like "taking an implicit sexism test online"), people find it quite appealing[6] and soothing. Focusing on individual behavior makes big systemic issues feel more controllable.[7] Taking action can make you feel powerful, especially when all you've known is abstract powerlessness. That sometimes holds even when the action is small or relatively meaningless in the long term.

When looked at from a Construal Level Theory perspective, the reactions of the women who publicly dogpiled West Elm Caleb make emotional sense. An individual woman might not be able to fix the culture that trains so many men to lie to her and ghost her, but by personalizing and shaming the actions of one random asshole, she can feel like she is doing something to discourage bad behavior. And while being unceremoniously dumped on a dating app doesn't really count as "abuse," we do know that abuse victims often find it healing to provide support to other survivors and prevent future mistreatment.[8] So if you've experienced a lifetime of objectifying slights, it might be tempting to project your wounds onto all of West Elm Caleb's exes and see yourself and them as part of some broader feminist community. It's true, even though, as Sarah Z points out in her video, "women aren't collectively benefiting from any of this." Attacking one guy and getting him fired doesn't change the culture. It doesn't give women the economic power or social support they need to escape from the people most likely to abuse them— typically, men they are related to, live with, or work for.[9] The only ones profiting from all this fervent posting is TikTok and its many advertisers.

I have often found myself engaging in behavior quite similar to that of West Elm Caleb's online haters. As a gay transgender man, I feel deeply wounded by America's pervasive homophobia and transphobia. I have tried to cope with how suffocated and afraid I feel by blaming my conversative mom and other relatives for the rise of transphobia across the country—as if they are a driving force in the movement rather than ill-informed pawns. My mom has always claimed to be tolerant of queer people (and has said that she only votes Republican for economic reasons), yet with her political choices, she's repeatedly sided with powerful figures who attack my community. The same is true of nearly all my Republican family members. Most of them treat me with basic decency. But they also find it acceptable, and even desirable, to elect politicians who have repeatedly made my life and the life of my loved ones worse.

In my pain and outrage, I've snapped at my family and insulted them. I've written angry letters and essays about their political views and shared that writing with the world without bothering to even initiate a real conversation first. I've called my mom sobbing, and ranted at her for an hour or more, believing that if she would only feel some *shame* about how her actions have affected me, she might finally realize that she's wrong. What I'm really longing for, on some level, is to stop feeling as if I'm broken and trapped inside a world that was not built for me. I want the pain of having grown up closeted to go away. I shame my mother and family to offload the immense Systemic Shame dwelling inside myself. I can't fix the United States, so I focus on the individual people who represent my pain.

The problem is, if inconsiderate guys like Caleb are the product of larger systems such as sexism and the impersonal nature of dating apps, holding one individual accountable won't stop the problem at its root. And if my mom and the rest of my family's politics have been influenced by decades of media misinformation and online hate movements, haranguing them for their ignorance won't change things much either. My years of failed attempts are proof of that.

In fact, devoting too much mental energy to individual blame can make it harder for us to really think systematically about why the same damaging behaviors keep cropping up in different people. But it's hard for many of us to see past this, because shame is so firmly embedded into our culture. Morally condemning other people often feels like it's simply the right thing to do. Plus, when you've experienced intense Systemic Shame about your own identities, pushing that shame onto others feels only fair. Sometimes, I just want to make others feel as hurt as I've felt. When you have no hope of the world getting better, all you want to do is take others down with you.

Even though I know intellectually that shaming my mom is kind of missing the point, for years I could not keep myself from being angry with her. I know from experience that when I get vulnerable with my mom about my hurt feelings and explain to her how her actions have created a distance between us, she is more likely to be sympathetic and alter her behavior. It's especially effective when I acknowledge the political concerns she and I do have in common. We both feel completely unrepresented in the current political system. We both see that most people's economic futures are on the verge of collapse. We both care about the planet, and finding an end to racism and sexism, and we both find it disturbing that so many people with nearly unchecked political power have sexually abused other people.

My mother and I don't share a clear view on what the solutions are to these problems, but we do share many values. In recent years, I've persuaded her that it's better not to vote at all than it is to elect a conservative whose policies would hurt me. She's agreed with me on that and sworn off voting for the rest of her life. That's more progress than I ever thought to expect. We arrived at this truce through honest conversation,—yet most of the time, I'm still too swept up in anger (at her actions) and self-loathing (over my own identity) to reach out in ways that help heal our rift.

This is how Systemic Shame works on so many of us. Because it convinces us that individual people are responsible for making change happen, it fills us with negative feelings toward other people that we perceive as not doing "enough." This makes it very difficult for us to connect. From there, Systemic Shame encourages us to pin sole responsibility for our suffering on ourselves and other individuals, rather than looking to the systems that got us all here.

In this chapter, we'll define what Systemic Shame is, and come to better understand how it functions in our world. We've already discussed how Systemic Shame is a personal taking-on of all the pressure and blame society directs at individuals. But as the examples of West Elm Caleb and my own family show, Systemic Shame doesn't *end* with internal feelings of anguish. It also radiates outward, and impacts how we relate to others and even how we think about humanity as a whole.

The Levels of Systemic Shame

Systemic Shame is a painful social emotion. It's also a set of beliefs about how change in the world can occur. Because it is so far-reaching and yet also so deeply felt, it can affect each of us on three different levels:

1. *Personal Shame:* Feelings of self-loathing over our identities, our limitations, or our perceived failings.

    How it affects us: Personal Systemic Shame leads us to hide ourselves from others. Because we fear being judged, we turn away from others, not trusting that anybody could ever accept us fully. This leads us to developing interpersonal shame.

2. *Interpersonal Shame:* A belief that other people are unsafe and untrustworthy, and that most people are basically immoral, lazy, and selfish.

   How it affects us: Interpersonal Systemic Shame leads us to harshly judge the actions of other people—the exact same way that we fear being judged. Because we don't feel comfortable opening up to others, Interpersonal Systemic Shame forces us to become hyper-independent and focus only on our own self-preservation and safety. This isolation and individualism makes it even harder for us to accept the aid of other people, or to work with a broader community to address injustice on a systemic level.

3. *Global Shame:* A belief that humanity is filled with selfish, apathetic, or morally "bad" people—to the degree we might not even believe the species is worth saving. In our disconnection and helplessness, we may start to think that life can never truly be rewarding or have meaning.

   How it affects us: Global Systemic Shame makes us cynical and discourages us from trying to improve our communities and our relationships. By convincing us that all the world's problems are caused by individuals behaving badly, global shame makes it impossible for us to imagine a way out of the pain that so many other people are in.

We can think of Systemic Shame's three levels as concentric circles, or as a snowball that begins with a small core of personal shame, and then builds outward:

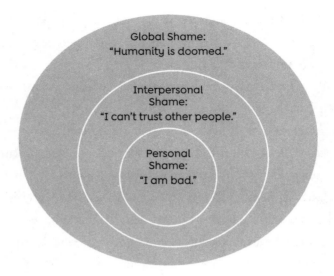

In the next few sections of this chapter, we'll break down these three layers and explain how they often develop inside us—and then spiral outside of us and beyond us, with disastrous social and political consequences. Personal shame is what's pushed on us the most directly when we are young—in our education, our upbringing, the thoughtless comments that friends and neighbors toss off at us, the seemingly well-intentioned corrections our families offer us, and even via the media that we consume. These many tiny rejections and social judgments slowly develop within us, and as we notice patterns in where they appear and who bears the brunt of them, they can develop into a broader worldview. Even if we happen to outgrow some of our own shame later on, the worldview of Systemic Shame can still linger within us. We might still believe that people outside our small social circle cannot be trusted, or that improving how society runs is still hopeless. In this way, though Systemic Shame starts as a personal, internal experience when we're very young, recovering from the damage it does to us can't ever be done in isolation.

Level 1: Personal Shame

Systemic Shame begins with personal feelings of self-loathing and self-blame. If we fear that we are fundamentally selfish, weak, and immoral people deep down, we become desperate to hide our real feelings and needs from others, and to perform the appearance of goodness any way we can. Yet the more we try to cover up who we are, the less authentic love and acceptance we are able to experience.

Personal Systemic Shame starts young. People who have been unfairly stereotyped or marginalized learn to view themselves with suspicion from very early on in life. But even children who are not visibly marked as different or divergent in some way absorb countless damaging messages about how they ought to look and carry themselves, what they should be capable of, and even how hard they ought to be working and sacrificing in order to be worthy of love. For instance, long before I had any clue I was trans and Autistic, I had noticed that my parents seemed very lonely and depressed, and that rather than taking steps to meet new people or expand their life with new hobbies, my dad confided in me as his sole confidant and proto-therapist. I was a small child, and I learned rapidly that my access to affection and to feelings of safety would come from being emotionally available and supportive, and by not clouding the already fraught family dynamic with my own worrying or tears. When my father cried, the rest of the world stopped moving, and I jumped into action, providing reassurances and listening deeply to figure out what kind of aid I could provide. When I cried, everybody got angry with me. To this day, I am consumed with shame over my "selfishness" nearly every time I do have to cry.

Many children live out this same pattern—one that the psychologist and therapist Lindsay Gibson has described in detail in her book *Adult Children of Emotionally Immature Parents*. When the children of emotionally immature parents grow up, we tend to be self-effacing to a fault, and so deeply mistrustful of our own moods and needs that we feel completely incapable of revealing any aspect of our inner lives to people. And emotionally immature parents, as Gibson writes, do not have to be abusive in order for their actions to have such a devastating impact. Quite frequently, they're just flawed people who were never educated about emotional coping skills or healthy boundary setting, and who lacked support so thoroughly that the only friend they thought they could find was their child.

My parents' loneliness was systemic. Both of them had invisible disabilities that wearied them and put them in frequent pain, but they both moved through the world looking and passing as "normal." They both got stuck working backbreaking, unfulfilling jobs that left them constantly fretting about money and feeling that they'd been trapped in a dead end. We lived in the suburbs of Cleveland, a city that was rapidly deteriorating and bleeding out both career opportunities and people, which made it even more difficult for them to find other opportunities and ways to connect. And they both held inside them a great deal of trauma that they never sought help for, other than by offloading pressure onto their child.

My parents were white, suburban people with a mortgage, two cars, two kids, and two pets. Yet for all their privileges, their suffering was systemic—completely molded by a lack of economic opportunities, limited educational and childcare options, no access to quality therapy, and a legacy of familial issues that reached back decades into the past. As their child, I bore the brunt of this, but I just thought that meant I was personally broken. A similar dynamic plays out for kids who are penalized for learning in ways their schools aren't designed for, for girls who observe their mothers obsessively dieting and then learn to scrutinize their own bodies, for kids from poor families who can't help but compare themselves to families who come from more wealth, and so many other groups that have been led to feel inadequate. Because Systemic Shame is a belief system that teaches that individual bad behavior is the root of all problems, it touches the life and warps the perceptions of just about anybody who is struggling under forces beyond their personal control.

Kids are very good at trying to figure out what society's unspoken rules are, because learning those rules protects them from being rejected or abandoned by their caregivers. Conformity is truly a life-and-death matter for many young people, and they can't help but form a connection to the forces they depend upon for survival. This is why children typically learn gender stereotypes by the time they are eighteen to twenty-four months old,[10] and absorb racial stereotypes by as young as two years.[11] By age three, children are capable of realizing when they have violated gender or racial expectations and show signs of feeling shame when they do.[12]

Children appear to be hardwired to find and adopt the attitudes of the culture that surrounds them, even when those attitudes are cruel or unfair. Society is guided by a stunning number of rules that we never explain to children directly, including many rules we are barely consciously aware of ourselves, because they have become so second nature to us. We divide children up by gender starting when they're very young, for example, having them use separate restrooms, draping them in gendered clothing, or even by asking them to line up girl-boy-girl-boy at school. Usually, we don't even bother to tell children why we are doing so—and in fact, we might not be aware why we're doing it ourselves. Gendering kids is just a thing that is done, one of the rules of society so pervasive and invisible it's practically in the air that we breathe.

Kids' minds have to adapt to all these unspoken expectations by noticing patterns quickly and conforming to them as though their life depended on it—because it often does. Children who cross gender lines are at risk of being criticized or even abused by the very adults who should be promising them unconditional acceptance. It's no wonder, then, that so many children learn to become aggressive policers of gender by the time they're in school. They believe that by shaming the boy who dances too femininely, and recoiling from the masculine girl with disgust, they're helping preserve rules that are so sacred they can barely be spoken of.

As the psychologist Lawrence Hirschfield writes in the *Handbook of Race, Racism, and the Developing Child*, a kid doesn't have to be brought up in a bigoted environment in order to wind up holding prejudiced attitudes. Just as a child born to immigrant parents learns to speak with the accent of the place they grew up rather than their parents' accent, children raised by antiracist, feminist parents still learn the racism, sexism, transphobia, and other biases that surround them in the culture. This makes Systemic Shame very difficult to escape.

My good friend Kelly is a fat liberationist, and they've spent years disconnecting from weight loss culture and healing their own internalized fatphobia. They've strived to raise their two children to see fat bodies as equally worthy of love and respect as thin ones. They celebrate their own body, and the bodies of other fat people, in their own photography and visual art. But none of this has prevented society's fatphobia from infecting Kelly's kids.

One day, Kelly was watching their eldest daughter play a video game, who shared that she would never make her character fat.

"I don't like fat characters," Kelly's daughter stated simply, as she fiddled with the character customization screen. "Your body is fine, Mom. But I don't want to be fat—being fat is worse."

"It's the kind of statement that if an adult said it to me, it would drive me up the wall," Kelly tells me. But rather than reacting in anger, Kelly asked their daughter why this was the case. Why did she think fat bodies were worse?

"My daughter told me she would be sad if she were fat, because people treat fat people far worse," Kelly explains. "And I didn't have a good comeback for that. I tried to teach my kids that all bodies are good bodies, and here's how you treat people with respect . . . but my kids started talking about fat bodies being worse by the time my eldest was age four."

Shame exerts a dramatic influence on how kids feel and behave. Researchers have repeatedly observed that kindergarten-age girls often get anxious and underperform in math when they are reminded of the stereotype that math is a "boys" activity, for instance.[13] This effect is equally common among adults, and it is unrelated to one's actual mathematic ability. Even women and girls who enjoy math suffer a dip in performance when they are faced with sexist stereotypes. Similarly, Black children are often hyperaware of racial stereotypes about their intelligence, which in turn hinders their standardized testing performance.[14]

This pattern, often referred to as the "stereotype threat" effect, can hit particularly hard when a stereotyped person cares a great deal about doing well. The higher the stakes of the test—and the more symbolic significance it carries—the more the fear of failure can hurt.[15] Stereotype threat has been extensively studied, and researchers have found that it can strike absolutely any group of people that has ever been negatively stereotyped or blamed for their social position. Girls experience stereotype threat when facing the fact they've been excluded historically from science and math,[16] Latinx people face stereotype threat when confronted with the expectation that they'll take longer than their white peers to complete their education,[17] people from lower-class backgrounds go through it when thrown into high-pressure performance situations such as job interviews, and much more.[18] Even when people recognize that the stereotypes being applied to them are unfair, the literature shows that stereotype threat still can impact how they behave and how they view themselves.

One way that young Black girls often cope with sexist and racist stereotypes, research shows, is by leaning hard into perfectionism and achievement.[19] This is a very common way individuals attempt to process Systemic Shame. When society conditions us into thinking that our identities are undeserving of respect or that we're fundamentally bad people, we try to overcompensate and earn our way into acceptance by being as impressive as we can possibly be.

Black women are the most highly educated group in the United States[20] and also the group with the greatest gains in entrepreneurship. Despite these facts, they are also one of the most poorly paid groups, making far less than white men, white women, and Black men in similar lines of work.[21] This illustrates pretty clearly that individual effort does not offer a handy solution to internalized shame or oppression. Systemic Shame teaches marginalized people that they must do great things and be incredibly strong and reliable in order to overcome their social position—but no amount of individual effort (or self-love) is actually enough.

How do you know if you're experiencing personal Systemic Shame? Here is a brief questionnaire to get you thinking about how it might manifest in your own life.

PERSONAL SHAME CHECKLIST

Read each of the following statements and check off any statement that feels true to your experience.

1. I often feel intense negativity toward myself. ___
2. I'm disgusted or embarrassed when I recognize traits in other people that remind me of myself. ___
3. I don't ever feel like I could really be a good person. ___
4. I can't seem to take pride in any good things that I've done. ___
5. I'm constantly telling myself to stop screwing up and be better. ___
6. I have to do everything on my own, because nobody else ever has my back. ___
7. I'm always worrying about how my actions might look to other people. ___

Level 2: Interpersonal Shame

Personal feelings of Systemic Shame can very easily develop into interpersonal shame, the second and middlemost layer. Once you have internalized a number of negative views and attitudes toward yourself, directing that same judgmental view toward others can become reflexive.

It's quite sensible to pull away from others when we have no expectation of being loved or believe that we are undeserving of love. The more a person hates themselves, the less likely they are to reach out for help. There is perhaps no better example of this problem than in the realms of public health and mental health stigma. In a systematic review of more than 140 previously published studies, Sarah Clement and colleagues found that when a person feels ashamed of their mental illness and believes on some level that they are at fault for their symptoms, it prevents them from seeking therapy or asking for support.[22] Similar findings emerge when we look at what prevents people with substance addictions[23] and people experiencing domestic violence[24] from reaching out.

Systemic Shame offers us a ruggedly individualistic worldview that says our lives can only get better if we personally work (and suffer) very hard. And if anyone does check in on us or offers aid, Systemic Shame will tell us to view it as an intrusion or an insult.

One person that I interviewed for this book, Connor, told me that when he was in elementary school, his family briefly became homeless. For several months, his small family of three crowded into a tent in a national park several miles from their old home—a position Connor's dad was absolutely incapable of acknowledging. When members of their church noticed that something was up and asked Connor if he needed food or somewhere to shower, Connor's dad fumed in outrage and insisted they all stop attending church services.

"He was a second-generation immigrant who carried baggage about being self-sufficient," Connor tells me. "If I would have taken food from other people, he would have seen that as some kind of debasement."

Later, after the family was lucky enough to get back on their feet, Connor's dad and mom became ardent conservatives. They'd always been right-leaning, he says, but after they escaped homelessness they spoke of other homeless people and the welfare system as if it were a national disgrace.

"There was this feeling in the household that if they could claw their way up from living in a tent and never wound their pride by telling anybody, then everyone else should do that, too," he says.

Rather than recognizing they shared the traumatic experience of homelessness with millions of other people, Connor's parents focused on psychologically separating themselves from other homeless people. They were ashamed of their condition, found it unspeakable in fact, and so they could not face looking at anyone else who reminded them of their own lowest point.

When we shame and judge ourselves, we become more likely to assume that other people are untrustworthy, too. If I see a parent in the park ignoring their agitated kid, I might judge them as neglectful without wondering how late they were up working the night before and how little support they might have. If an old high school buddy posts a photo of herself throwing a small party during the pandemic, I might grumble to myself that she is responsible for Covid's spread, because it feels more satisfying to point the finger at her than consider all the ways my local and federal government have failed to protect me. Interpersonal Systemic Shame makes it easy to see people's laziness, sloppiness, or apathy as the source of the problem rather than a consequence of repeated structural failures.

Interpersonal Systemic Shame often involves blaming and shaming people who share identities or experiences with us, because they reflect the qualities we've been conditioned to hate in ourselves. Thousands upon thousands of abuse survivors did precisely this in the spring of 2022, when actor Johnny Depp sued his ex-wife Amber Heard for defamation because she had referred to herself as a survivor of sexual violence.[25] Thousands upon thousands of DV survivors flocked to Johnny Depp's defense online, claiming in comment sections and livestream chats that Amber Heard was giving "a bad name to victims everywhere."[26]

This, unfortunately, is not a rare occurrence. Many women and abuse survivors wish to believe that the world is just and fair, and that they can avoid future violence if they only make the right choices.[27] Many people are taught to think in this way as they're growing up. Most college "rape prevention" programs focus on what actions potential victims should take if they wish to stay safe, rather than looking at which steps the institution can take to make people less vulnerable to assault,[28] for instance.

If you're a woman riddled with Systemic Shame regarding your own abuse and you want to find a way to distinguish yourself from Amber Heard, you'll find plenty of personal failings to latch on to. In audio recordings of the couple's fights, Heard mocks Depp, laughs in his face, and discusses having hit him. She uses drugs and appears to have jealous meltdowns when she feels abandoned. She's not a likable victim. Unfortunately, many survivors are primed to pick these imperfections apart. Research shows that when presented with the details of sexual assault cases, many women attempt to empathize with the *perpetrator* rather than the victim, because identifying with victimhood is far more emotionally threatening.[29]

There's a sick, twisted resentment of other people that interpersonal Systemic Shame creates in us. We learn to beat up others the same way we brutalize ourselves. We hate any signs of weakness or imperfection that reminds us we cannot always act perfectly and protect ourselves from all harm.

Here is a brief tool to help you examine whether you experience interpersonal Systemic Shame.

INTERPERSONAL SHAME CHECKLIST

Read each of the following statements and check off any statement that feels true to your experience.

1. When someone checks in on me or asks if I'm "okay," it fills me with rage, embarrassment, or defensiveness. ___

2. I don't trust other people to know what they're doing. It's better to just handle things myself. ___

3. I really hate it when someone of the same identity group as me (people of the same race, gender, class, sexual orientation, or other identity) behaves in a stereotypical way that makes us "look bad" to everyone else. ___

4. It feels like nobody around me has any idea of what I'm going through. ___

5. I'm terrified that the stereotypes others apply to me and to people like me might actually be true. ___

6. Most people seem to make the same mistakes over and over again without ever learning. ___

7. Being around other people is stifling. I only feel at ease when I am alone and can't be judged. ___

Level 3: Global Shame

Global Systemic Shame convinces us that humanity as a whole is filled with "bad" people, and that working together or building a better society is basically hopeless. It takes all the mistrust, victim-blaming, and isolation that we see in the other two layers of Systemic Shame and applies it on an even wider scale, to all of society.

We see global Systemic Shame at work when people discuss issues such as climate change and global pandemics through the lens of personal choice. We have been *trained* to see such issues in this way. Messaging from both large corporations and many of our governments have convinced us to focus on individual habits rather than the laws and economic incentives that actually cause temperatures to rise and deadly viruses to spread.

In her essay "Confessions of a Former Pandemic Shamer," the comic illustrator and author Shelby Lorman describes how she initially coped with the stresses of the pandemic by blaming individuals for taking too many risks and spreading Covid. She remembers combing through her friends' social media posts in the spring of 2020, looking for risky decision-making and irresponsibility to obsess over and condemn.

"In the first few months of the pandemic, I was an eternal Charlie from *It's Always Sunny* with his wall of suspects and red string," she writes.[30] "Assessing who was trustworthy and who had moved down the rankings."

Lorman made social media posts reprimanding people who held small social gatherings or didn't wear the right kinds of masks. When she did share genuinely helpful information about Covid mitigation, she still wrapped it in a judgmental tone: "You are failing. Here is why. Part $^1/_{100}$." She says that for herself and for many of her friends, speaking from a place of "moral superiority" felt satisfying. But as time went on and governments and corporations continued to make decisions that put lives at risk on a larger scale, Lorman started doubting whether an individualistic approach made any sense.

"I felt myself toggling mightily between the weight of what was happening around us and the smaller, more textural sins," she writes, "the ones I felt I could control or understand."

That tricky toggling helps explain how Global Systemic Shame can make us both anxious *and* apathetic at the same time. Global Systemic Shame holds that individual people are at fault for all the world's problems. It's not much of a logical jump to conclude from there that "humanity is the real virus,"[31] or to believe humans *deserve* to die out in the climate apocalypse. Such statements might sound extreme, but they pop up shockingly often in conversations about these issues. Social scientists and environmental activists have been sounding the alarm for years about the rise of ecofacism, the belief that in order for the planet to be saved, a large number of humans need to (and *deserve to*) die.[32] During times of crisis, such as early into the Covid-19 pandemic, these beliefs tend to become even more popular in the news media and online.[33] If the suffering that's all around us was caused by bad people making stupid or evil decisions, then humanity is due for a moral reckoning.

Ellen tells me that by shaming herself for her daughter's self-harm—and by coping with the shame by then holding herself responsible for saving all self-harming kids—she collapsed into a profound depression. She was consumed by thoughts of the silent suffering that must be lurking around her, and of all the children lacking mental health support throughout the world, that she'd never get to help. Her family's personal tragedies had become symbolic of a far larger societal ill—one she couldn't ever possibly mend. Imagining a way out of her grief and self-loathing seemed impossible, because the pain of the world was too big.

"Ironically that made me about as depressed as Jenna had probably been," she says. "Nobody was doing anything right by these kids, least of all me. There was no light in the world anymore, no light."

If we believe that individual action is the only way to change the world but that it's already too late to do so, our minds can go to some incredibly dark places. Global Systemic Shame is a cynical, despairing feeling, a rejection of hope and sometimes even life itself.

Here is a short checklist to help you examine whether you are impacted by global Systemic Shame.

GLOBAL SHAME CHECKLIST

Read each of the following statements and check off any statement that feels true to your experience.

1. One of the biggest problems in the world right now is that most people do not care enough. ___

2. It is difficult for me to imagine leading a life that truly matters. ___

3. It seems impossible to keep up with all the obligations I would need to, if I truly wanted to be a "good person." ___

4. I don't have warm feelings toward most of humanity. ___

5. I don't feel like I belong to any kind of meaningful community. ___

6. I don't really know what I stand for in life, or what truly matters to me. ___

7. Sometimes, I get to thinking that humanity deserves all the terrible things that are happening to us. ___

Life Does Not Need to Be Like This

I recognize that the last few sections of the book have been really bleak. I thought it was important to take a moment here to emphasize that even with Systemic Shame being as widespread as it is, and despite how much damage it has caused us, living this way is not inevitable. Throughout most of human history, and across a variety of cultures, people did not approach social issues or think about shame in this way. And for each level of Systemic Shame that we might experience, there are many equally powerful, counteracting feelings we can learn to harness. Here's some alternatives to Systemic Shame:

Level of Systemic Shame	Healthy Emotional Alternatives
Personal shame (Hatred of self and fear of judgment)	Radical self-acceptance Compassion Neutrality Joy Pleasure
Interpersonal shame (Mistrust of others and isolation)	Vulnerability Trust Identification Curiosity Pride
Global shame (Anxiety and despair about humanity's future)	Humility Hope Shared mourning Shared celebration Collaboration Finding one's purpose

Systemic Shame has become a worldwide source of emotional suffering only in the last few centuries, and it's taken a firm hold over our political discourse really only in the last few dozen years. Even today, it is possible to navigate the world as a marginalized person (or to care about structural issues like climate change or racism) without descending into self-hatred, social isolation, and global pessimism. In our recent history, there have been influential social movements that did not rely on shaming individuals for their choices—and they were far more successful for it. And there are numerous healthy and vibrant communities in the world that support marginalized people in their full, messy complexity rather than holding each person to some impossible benchmark of perfection. We'll take lessons from these groups and movements in the latter half of this book.

In the next chapter, we'll examine the origins of Systemic Shame and explore how it gained such a foothold in our society.

CHAPTER 2

The Origins of Systemic Shame

Choosing to Get Hit

In the early 1920s, a new public health crisis was emerging. Many consumers were buying automobiles for the very first time and receiving absolutely zero training for how to handle them safely, as driver's licenses were not introduced in most American states until about 1935. In addition, most roads had not been built with automobiles in mind, and instead were developed for horse-drawn carriages as well as pedestrians. As the number of unprepared drivers on too-narrow roads expanded rapidly, so did the number of accidents and deaths. From 1910 to 1915, the number of car-accident-related deaths jumped from about 1,600 to 6,800. From 1915 to 1920, it nearly doubled to 12,155.[1] As the historian Peter Norton reports, the majority of victims were pedestrians, many of them children and elderly people.

Before the rise of the automobile, people walked in the middle of roads, gathered on roadsides to chat and trade goods, and even let their children dash along the sides of the streets.[2] But the introduction of cars changed all that. In just a few short years, roads morphed from multiuse public spaces similar to parks to the sole territory of hulking, fast-paced machines.

At first, the American public blamed the automotive industry for the resulting upsurge in accidents. Political cartoons from the period depict cars rolling over piles of bodies, or show the Grim Reaper creepily oozing from a vehicle's grille to claim the lives of women and children.[3]

"The horrors of war appear to be less appalling than the horrors of peace," read a front-page piece in *The New York Times* on November 23, 1924. "The automobile looms up as a far more destructive piece of mechanism than the machine gun."[4]

This messaging was bad for the car-selling business—and for developers who wanted to expand cities and reshape them to give priority to cars. So across the country, car manufacturers began lobbying the government, downplaying their role in the pedestrian death crisis—and laying the blame on *individuals* for having gotten hit. The problem wasn't the rapid expansion of car culture and the lack of wide roads and sidewalks built to support it, nor was it an issue that the car industry and drivers were almost completely unregulated.[5] No, the real issue was that pedestrians were *jaywalking*, a new term the automotive industry had just invented.[6]

In the mid-1920s, auto industry groups began meeting with lawmakers throughout the country, offering them example traffic ordinances making jaywalking a punishable crime—and marking jaywalkers as culpable for their injuries and deaths.[7]

"In the early days of the automobile, it was a driver's job to avoid you, not your job to avoid them," says Peter Norton.[8] But after the passage of these ordinances, the legal status reversed. It was pedestrians who now were legally obligated to "do the right thing" by looking out for cars. Government safety posters from the 1920s and '30s depict jaywalkers as reckless, ignorant clowns. In 1925, the AAA staged a public mock trial for a child who had jaywalked; hundreds of Detroit schoolchildren watched as he was publicly shamed and sentenced to cleaning chalkboards for his crime.[9]

The blame for a system-wide failing had effectively been shifted onto the people most harmed by it. In the years to come, corporations and the American government would work to give everything from smoking to seatbelt-wearing to getting vaccinated to purchasing a gun the jaywalking treatment, usually with great success. For a variety of historical and cultural reasons, American culture was uniquely primed to accept the victim-blaming logic of Systemic Shame.

The History of Shame

The word *shame* comes from the Proto-Indo-European root word *skem,* which means "to cover or hide."[10] Across a wide variety of cultures and time periods, people experiencing shame are described as turning away, being covered, or withdrawing themselves.[11] This is a theme that will reemerge many times in this book: Shame is a hiding-away, a separating of a person from the society that surrounds them.

In writings from ancient Greece, to ancient Rome, to Confucian China, to medieval Europe, shame is described as both an inward feeling that you are bad *and* the recognition that your community would look down on you for your actions. Shame has always had a lot to do with a person's social position:[12] Children are more likely to be described as deserving shame than adults, historically, as are people who are enslaved, or in a lower class or caste.[13] People who feel shame exhibit the behaviors that signal being low status in their society: hunched shoulders, eyes that avert the gaze of others, and modest dress. To owe a debt is also, historically, to experience shame,[14] marking you as lesser than the person you owe money to.

Social stigma and shame have always been connected. Originally, the word *stigma* referred to the markings or brandings put on the skin of criminals, permanently identifying their crimes to others.[15] *Stigmatizing* was the physical act of marking someone as a rule-violator and a person deserving of shame. Similar forms of public shaming included the throwing of thieves into stocks in the town square during the Middle Ages, or the placing of painful mouth gags on rude or "scolding" women in England during the sixteenth and seventeenth centuries.[16] The idea that people who cross society's boundaries deserve to be publicly marked and punished has been with us for a very long time.

Historically, many philosophers believed shame was necessary to rein in bad behavior. Roughly ten percent of Confucius's writing discussed why society needed to teach people to feel shame in order to help them adhere to social standards.[17] Aristotle claimed that while shame could be painful, it was necessary to help people control childish or immoral impulses. There's this recurring idea we see throughout human history that holds that deep down humans are amoral animals that must have their worst desires contained by shame. We even see it in Sigmund Freud's claim that all humans carry a wild, impulsive id within them that must be reined in by the rule-abiding, shame-filled superego. Though the belief that shame is necessary has existed in many human societies for a very long time, it became far more prominent under Christianity[18] and with the rise of agriculture, industry, and income inequality.[19] Generally, we see that the cultures that tend to rely on shame the most are the ones that are the most unequal and stratified.

Why Societies Shame

In his book *Shame: A Brief History*, the historian Peter Stearns describes how shaming became a far more widespread practice in cultures that moved away from communal living and hunting and gathering for food, and toward farming, accumulating private property, and living with more isolation and inequality.[20] As a general rule, when a society is more interdependent and egalitarian, fewer activities are seen as shame-worthy. But once groups of people start cleaving off from one another and class divides begin to appear, shame emerges as a tool that societies use to hold people in their proper place. Eventually, shame becomes systematized, and gets built into a culture's core belief systems, teachings, and laws.

More egalitarian cultures are less likely to attach shame to sex or nudity, Stearns observes, and are less likely to publicly punish community members for failing to "pull their weight" when it comes to gathering food and resources. When European colonizers began invading what eventually became North America, they noticed many of the Native cultures they encountered did not practice public shaming in the way European Christians did. This dismayed and confused them, and they took it as evidence of Native people's moral inferiority.[21] Native philosophers, for their part, often viewed the harsh judgment and inequality of European cultures to be inhumane.[22]

Stearns describes shaming as downright "ubiquitous" in agricultural societies.[23] And there's a reason shame was a more prominent tool in cultures where food is grown[24] (especially grown privately) than in ones where it's collectively gathered. Foraging and hunting is a large numbers game. An individual person's odds of success on any given day are pretty low and subject to chance. The hunter who works the "hardest" isn't necessarily the one who kills the biggest prey, or even makes any kill at all. It's only by working together and pooling the fruits of everyone's hard work (and luck) that hunter-gatherer societies keep everyone fed.[25]

Hard work and shame are looked at quite differently in most agricultural cultures. One reason for this is, as a great deal of anthropological research shows, farmers have to work far longer hours than foragers in order to survive.[26] In societies where people farm, there is a much higher risk of famine and malnutrition than in hunter-gatherer societies, and a much higher infant mortality rate.[27] At the same time, humans who farm their food tend to have more children than hunter-gatherers do, in part to use their children as a source of free labor.[28] Whereas hunting and gathering for food is often a non-hierarchical process, in farming there is often a clear status divide between the people who are forced to work the land and the people who manage it or own it. In humanity's shift toward agriculture, then, we see some of the first seeds of inequality taking root.

In more egalitarian cultures there is less privacy, and less wealth being hoarded; there's less to be protective of, in other words, or to be secretive about. There is also less need to use shame to influence how people act. In an article for the journal *Nature*, the anthropologist Daniel Smith and his colleagues write that many hunter-gatherer societies use storytelling to pass down important values and encourage social collaboration, instead of shaming people and making examples of them.[29] When everyone in a society knows everybody else, and everyone gathers regularly to share food and celebration, it's far easier to spread social norms.[30]

Hallmarks of a Shame-Based Culture	Hallmarks of an Egalitarian Culture
Competition	Cooperation
Extreme wealth inequality	Moderate or negligible wealth inequality
Private property ownership	Shared or public resources
Isolation	Interconnectedness
Anonymity	Recognition
Strict standards for behavior	Many ways of behaving are "normal"
Rule violators are seen as "broken" or "sick"	Rules are regularly questioned and reevaluated
Bureaucracy and laws maintain the group "order"	Debate, discussion, and social teachings maintain the group norms
Denial of diversity	Difference is tolerated or accepted
Sex negativity	Sex positivity or neutrality
Suffering is moral, pleasure is sinful	Pleasure and rest are celebrated, mourning is shared

Agricultural and industrial societies are often larger and more diffuse than hunter-gatherer ones, so social norms can't spread as easily within them. Instead, social values get transmitted by force—often using processes like incarceration, banishment, stigmatization, and shaming. In Europe in the Middle Ages, jails and sanitariums emerged as a way to punish people for failing to pay debts, disturbing the peace, refusing to work, or physically attacking others. Breaking the rules of society now meant you were hidden away rather than tended to and cared for by your community.[31] Around this same time, the concept of people being mentally *disordered* began to emerge.[32] Debtors, criminals, and persons with mental illness were all housed in the exact same facilities as one another, and generally were seen as suffering from the same moral disease. The idea that some people were innately sick and needed to be kept out of the community became increasingly popular.

Christianity became far more shame-based during the medieval period as these changes happened. Though early Christians had believed in the importance of grace for all people, in the Middle Ages, Christian teachings began relying heavily on the need to use shame to reinforce the social hierarchy and keep people in line.[33] Christian leaders from St. Augustine to Martin Luther preached that shame was necessary to make people atone for their sins and follow society's rules.[34] Public-shaming rituals and punishments exploded in popularity during this time, and the word *shame* started appearing in books and pamphlets somewhere between three times and six times more often than it had in prior centuries.[35]

A culture with a great deal of wealth inequality is also one that's more likely to shame women for their sex lives, according to Stearns, because the more wealth and property a person owns, the more they'll want to control who inherits it. It's perhaps for this reason that medieval European societies became increasingly obsessed with preserving female virginity, and with arranging and documenting marriages and official heirs.[36] A variety of new legal systems emerged during this time to keep track of property ownership, tax payments, citizenship, and class status as well. In this we can see how shame and bureaucracy so often become intertwined with each other, both being used to uphold an increasingly divided social order.

Once a culture of stratification and shame overtook Europe during the Middle Ages, it never really went away. Shame continued to play an integral role in the legal system and the church and became a core part of how people explained the causes of social ills like poverty, addiction, and disease. Eventually, this worldview culminated in the rise of the Puritans, whose belief in the moral power of shame would become the backbone of American culture.

Shame in the American Psyche

The Puritans who colonized North America were religious extremists who believed in personal responsibility above all else. They saw self-discipline and self-denial as the ultimate virtues and believed shame motivated people to behave correctly in every realm of life, from sexuality, to child-rearing, to having a strong work ethic.[37] And it's in their teachings and practices that we see the beginning of Systemic Shame's presence in the United States.

Puritans lived in isolated communities that ostracized anyone they saw as weak or lazy. If you couldn't behave "correctly" and pull your own weight, you were pretty much on your own. Even though early Christianity preached the importance of community building and mutual support, by the seventeenth century Puritan Christianity had adopted the exact opposite value system. Puritans believed independence was the mark of being a good person, and that needing support was a sign of depravity. As the economic historian R. H. Tawney put it, Puritans saw poverty as "not a misfortune to be pitied and relieved, but a moral failing to be condemned."[38] They also believed individual people had a moral obligation to accumulate as much wealth as possible, and that receiving charity made a person weak.

One thing that's particularly fascinating about the Puritanical approach to shame is how long it persisted despite all evidence it wasn't working. Puritan communities struggled and starved due to their isolation and obsession with independence. They experienced elevated infant mortality rates[39] and rampant poverty and malnutrition.[40] In their child-rearing, Puritans expected kids to behave like little adults, even forcing their developing bodies to sit in adult postures. When children proved incapable of doing the developmentally impossible, they were punished, reprimanded, and shamed for it anyway.[41] It's astonishing how often human beings reach for shame as a tool of social control, see it failing, and conclude that more shame is what's needed.

American culture was built upon the Puritan idea that individual hard work is what makes a person good.[42] Our laws, national myths, and much of the media we consume is rooted in the idea that any person can succeed in life, so long as they exercise a ton of willpower and work very hard. This ideology makes it extremely difficult to talk about systemic barriers to success, such as structural racism, ableism, or the patriarchy.

To this day, far more Americans endorse Puritanical beliefs than do people in other countries.[43] We're more likely to believe that the world is basically fair and that our legal and economic system is just.[44] We have more conservative views about sex compared to people in most other countries,[45] and if a person does accidentally get pregnant or contract a sexually transmitted infection, we are more likely to think of them as "irresponsible." Many Americans also think that victims of sexual assault, abuse, and homelessness deserve their fates.[46]

Like our Puritan predecessors, Americans take a more punitive approach to child-rearing than much of the world does, spanking our kids more often and verbally reprimanding them at higher rates.[47] We also arrest and jail a far larger percentage of our population than most other nations do. Forty-five percent of all Americans have an immediate family member who has been incarcerated; for Black families, that number jumps all the way up to 63 percent.[48]

This is true despite decades of psychological research showing that corporal punishment and incarceration do not change a person's behavior for the better,[49] and only cause children and adults alike to feel more traumatized, unsupported, and ashamed.[50]

Though the punitive approach to social problems has never really paid off for us, many Americans continue to believe that shame is the answer. Shame is a huge part of the religious history and culture of America (as well as many other countries shaped by colonization), and it's infused into our legal, economic, educational, and criminal justice systems.

Psychologists have been studying the effect of Puritanism on the American consciousness for decades and developed a well-validated measure of Puritanical attitudes called the Protestant Work Ethic Scale.[51] Originally created in the 1970s, the Protestant Work Ethic Scale is still popular with researchers today, because it's such an effective predictor of a person's social outlook and their political attitudes. People high in the scale look down on those who receive unemployment and welfare benefits,[52] and are endlessly dedicated to their own jobs.[53] They believe convicted criminals should serve longer sentences,[54] and that the government should not intervene to address matters of prejudice or structural inequality.[55] Generally speaking, people high in the Protestant Work Ethic Scale believe that the world is fair, that hard work is the key to living a meaningful life, and that taking time for leisure or requiring help from others makes you a weak, immoral person.

The Protestant Work Ethic Scale is nineteen items long, and is separated into four subscales, which measure a person's attitudes toward hard work, independence, leisure, and self-discipline, respectively. Completing this measure may help you reflect on how much you've internalized Puritanical values.

THE PROTESTANT WORK ETHIC SCALE

Adapted from Mirels & Garret (1971)

Please read each of the sentences listed below, and indicate how much you agree with each statement by selecting a number from the following scale:

5 Strongly Agree

4 Agree

3 Neither Agree nor Disagree

2 Disagree

1 Strongly Disagree

Hard Work

I believe most people who fail at their jobs have not really tried hard enough. ___

Doing my best at work gives me great satisfaction. ___

Hard work almost always offers a guarantee of success. ___

In general, anyone who is willing and able to work hard has a good chance of succeeding. ___

Most people who don't succeed in life are just plain lazy. ___

Distaste for hard work usually reflects a weakness of character. ___

Independence

Cheap loans are often just a ticket to careless spending. ___

I personally believe that the self-made person is likely to be more ethical than someone who is born to wealth. ___

I believe that money acquired easily is usually spent unwisely. ___

Most people will have a good life if they work hard enough. ___

Leisure

Life would be less meaningful if we had more leisure time. ___

Most people spend too much time on unprofitable amusements. ___

I feel uneasy when I have not worked for a long time. ___

People in my country think too much about fun and vacations and too little about working harder. ___

Self-Discipline

I often feel that I would be more successful if I sacrificed certain pleasures. ___

Suffering makes life more meaningful. ___

The person who can approach an unpleasant task with enthusiasm is the one who gets ahead. ___

The most difficult challenges often turn out to be the most rewarding. ___

Interpreting your results: Total scores on the Protestant Work Ethic Scale range from 18 to 90, with the average respondent scoring around 61 points.[56] The more 4s and 5s you list within a particular subscale, the more highly you endorse that particular value.

As you read through this scale, you may also find it useful to contemplate your upbringing, the lessons your caregivers and teachers might have given you regarding such ideals. Even if you don't consciously agree with many of these items, you might notice they feel intuitively or emotionally true, particularly when you're disappointed in yourself or someone else. Later on in this chapter, we will reflect on how attitudes like these may have shaped our opinions on various social issues. But for now just keep these statements and values in mind, and as we continue to move through American history, notice how the obsession with personal responsibility and independence continues popping up.

Systemic Shame: Where Markets Meet Morality

Because of its deeply rooted Puritanical history, the United States has always defaulted to treating public crises as personal problems. For example, for the first hundred years that the United States existed, there was zero government regulation of who got to call themselves a doctor.[57] There wasn't any oversight over medical schools, either.[58] Selecting a reputable doctor was an individual patient's responsibility.[59] Of course, most Americans could not afford to hire a doctor at all, and that too was not considered the government's problem to solve. Individual consumers held all the power to decide what was legitimate medical treatment—and could only earn access to any treatment at all through considerable wealth.

The public health philosopher Daniel Beauchamp writes that the United States approaches social crises using a framework he calls market justice.[60] Under market justice, a person's only real source of power in the world is their wealth, and that the only way to wield that power is by exercising the freedom of consumer choice: "voting with your dollar" rather than in the polling booth. According to the logic of market justice, the government shouldn't step in to protect vulnerable groups of people, and it shouldn't tax the wealthy or regulate large industries to benefit the larger community, either. Every problem should be solved by individuals behaving responsibly and spending their own money well.

Market justice, Beauchamp says, is a strong counterpoint to social justice. A social justice issue, he says, is one where individual choice can never do enough to reduce risk. Take, for example, a massive power plant that fills an entire community's air with dangerous smog. If you live near the power plant, you can't just *choose* not to inhale toxic air. And even if a few people in the neighborhood can afford to decide to move away, an entire community probably can't pack up and get away from the power plant either. The pollution will take a visible toll on the whole area, filling hospitals with sick people and making it difficult for anybody to come into work.

In a situation like this, Beauchamp says, people will eventually recognize pollution is a problem that requires collective, systemic solutions—not individual willpower. Members of the community might organize protests against the power plant or sue the power company to get compensation for illnesses or disabilities they've developed. With enough public pressure, the government might step in and force the power plant to install air filters. Through this process of collective action, pollution is forcibly changed from market justice issue to a social justice one.

Unfortunately, when it comes to most public health problems, there's usually some element of personal choice involved in who experiences a risk and who doesn't. This makes finding a collective solution and pushing for social justice then becomes a lot more difficult. Take for example another major source of air pollution in the United States: cigarette smoke. The tobacco industry is responsible for manufacturing cigarettes, advertising them, and filling them with deadly chemicals. And the federal government got millions of Americans hooked on nicotine by giving away free cigarette rations to soldiers from 1918 until the 1970s.[61] Despite these external, systemic causes, it's true that every smoker physically *chooses* to put cigarette smoke in their body, and because of this, they can be blamed for the consequences of that decision.

Market Justice	Social Justice
Health is a personal responsibility	Health is a community responsibility
Access to resources is determined by one's ability to pay	Essential resources are provided to all
Government regulation is limited or nonexistent	Government regulation is necessary
Individual willpower determines morality	Community well-being determines morality
People are only responsible for themselves	All people's actions affect one another
If a person suffers, it's because they lack money or willpower	If a person suffers, it's because society has failed them

Hallmarks of the market justice and social justice approaches to public health, adapted from Beauchamp (1976)

"Market justice forces a basic distinction between the harm caused by a factory polluting the atmosphere and the harm caused by the cigarette or alcohol industries," Beauchamp writes, "because in the latter case those that are harmed are perceived as engaged in 'voluntary' behavior."[62]

Beauchamp began writing about market justice in the 1970s, just as Big Tobacco was facing increased government scrutiny. The link between smoking and cancer was proving harder than ever to deny, and the industry was desperate to dodge the social justice consequences of increased regulations and fines. And in order to do this, Big Tobacco leaned heavily into market justice's view of smoking as a voluntary choice—and began systemically shaming consumers by claiming they were morally to *blame* for their choices.

Assuming the Risk

In 1965, Congress passed the Cigarette Labeling and Advertising Act, which required that all consumer tobacco products bear warning labels about the risks of smoking. This law came into effect just one year after the federal government finally banned tobacco companies from claiming cigarettes had health benefits. Both these policy changes were a long time in the making. Medical experts had known smoking caused lung cancer since at least the early 1950s; so had tobacco executives.[63] Yet for years the industry poured millions of dollars into hiding this fact, promoting smoking to doctors, misrepresenting the data on the health risks, and marketing certain cigarette brands as "safer" than others. But finally, in the 1960s, this was no longer allowed.

Since they could no longer deny the danger of smoking, the tobacco industry began to emphasize the liberating power of personal choice.[64] Everybody *knows* that smoking comes with risks, the industry claimed (even though they'd tried to prevent everybody from knowing that for years). And there were many resources available for those who wish to quit (including smoking cessation hotlines, developed by tobacco companies themselves).[65] When all these facts and resources were made available to consumers, Big Tobacco argued that each person could freely "assume the risks" of their own decisions. Cigarette ads from this period linked smoking with images of freedom, masculinity, and rugged independence, such as the Marlboro man, a stoic cowboy who can't be told what to do or how to live.[66]

As the documented health risks of smoking kept mounting, more and more strident anti-smoking laws continued passing all across the country. In the 1980s and '90s, smokers started suing Big Tobacco for its role in their illnesses. To try to get in front of this public relations disaster, Big Tobacco looked to American history—and learned from the example the automotive industry had set in the 1920s when they invented jaywalking.

Big Tobacco slowly shifted its messaging away from just celebrating *freedom* and into blaming individuals for getting sick.[67] For example, in the Supreme Court Case *Cipollone v. Liggett Group, Inc.* in 1992, the defense attorney Robert Northripp claimed that the tobacco industry could not be responsible for the death of lifelong smoker Rose Cipollone (or others like her), because she knew cigarettes were dangerous. After all, Cipollone only smoked cigarettes branded as "safer." *The New York Times* quoted him as saying:

"Our position is that when someone is bright, well-read and independent like Rose Cipollone was, and believes smoking causes lung cancer, as Rose Cipollone did, but enjoys smoking, that is her choice to make and we shouldn't second-guess her."[68]

At one point, this personal responsibility rhetoric was even applied to young children: Speaking to an anti-smoking activist in 1996, the R. J. Reynolds Tobacco Company chairman Charles Harper stated, "I will not restrict the right of anyone to smoke. If the children don't like to be in a smoky room . . . they'll leave."[69]

Of course, the tobacco industry lost quite a few lawsuits and wound up eventually becoming heavily regulated. But their personal responsibility rhetoric held off the passage of such laws for years, even decades in some cases, and muddied the moral waters enough to confuse many Americans about who was really at fault for lung cancer deaths and other health complications. In public opinion surveys, respondents increasingly came to view smokers as undesirable and irresponsible rather than as victims of a predatory industry.[70] In several studies, even ex-smokers were viewed less favorably than people who had never smoked, as if the choice to have ever used a carcinogen substance tainted them socially. Additionally, in several studies, smokers report that the stigma associated with smoking actively made it harder for them to quit (for example, by making it more difficult and costlier to be open with their doctors about their smoking status).[71]

Big Tobacco's strategy of blaming individuals for their own illnesses was wildly successful—and it had a massive impact on the cultural conversation, which other corporations quickly took note of. Beginning in the 1990s, a variety of different industries began blaming and shaming individual consumers for problems that their own deeds had created.

The Systemic Shame Boom

Throughout the 1990s, the American public was becoming more and more concerned about the health effects of foods high in trans fats, and the high sugar content of sodas and prepackaged snacks. In 1995, public health researchers coined the term *food desert*, drawing attention to the fact that impoverished people often live miles away from grocery stores and fresh produce.[72] The food and beverage industries were facing stiff criticism, and with it the risk of increased taxation and regulation. And so they adopted the very same strategy of individual blame and Systemic Shame that the automotive industry and Big Tobacco had pioneered, claiming that irresponsible and greedy people were at fault for such problems.

Representatives of the food and beverage industry began claiming in the 1990s that the health risks of high-trans-fat foods and sugar[73] were "common knowledge," just as the tobacco industry had claimed the public health risks of smoking were well known years before. If everybody already knew the hallmarks of good nutrition, they argued, there was no need for the government to intervene and change how food was produced.

Corporations like Nestlé worked alongside the meat and dairy industries, lobbying the federal government to edit the food pyramid to promote their products.[74] Foods were increasingly packaged as "fat-free," "diet-friendly," and "part of a balanced breakfast," which fed into the idea that a person's health is determined by what they freely choose to consume.[75] Public service announcements and news segments encouraged the public to eat healthfully and purchase the right foods for their kids. On daytime talk shows like *Ricki Lake* and *The Maury Povich Show,* fat people and people in poverty were vilified for how they ate and dressed, and parents of fat children were treated as abusive and publicly shamed.[76]

As a child of the 1990s I still vividly remember witnessing a *Maury Povich* segment where a bariatric physician tore into the parents of several large infants (nearly all of them Black), telling them it was their fault their children faced an increased risk of cardiac problems, breathing difficulties, and early deaths. Several of the women and children sobbed openly on the air while they were being reprimanded and most of the audience looked on with disgust.

The intended takeaway of all this messaging was clear: Problems like heart disease and high blood sugar were caused by lazy, gluttonous people who needed to be shamed into eating better. Unfortunately, this rhetoric lined up very closely with what many doctors already believed about poor, fat, or Black patients: they were careless, irresponsible, and did not follow medical instructions, and if they didn't improve their behavior, they deserved whatever negative health consequences they got.[77] Unfortunately, many studies find that both doctors and members of the public still feel this way.[78] Even as discussions of regulating the food and beverage industries have moved forward, and the impact of medical fatphobia has been more openly critiqued, public stigma against fatness, Blackness, and poverty have not gotten any better. The health outcomes for the people on the receiving end of all this bias have not improved, either. Not only do fat, Black, and poor patients still face massive disparities in healthcare access, but they also have always reported (and continue to report) a reduced motivation to exercise or to seek out preventive healthcare, in large part due to the Systemic Shame that they face. If society tells you repeatedly over the course of your life that you are nothing but lazy and careless and to blame for your illness (but also that overcoming such "laziness" and improving your health is hopeless), you'll probably wind up believing it.[79]

The fossil fuel industry adopted the Systemic Shame approach during the 1990s, too, blaming individual drivers for the environmental damage caused by gasoline use.[80] Companies like Exxon-Mobil closely studied and then copied Big Tobacco's tactics. In advertisements, they encouraged consumers to choose to drive less, track their carbon footprint, and buy more environmentally friendly products.[81] Fossil fuel companies promoted the idea that by purchasing the right "green" items (such as an energy-efficient dryer or a reusable tote bag), a consumer could cancel out any damage to the environment they'd already done. In other words, these companies promoted *more* consumption as the solution to feeling ashamed about past consumption.[82]

Unfortunately, psychological research shows that many consumers bought into this logic and began believing in what is called the negative footprint effect: the idea a person can undo a morally "bad" purchase by also making a "good" one. This belief is not actually true, of course. In many cases, buying a brand-new energy-efficient appliance or tote bag is a lot worse for the environment than using what you already have. But in an economic system where people are taught to vote with their dollar, and where consumption is assigned moral and symbolic value, buying a "good" thing feels like the only way to make a proactive difference. In this way, Systemic Shame proved to be more than just a way to offload corporate blame: it helped to line the pockets of fossil fuel companies by filling regular people with so much anxiety and grief about the future of the planet that they went rushing to stores to try to atone for it.

By the end of the 1990s, Systemic Shame had become the prevailing approach to a wide variety of inequalities and crises. And as we moved into the new millennium, it took one final turn that was especially bleak. With deadly mass shootings becoming more common across the United States, gun lobbyists began defending their industry by pinning the blame on individuals—usually persons with mental illness.[83]

In the wake of the Columbine massacre in 1999, gun control opponents zeroed in on the video game and music tastes of the shooters, Eric Harris and Dylan Klebold, as well as their antidepressant prescriptions, claiming these were signs of the boys' sociopathy and evil. The news media and American public lapped this up, discussing at length the risks of teenagers wearing trench coats, listening to Marilyn Manson, and taking fluvoxamine. I can recall peers of mine with similar styles of dress and interests getting bullied for resembling members of the "trench coat mafia." Even teachers looked at them with suspicion. Many of them were shy or awkward Autistics, much like myself, who didn't deserve and certainly didn't benefit from such intense vilification and scrutiny of their every move. And even while the media habits and mental health of the shooters were scrutinized, their white supremacist sympathies (which certainly played a greater role in their attitude toward mass violence than gaming did) were all but swept under the rug.

Blaming evil individuals and mental illness quickly became a part of the National Rifle Association's playbook. After the shooting at Sandy Hook Elementary School in December of 2012, NRA president Wayne LaPierre stated that "delusional killers" were to blame. He called for the government to create a national registry of people with mental illnesses,[84] advocating that immense stigma and shame be attached to a group that was already unfairly feared. Gun lobbyists also blamed mental illness for the 2012 mass shooting at a movie theater in Aurora, Colorado,[85] and the attempted assassination of the US congresswoman Gabrielle Giffords.[86]

When Elliot Rogers shot and killed six people in Isla Vista, California, in 2014, Rogers's Autism was presented by news outlets as a contributing cause.[87] Autism was yet again blamed (along with transness) in the 2023 shooting at the Covenant School, just outside Nashville.[88] At an NRA conference held shortly after the 2022 mass shooting at Robb Elementary School in Uvalde, Texas, gun advocates echoed that "evil" people and mental illness were the true cause.[89] By explaining mass shootings as a phenomenon of mental illness rather than one of hopelessness, hatred, and easy access to guns, the NRA managed to effectively distance itself from holding responsibility for the ongoing crisis. And by linking mental illness and disability with violence, they managed to worsen the stigma that already leaves so many neurodivergent people lonesome and disaffected.

The Wounds of Living Under Systemic Shame

I'm an Autistic person who spent many years of my life feeling immense shame about my differences. And in my work, I've closely studied the impact that mental health stigma has on neurodivergent people. So the idea that mentally ill and disabled people like me are somehow the source of mass shooting violence is unspeakably heart-breaking to me.

From empirical research, we know that people with mental illness are far more likely to be in danger of violence than to be violent ourselves.[90] We also know that mentally ill folks suffer from theft, sexual assault, battery, and police violence at extremely elevated rates.[91] Nearly *half* of all people with mental illnesses experience at least one of those acts of violence in their lives. On the flip side, only 3 percent of all violent crimes are committed by someone with a mental health diagnosis.[92]

It feels absurd that I even have to point to such figures, because it should be pretty self-evident that branding an entire community of marginalized people as dangerous will render them vulnerable to further abuse. Neurodivergent people experience exploitation, poverty, homelessness, and domestic abuse at very high levels,[93] and many people are resistant to us receiving any government benefits or resources that could help prevent such experiences.[94] As a class, we are viewed as complainers, liars, and dangerous freaks, and are instinctively disliked by most non-disabled people when they first meet us.[95]

Public stereotypes of mentally ill people as "dangerous," "dishonest," and "evil" can have a big impact on the course of our lives. On the podcast *Reply All*, the reporter Sruthi Pinnamaneni described how mental illness stigma led to the lifelong incarceration of one Autistic murder suspect, a man named Paul Modrowski. The judge in Modrowski's murder case, Sam Amirante, admitted in an interview that he chose to sentence Modrowski to life in prison because the Autistic man "looked like a murderer" to him. Modrowski avoided eye contact throughout the trial proceedings. During particularly fraught moments in court, he just sat completely still and stared ahead.[96] Judge Amirante determined that this meant Modrowski was a cold-blooded killer without remorse. These are all, of course, very common behaviors in Autistic people, especially those who are overwhelmed or whose lives are imminently under threat.

No matter a person's identity or position in society, it's likely they have been taught by Systemic Shame to assume all of society's problems have been caused by individuals behaving badly—and that as a consequence, the solution is to just exercise more willpower, leverage more shame, and push themselves and others to make better decisions. But as the next chapter of the book will illustrate, the data is unequivocal: Shame does not work.

Identifying the Roots of Your Systemic Shame

Throughout this chapter we've discussed where Systemic Shame comes from, on a historical and cultural level. I wanted to wrap up by encouraging you to ponder the origins of your own Systemic Shame, and the variety of social and cultural forces that might have led you to blame yourself and other individuals for far-reaching societal problems.

I've already discussed how I absorbed messages early in life telling me that queer folks were perverse and that Autistic people were unlikable. These attitudes have haunted me for the rest of my life, and caused me to erect sharp, self-protective barriers that kept a distance between me and other people. If you experience racism, sexism, ableism, fatphobia, transphobia, or any number of other injustices, it's likely that you internalized a lot of shameful messages about yourself, too. But even if you are someone with a decent amount of privilege, you have grown up in a culture and economic system that promotes shame as the solution.

To start thinking a bit more about where your own feelings of Systemic Shame may have originated, complete the activities in the following table.

INVESTIGATING YOUR SYSTEMIC SHAME
Where Does It Come From? What Do You Feel Systemic Shame About?

Instructions: Complete the following self-reflection activity by answering the questions in the space provided.

1. When you were a child, were there any groups of people you were taught to view as greedy and selfish? What were those groups?

2. When you were a child, were there any groups of people you were taught to view as dangerous, unpredictable, or scary? What were those groups?

3. When you were a child, were there any groups of people you were taught to view as untrustworthy, or as liars? What were those groups?

4. Do you have anything in common with any of these groups? If so, what?

5. As you began growing up, did you ever feel that people were viewing you as greedy, scary, lazy, or a fraud? Try to describe one experience that triggered that feeling.

6. When you were growing up, what did the adults teach you about the causes of problems like addiction, poverty, or violent crime?

7. When you were young, were you ever publicly shamed by adults or other children? What unfair standards were being pushed onto you at that time?

In the chapters to come, we'll unpack this cultural conditioning further, and look into some tools that can help a person unlearn Systemic Shame's damaging messages. But in order to move beyond Systemic Shame, we have to genuinely believe that letting go of our self-loathing and judgment is worth it. And so, in the next two chapters, we will review the abundant social scientific evidence that reveals why shame never helps people grow, change, or combat systemic issues—and take a look at how the very logic behind Systemic Shame as a belief system is fundamentally flawed.

CHAPTER 3

The Values of Systemic Shame

In the last chapter, we reviewed Systemic Shame's political and economic history, and the enduring legacy that it's had on each one of us. In this chapter, we'll delve a bit deeper into the core values that Systemic Shame has upheld throughout that history, so we can further understand how it operates and why it continues to ravage conversations about social issues and poison our self-concepts.

Systemic Shame is more than just a feeling of debilitating self-blame—it's also a worldview about how change happens and what it means for a person to lead a meaningful or moral life. But by prioritizing the values of perfectionism, individualism, consumerism, wealth, and personal responsibility above all other things, Systemic Shame actually trains us to preserve the status quo rather than disrupt it. And by preaching that a person can only be moral if they fully align themselves with these values, Systemic Shame leaves us feeling isolated, mistrustful, and completely stuck when it comes to imagining a more enriching, more connected way to lead our own lives.

So, let's take a look at the core values of Systemic Shame, and the many contradictions and double binds it creates for us. We'll also take several breaks throughout this chapter to look at some self-reflection tools that can help us better understand the role Systemic Shame plays in our daily lives and thinking—and how much it takes away from us.

Perfectionism

In December of 2020, pop singer and flautist Lizzo was publicly criticized by thousands of people because she posted online about going on a ten-day "smoothie cleanse."[1] Fans accused Lizzo of "betraying" the fat positivity movement by dieting[2] and putting people's lives at risk by promoting a potentially dangerous weight-loss method.[3] A few days later, Lizzo responded to the controversy, clarifying that she was not in fact setting out to lose weight or promote dieting to her fans, but that she didn't consider herself an activist for the fat positivity movement, either.

This wasn't the first time Lizzo faced mass criticism for choices she'd made regarding her own body. Earlier that year, after posting a video of herself exercising, Lizzo also had to reassure thousands of dismayed fans that she wasn't trying to lose weight. On the opposite end of the spectrum, throughout her career Lizzo has faced almost constant public scrutiny for "glorifying" being fat, simply by virtue of being a famous plus-size woman who doesn't openly hate herself.[4]

On August 1, 2023, three of Lizzo's former dancers filed a lawsuit accusing the performer of creating a hostile, sexually charged work environment and making critical remarks about their bodies. This further revealed the problems with equating Lizzo's identity and body size with her politics. Being a fat woman was no guarantee that Lizzo personally held fat liberatory beliefs, or lived up to them. But because of her identities she was assumed to stand for ideals that existed completely outside of her. If Lizzo exudes confidence, fatphobes shame her for supposedly promoting being fat, as *The Biggest Loser* host Jillian Michaels did when she declared of Lizzo, "There is nothing beautiful about clogged arteries."[5] Yet when Lizzo does broadcast herself exercising or consuming fruits and vegetables, she's a failure of self-acceptance according to a vocal subset of her fans. If she mistreats other people, Lizzo's fans are shocked at her for not being a perfect symbol of the ideals they've projected onto her brand. Lizzo isn't permitted to be a person who is capable of harm, or who makes private decisions regarding her body for a variety of reasons. Instead, she is forced to represent every single prejudice she lives under in America—fatphobia, sexism, and misogynoir—and serve as a model for how those problems ought to be handled.

Systemic Shame politicizes every choice that a marginalized person makes, until their entire existence becomes an object of public criticism. Every single act they take can be picked apart, judged, and assigned a moral value. To an extent, Systemic Shame politicizes the choices of just about everyone—that's why any of us can feel flooded with shame when we're at the grocery store, after all, or as we linger holding an aluminum can over the garbage bin. But because the very lives and bodies of the marginalized are viewed by Systemic Shame as inherently political, for oppressed people there truly is no escaping judgment of their every choice. The more marginalized a person is, according to Systemic Shame, the greater the pressure there is upon them to forever behave perfectly—because they exist as a symbol of every injustice that they've ever lived, and they are solely responsible for fixing their own oppression.

Often, Systemic Shame loads judgment onto marginalized people for behaviors that would go completely unquestioned and unshamed among the relatively more privileged. Thin white celebrities discuss their fitness regimens and starvation diets openly all the time. When they mention gaining a few pounds or suffering blows to their self-confidence, magazines and comment sections celebrate their "bravery." But if a fat Black woman does either of these things, she is a betrayal of public health *and* fat self-love all at once.[6] Just by existing in her Black plus-size body, she is assumed to stand for something beyond herself, and to be more moral than other people.

In a similar vein, I have often witnessed the trans women in my life being held to impossibly high standards of perfection. In the early 2010s when I was still exploring my gender identity in private, I befriended a lot of trans people on the blogging site Tumblr. Over the ensuing decade, I witnessed as, one by one, nearly every single trans woman I followed was accused of some sexual offense, usually for which there was absolutely zero evidence. It happened to almost every trans woman I know, including many who were not public or political figures at all—except insofar as their very *existence* became a symbol of transgender "depravity" to the people that hated them.

Trans women are unfairly stereotyped in our culture as being predatory and hypersexual. For decades, the media has portrayed trans women as dangerous "men" who are merely pretending to be female in order to prey on children and cis women. And as a result of all this stigma and Systemic Shame, individual trans women have their every action ruthlessly torn apart for evidence of danger or perversion. As the writer Ana Valens observed about her own experience, nearly every trans woman who is well known online will eventually get burned by this system of sexism and violent transphobia. Even fellow trans people pick up the torch.[7] We hold our own kin to higher standards than we do cis people because we want trans individuals to "represent" our community well and earn us more collective respect. But perfection has never earned any of us equality or safety. No matter how hard you work or censor yourself, as a marginalized person, your very life will be politicized.

Research shows that the double standards of Systemic Shame begin affecting marginalized people very early on in life. An article published in the journal *Cognition and Emotion* in 2021 found that Black children are perceived by adults as older than white children of the exact same age.[8] This misperception comes with a higher burden of obligations. Black children are expected to behave more maturely and are viewed as needing less nurturing, protection, or guidance than white children of the same age.[9] Our society truly does demand that Black kids accomplish more when given far less. When Black children fail to live up to those unrealistic expectations, they are shamed and sometimes even violently punished.

That same study found that adults view Black children as angrier than white kids, even when no emotional displays of anger are present. Simply having a neutral facial expression is taken as a sign of hostility in a Black child—meaning that Black children have to smile and radiate fake happiness if they want to be seen in a merely neutral light. Other data reveals Black kids are expected to be more compliant and agreeable by their teachers, and are more likely to be punished if they even step slightly out of line.[10] This all begins as early as preschool.

In a study examining how members of a national feminist activist group spoke to one another, the authors Audra Nuru and Colleen Arendt found that Black female activists were repeatedly corrected on their "tone" by the white women around them.[11] When Black women pointed out instances of racism within the group, white women told them to remain patient, asked them to "cool it," and instructed them to be gentler in the way they spoke. The study authors also found that for Black women, what crossed the threshold and counted as "anger" in people's eyes was much lower. White women could be snarky or disagreeable without pushback, but if a Black woman showed any sign of tension, her behavior was seen as hostile.

Systemic Shame leads us to scrutinize the actions of the marginalized far more severely than other people, and consequently, we find more faults with their actions. White people tell themselves that we'd do more to fight racism if only Black people would explain what they need (in a judgment-free tone). If we can find any flaw in the responses we hear from Black people, we have a ready-made excuse to not take them seriously. Our obsession with perfection gives us license to preserve the status quo.

The following exercise is designed to get you thinking about the double standards that you face and the unfair standards of perfection that Systemic Shame demands of you. Keep in mind that there are many different ways that a person can be marginalized, and even if you also hold some privileges, many of these challenges might still apply to you.

DOUBLE STANDARDS REFLECTION TOOL

Below are some common double standards that marginalized people are commonly held to. Check off each statement that resonates with you, and in the spaces provided, reflect on how this standard has affected your life.

☐ Other people get to speak their mind, but I'm never given the space for my voice to be heard.
How has this double standard affected you?

☐ Other people's emotions are taken seriously, but when I share how I feel, people think I am overreacting or wrong.
How has this double standard affected you?

☐ No matter how much work I take on, someone is always angry with me for not doing enough.
How has this double standard affected you?

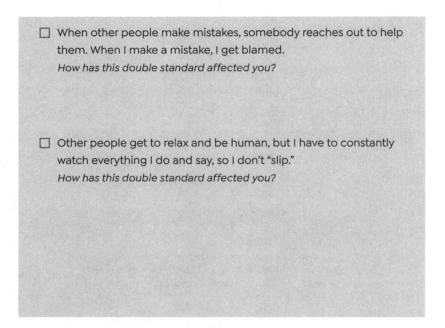

☐ When other people make mistakes, somebody reaches out to help them. When I make a mistake, I get blamed.
How has this double standard affected you?

☐ Other people get to relax and be human, but I have to constantly watch everything I do and say, so I don't "slip."
How has this double standard affected you?

If you experience racism, classism, fatphobia, homophobia, or any other bias, you are quite used to living under these double standards every single day. But even if you are relatively privileged, you may notice that as an individual you are expected to take on more responsibility and behave more perfectly than the powerful institutions that surround you. If your company's CEO cuts your hours or reduces the number of people working in your department, you as an employee are still on the hook for completing all your duties. When the federal government cuts public funding for Covid tests or vaccine boosters, you're stuck with the bill if you want to keep mitigating risk.

Individualism

Systemic Shame holds that the individual person is the sole agent of change in this world. According to this worldview, social pressure is never an adequate explanation for bad behavior, and there are no economic incentives or legal exclusions that can help us understand any social ill. Under Systemic Shame, violent crime happens because the world is filled with unruly and despicable people, and theft is caused not by poverty or deprivation, but by personal greed. Naming the structural factors that contribute to such problems can get a person accused of lacking morality, or "excusing" inexcusable acts. This helps explain, in large part, why Systemic Shame moves us to seek out a seemingly acceptable target to offload all our blame when we do become aware of a widespread crisis in need of addressing. We often believe, on an intuitive level, that shaming an individual symbol of a larger social problem is our only route to enacting meaningful change.

If you're a lover of psychology or self-help books, you've almost certainly encountered Amy Cuddy's work. She's perhaps most famous for a 2012 TED Talk that went massively viral and has been seen by more than 65 million people. In it, Cuddy discussed how she struggled following a car accident that gave her a traumatic brain injury.[12] Following her injury, Cuddy floundered in college and graduate school. She'd lost many of her cognitive abilities and wasn't sure she had what it took to be a success anymore. But things finally shifted when one of her mentors, a psychologist named Susan Fiske, gave Cuddy an uplifting pep talk: She instructed Cuddy to say yes to every speaking opportunity that came her way, no matter how anxious it made her, and to fake confidence until one day she finally really felt it. Following Fiske's advice paid off, and eventually inspired Cuddy to conduct research on the benefits of feigning confidence via something she called "power posing"—which involves standing in a dominant or self-assured way.

In her TED Talk, Cuddy discusses her research showing that when people "power pose" a few moments before a stressful situation such as a job interview, their confidence goes up, their physiological stress response reduces, and their performance improves. She explains how power posing could be especially beneficial to women and people of color, who are used to being underestimated in high-pressure situations. Cuddy's TED Talk is a masterclass in the format: It's personal yet scientific, with a tidy, happy resolution, and it all feels quite empowering to take in. Cuddy's "power posing" offers a solution to sexism, racism, and disability that's straightforward and achievable: Just stand more confidently. Act like a privileged white man, and you will embody the courage it takes to succeed. I used to assign Cuddy's TED Talk in my own social psychology classes because I found it so compelling.

But there was a big problem with much of Cuddy's research: Other scientists could not reproduce nearly any of her findings.[13] As her popularity grew, scrutiny of how Cuddy conducted her studies rose.[14] Many of her statistical techniques came into question. Eventually, one of Cuddy's collaborators publicly admitted they had used a variety of what are now known in the field as questionable research protocols to arrive at their stunning, TED Talk–ready results.[15]

Questionable research protocols (also known as QRPs) involve taking steps like testing the same potential effect multiple times, but only reporting the results when they "work," collecting additional data and retesting analyses repeatedly until the desired effects appear, failing to report key elements of a study's methodology, and throwing variables in and out of an analysis in an unfocused "fishing expedition" until any significant and publishable effect appears.

Using QRPs is not quite so ethically problematic as committing outright data fraud, but it does taint the validity of a researcher's results. And the more regularly and widely QRPs are adopted, the more doubt has to be cast on the entire scientific literature that surrounds it as a whole.

At the time that Cuddy's research collaborator spoke out, social psychology was facing a replication crisis. Numerous well-known psychological effects that had been written about in the popular press and published in books were failing to be reproduced by any other scientists, and a wide variety of data fraudsters, shoddy scientists, and QRP users were getting publicly revealed. And so Cuddy was transformed instantly from a mainstream media darling to an icon of everything wrong with pop psychology. Articles in scientific journals and the mainstream press alike excoriated Cuddy and her work. She began receiving harassing messages and death threats. Professional colleagues distanced themselves from her. On blogs about the replication crisis, some users even speculated that Cuddy had fudged her study results *because* her brain injury had made her incapable of doing good science.[16]

"I love social psychology, but I don't feel at home here anymore," Cuddy later confessed at a conference. "I don't feel like this is my group. People have not stood up for me."[17]

When I first saw Cuddy being discredited, I remember feeling a sick sense that justice was being served. I was dismayed by the replication crisis, and rapidly losing faith in my own field of study and work, and even one of my own studies failed to be reproduced by other scientists. It felt like a relief to see one person being passed the baton of blame. With her high-profile results and her inconsistently conducted studies, Cuddy reminded me of every hyper-productive careerist psychologist I had ever envied and secretly told myself I was better than. She also reminded me of my own nervous, awkward self, who often had to hide how much I was battling to get by in the academy. It felt good to see Cuddy bearing the shame of being a lying imposter—a shame I didn't want to feel.

Ultimately, though, there were a lot of problems with that interpretation of the situation. Cuddy hadn't deliberately lied or made up any data. In fact, nothing that she had done was unusual for the time. The questionable research practices she'd adopted were considered normal. A survey of researchers in the field conducted by John, Loewenstein, and Prelec in 2012 had found that fully 66.5 percent of social psychologists admitted to having used QRPs at various points in their careers.[18] Some of the most common questionable practices, in fact, were ones I'd actively been *instructed to use* back when I was in graduate school. One of my research mentors had sat me down in front of a statistical analysis program and showed me step by step how to go about conducting a "fishing expedition" on a fresh set of data. These and other methods were taught without controversy in many of my labs. The lead editor of a prestigious journal had openly endorsed QRPs at a national conference during the first year of my graduate program. The problem of QRPs was systemic—embedded into the very backbone of social psychology. Yet as soon as the public began criticizing these issues, it was individual "bad" psychologists who were assigned all of the responsibility.

Once she began being criticized, Cuddy cooperated with every replication attempt and inquiry done on her work. She answered questions about her methods and analyses openly, and behaved professionally and transparently toward researchers who challenged her. But that wasn't enough. She'd been identified as the main character of the replication crisis—and with that came the full force of Systemic Shame.

"As a young social psychologist, [Cuddy] played by the rules and won big," wrote Susan Dominus in a profile for *The New York Times*. "Then, suddenly, the rules changed."[19]

Systemic Shame treats people's "bad" actions as if they have happened in a vacuum—ignoring the incentives and norms that can push nearly any of us to act unethically. But if we really want to change those norms and incentive structures, we have to take collective responsibility for making it happen.

If social psychologists really want to decrease the use of questionable research protocols, we can't just attack the individuals who have engaged in them. Instead, we have to look to the root causes of the phenomenon.[20] And there are many structural reasons why social psychologists fudged our results for so long.

One reason that many scientists rely on QRPs is because academics face an intense pressure to publish as many studies as they possibly can. If you don't publish, your chances of getting a job as a professor (or of gaining tenure) dwindle to nearly nothing. And most academic journals will only publish significant results, in which a researcher successfully found the effect they predicted they'd find (or at least an effect they *claim* to have predicted in advance). People with robust publishing records get more funding, more graduate student assistants providing them with free labor, and lots more attention at conferences and in the media. If your results are intriguing enough, publicity turns into paid speaking engagements and book deals. So there's a strong incentive in place for scientists to write up as many "successful" studies as they can find—to pretend that surprising results were expected all along, and to hide how many times they tried to find an effect and failed.

The only way to prevent future Amy Cuddys is to stop rewarding people who behaved as she did—and to start encouraging the actions we actually want to see in our scientists. That might mean promoting scientists based on the quality of their work, or their collaboration skills, rather than how many publications they have bagged. We also need to reward researchers for finding nonsignificant results—because failing to find support for a hypothesis is just as valuable to science as finding it. We should provide consistent funding to junior researchers, particularly people of color, women, and disabled scholars, so that they can afford to invest years into building robust research programs. If our scientists-in-training have the time and means to build up a diverse program of research, they won't have to chase after quick, sloppy results.

With these kinds of top-down solutions in place, we could end the crisis of QRPs. But instead, Systemic Shame keeps us distracted with infighting and conflict—particularly directed toward marginalized people, who are the most likely to become symbolic scapegoats. It's not a coincidence that Cuddy, a woman with a brain injury, became the face of QRPs. Older, more established, and male social psychologists such as John Bargh had just as many of their studies discredited as Cuddy, but the public scrutiny and professional censure he faced was far quieter.

When we feel ashamed of ourselves, or frustrated with a sense of stuckness, we often cast out looking for another individual to blame. Here is an exercise to get you thinking about how you assign blame and responsibility for pressing issues that affect your life.

SYMBOLIC SACRIFICE EXERCISE
Where Do You Offload Your Shame?

Reflect on the following questions and leave a response in the space provided.

1. Try to think of the ways that you might use other people as symbols of larger problems. Is there anyone whose actions always annoy or infuriate you because they remind you of bigger issues happening in your life?

2. In the space below, list some of the individuals that come to mind, and some of the behaviors they engage in that frustrate you.

3. What do you have in common with this person (or people)? Try to list a few personal traits or aspects of your life situation that you share with them.

4. Why do you think this person (or people) behaves in the ways they do? Try naming a few benefits they might receive for their actions.

5. Do you fear that other people might see you as similar to this person (or people)? If so, in what ways?

When I dwell on these questions, I notice that I often hold the people close to me responsible for the much larger stressors I am facing. I get angry with my conservative mother because of the actions of Republican lawmakers, and I feel contempt for colleagues who put their career prospects ahead of scientific integrity. Once I take a minute to "zoom out," though, I can see that what's needed is a lot more complicated than punishing a single person who gets on my nerves. I need healthcare and body autonomy. I need a way to pay the rent that doesn't feel slimy and dishonest. Probably the person that I'm angry with needs many of those exact same things. Reflecting on this helps me behave a bit more compassionately, even if I'm still hurt or disappointed. It also forces me to put my focus back on the systems that have failed us, not the people whom I've decided are failures.

Consumerism

"I can't stop buying bisexual-flag-colored accessories and clothes," says my friend Carys. "The constant compulsion to broadcast my bisexuality is exhausting. I never feel queer enough."

Carys is a bisexual woman in a healthy, happy long-term relationship with a man. But when she is out in public with him, Carys feels alienated. She longs for acceptance within the queer community and wants to live in a way where her sexual orientation is fully recognized as a central part of her. But right now it feels like the only way to affirm her identity is via consumption—purchasing and adorning herself in queer-coded swag.

"It is a small thing, but I really want to share smiles, eye contact, and nods with fellow queers in the wild," she says. "I try, but when queer people avoid eye contact because I scan as hetero, I don't blame them."

Because of systemic homophobia and transphobia, queer people are usually pretty isolated from one another. In a world where our identities are regularly erased, or else framed as disgusting and predatory, it's still highly difficult for us to find one another or to express openly who we are. Systemic Shame then turns around and offers us consumption and personal branding as the remedy to being so alone and unseen. Instead of embracing other LGBTQ people, forming queer friendships, building up our communities, and having the sex and relationships we long to have, Systemic Shame tells us what we need is to find personal empowerment and pride in our identities—by purchasing the correct items and styling ourselves the right way.

Carys tells me, "I pour too much money into the capitalist pride machine, in a quietly desperate want to be known." She knows it is not a solution, but in the absence of real community support, consumption feels like all she's got.

I remember when I used to feel a whole lot like Carys. When I was in a relationship with a straight man, I did not permit myself to transition as "far" as I really wanted to. I knew that looking like a man and living as one would drive him away, and so instead, I played out my identity in the realm of fantasy. I spent a lot of time online role-playing as a gay man in video games and reading fanfiction featuring romances between men (such as Hannibal and Will from the NBC series *Hannibal*). I bought pronoun pins and bracelets in the colors of the transgender pride flag, and covered myself in these items compulsively. Any time a pronoun pin fell off my jacket or a trans flag bracelet withered in the washing machine, I felt naked—and I rushed to the nearest queer-affirming bookstore or Target to buy up all the pride gear I could find to replace it.

Wearing all this pride gear did nothing to curb my loneliness and shame. It sure didn't remedy the dysphoria of living as a woman in society's eyes while knowing I was a man, either. What did help was venturing out into queer spaces and making friends with other queer and trans people. I needed lots of quality time with fellow queer people, talking about our dreams, mourning our losses, processing our conflicts, and enjoying activities with one another in order for me to feel less unspeakably broken. Transitioning also made my own body feel like home, rather than an incomplete vessel I had to decorate with external proof that who I was was okay. Once I started moving through the world as a gay man, meeting other gay men at bars and cruising spaces, having sex and dancing with strangers and being treated as someone who belonged there, pride swag and pronoun pins ceased to hold any appeal for me. I was leading the kind of life I actually wanted, so I didn't have to buy things to represent who I was.

I've spoken to many queer people who have experienced a similar trajectory in their identity development. When they were closeted and cut off from really living their queerness, they felt a strong impulse to purchase and perform their identity in whatever ways they could. Some of them were stuck in remote rural areas, or with homophobic family members or partners, and so symbolic queerness was the only solace they could get. But consumption could never fill the hole that actual gay life would. Real gay life requires connecting to others.

Systemic Shame often encourages people to spend money consuming items that express their identities—and their belief systems. When attacks on women's rights and reproductive health ramp up, feminist-identified people reach out for bright pink "pussy hats" or sip from mugs with "male tears" printed on them. Following the election of Donald Trump, well-intended progressives began spreading social media posts instructing people to wear safety pins on their jackets to communicate to strangers that they were a "safe" person to approach in the event of an Islamophobic or racist hate crime.[21] Whenever news of racist police violence sweeps the country, anti-racist allies try to signal their beliefs by wearing Black Lives Matter T-shirts and wristbands.

Unfortunately, though, psychological research shows that symbolic gestures like wearing a BLM shirt or safety pin are not always harmless social performances—in some cases they actually make a person *less likely* to take more meaningful actions afterward. This is due to what psychologists call the moral licensing effect:[22] When a person takes a symbolic step to signal to other people that they have a virtuous moral identity, they may feel afterward that they've already satisfied the inner need to be a "good person" (or to *look* like a good person). Having already proven their goodness, they now have the moral "license" to lie, cheat, or sit still and witness a hate crime without intervening.[23] When we equate who we are with what we consume, we stop thinking of our values and morality in terms of what we can *do*.

Psychologists have observed that the moral licensing effect can reduce people's willingness to engage in pro-environmental behaviors,[24] as well as acts of antiracism or feminism.[25] Systemic Shame suggests to us that we can buy our way into a moral identity—but when all we focus on boosting our own personal branding, we often lose the momentum to fight for anything larger. Unfortunately, it often feels that consumption is the only option we've got for expressing our beliefs.

When a company wishes to brand itself as forward-thinking and friendly toward the environment, they often sell reusable cotton totes next to their cash registers, or give them away to consumers for free. For individual consumers, carrying a tote bag can be a symbol of one's liberal green-mindedness—and forgetting to bring your totes to the store can be a source of guilt. Unfortunately, this is all misplaced focus: As *The New York Times* reported in August of 2021, producing a single cotton tote bag is so resource-intensive that a person would need to use the same one every single day for *fifty-four years* to justify its purchase.[26]

The journalist Grace Cook writes that the tote craze was initially set in motion back in 2007, when the British designer Anya Hindmarch created a cotton bag with the words "I'm Not a Plastic Bag" printed on its sides.[27] The item was immensely popular among British grocery-store customers, many of whom lined up around the block in order to buy one, then began carrying it as an accessory and quasi-status symbol. Eventually, when studies began pointing to the environmental damage done by producing cotton totes, Hindmarch pivoted and created a new bag made from recycled plastic. The revised slogan? "I Am a Plastic Bag." Thanks to Systemic Shame and the negative footprint effect, grocery stores can now capitalize on consumers' guilt over buying cotton bags by selling plastic ones to them again.

As consumers, we are each offered a staggering litany of green and sustainable product options—and in the long run, seemingly none of them give us the power to make any actual difference. Instead, they provide us a temporary means for shaking off the shameful feeling that we aren't doing enough. And by encouraging us to identify with our purchases and view consumption as our primary means of expressing our beliefs to the world, Systemic Shame keeps us enriching the very corporations that are actually to blame for ecologic degradation in the first place.

The table below provides some prompts to get you thinking about your own relationship to consumption, and how your habits are shaped by Systemic Shame:

SYMBOLIC CONSUMPTION EXERCISE

Answer the questions below in the space provided.

1. Are there any companies that you feel guilty or ashamed about supporting? What are they, and why?

2. Are there items you regularly buy in your daily life that you feel reflect poorly on you? What are those items, and why does consuming them feel bad to you?

3. What are some factors that make it hard for you to stop shopping from these companies or buying these items?

4. Are there any TV shows, movies, or musicians that you feel ashamed about enjoying?

5. Do you have any consumption habits you feel like you have to hide from other people, in order to avoid judgment? If so, what are they? What steps do you take to hide them?

6. Do you ever use your purchases or consumption habits to communicate your identity or beliefs to others? If so, how?

When we focus on the morality of our purchases and consumption habits, we do so with the best intentions in mind. After all, most people wish to feel that with their daily existence, they are having a positive net impact on the world. That's a good impulse! Nobody wants to feel like their life is meaningless. But by convincing us that purchasing power is our primary source of social influence, Systemic Shame keeps us feeling overwhelmed with thousands of small daily decisions, and deeply guilty—this prevents us from keeping our attention on more collective solutions to the problems at hand.

Wealth

In her book *White Feminism*, the former *Jezebel* editor Koa Beck describes how the movement for women's liberation has often been undermined by a desire for "personalized autonomy, individual wealth, perpetual self-optimization, and supremacy."[28] Under white feminism, as Beck describes it, personal achievement matters more than solidarity with other women, especially women who might be poorer, darker-skinned, or otherwise more marginalized. This is an idea that Systemic Shame also thrives on.

White feminists have played an active role in spreading Systemic Shame—and that's because they had many financial incentives to do so. In the early 1900s, white, well-off suffragettes tried to earn themselves the right to vote by making themselves seem as virtuous and nonthreatening to the status quo as possible. They emphasized their traditional family values and commitment to domestic life in order to spare themselves from being seen as man-hating or radical. In other words, they internalized the Systemic Shame that said women shouldn't demand too much of the society around them and should do all they can to keep powerful men from feeling threatened or afraid.

Prominent white suffragettes like Susan B. Anthony and Elizabeth Cady Stanton silenced Black and brown feminists who wanted not only the right to vote, but broader economic and racial justice measures as well.[29] Women like that made the movement look *angry* and *radical*, white suffragettes feared, and for this they were excluded from organizing meetings and pushed to the back of parades and demonstrations. When white women successfully earned the right to vote, they left the concerns of Black and brown women aside. Their feminism was all about the individual right of white women to vote—not about addressing problems that harm a wide array of women such as poverty, domestic abuse, child labor exploitation, or the many deaths of working-class women in manufacturing plants.

Decades later, in 1977, the Combahee River Collective, a Black lesbian activist group, observed that mainstream white feminists were still leaving Black women and their concerns out.[30] White feminists of the "second wave" weren't interested in battling the economic and social forces (such as racism) that allowed so much power and wealth to be unjustly hoarded in the first place. Freeing white women just meant granting them the opportunity to own property, hire and fire people, and purchase whatever they wanted. But freeing Black women required, as the Black feminist Michele Wallace put it, fighting the entire world.[31]

Instead of fighting the entire world—working against complex networks of sexism, racism, transphobia, and economic injustice— white feminism suggests you just work very hard and become a "girl boss." It's a Systemic Shame–based approach, focusing on the virtues and costs of shaving one's legs, changing one's last name, wearing makeup, and aspiring to get a promotion at your job while raising children ("having it all" usually only being possible with the help of underpaid labor from other women). Every purchase, mannerism, vocal cue, and personal styling decision can be either feminist or unfeminist, and it's only by making all the correct choices that a woman can "win."

"[White feminism] positions you as the agent of change, making your individual needs the touchpoint for all revolutionary disruption," Beck writes. "All you need is a better morning routine, this email hack, that woman's pencil skirt, this conference, that newsletter."

Conversely, when women fail under a white feminist framework, they are at fault for it: They were too angry, too meek, too shrill; they had children too early, they put too much energy into their appearance, they chose to marry the wrong man. Not doing feminism correctly is a mark of shame.

This approach takes a massive toll on women. Psychological research shows that feminist-identified women frequently feel shame about all kinds of choices that they're forced to make,[32] from formula feeding,[33] to hair removal[34] to the kinds of sex they have and the pop music they enjoy.[35] Research in 2020 found that many feminist women felt ashamed for having to take on more child-rearing and housekeeping duties during the pandemic. Women experienced significant hits to their professional and academic careers during the pandemic,[36] but white feminism had little recourse to offer for it. Being forced to adapt to a global crisis felt, somehow, like an unfeminist "choice"—even though it really wasn't a choice at all.[37]

When we understand gender equality as a matter of personal choice and private shame, productive conversations about gender norms fall apart. Over the years I've watched in frustration as discussions about, for example, the professional expectation that women wear makeup devolve into fights over whether "choosing" to wear makeup is an antifeminist act that worsens sexism, or a bold, expressive act of feminine defiance. The "makeup wars" still routinely rack up tens of thousands of replies on social media platforms like

Instagram and Tumblr,[38] with women expressing frustration at being shamed for their choices on both sides. In 2020, the former beauty writer Jessica DeFino wrote in *The New York Times* that she was relieved that the pandemic was leading many women to question the time-consuming beauty regimens they'd been expected to adhere to all their lives, and that she welcomed the fact that manicures were no longer being seen as absolutely necessary.[39] She received an outpouring of outrage and criticism, mostly from fellow women who accused DeFino of not supporting women's freedom to make their own decisions and of attacking a multimillion-dollar industry that is largely woman-owned.

Women also face relentless scrutiny when they decide whether to have children, take the surname of a spouse, combine finances with a partner, or to get cosmetic surgeries. Often there are significant social and legal pressures directing a woman to make a particular choice in these realms—but making note of this tends to be read as being sexist and not allowing women to do whatever they want. Thanks to Systemic Shame, women often view a critique of sexist standards as an indictment of their own behavior under those standards. People identify with their choices, even when their options were restricted or coerced. After all, Systemic Shame teaches that our consumption is moral and that personal choice is the only tool of change.

Personal Responsibility

Systemic Shame is incredibly effective at derailing and nullifying powerful social movements. As soon as large groups of people start organizing to demand changes from their legal system, their government, or their employers, those same powers use Systemic Shame to replace carefully thought-out collective demands with a plea for personal responsibility. Systemic Shame tells us that change must come from within—that racism is solved by individuals choosing not to be bigoted, that unfair beauty standards can only be improved by women adopting more confidence, and that gun violence will only cease when every mentally ill person submits themselves to a cure. And when a person really does care about such social issues, examining their own attitudes and ignorance certainly isn't a bad place for change to start. The real problem occurs when Systemic Shame uses an obsession with personal responsibility as a replacement for a broader understanding of where social issues really come from.

When Branson, a social worker at a small mental health non-profit in Minneapolis came out as genderqueer, he was immediately tapped to become his organization's resource on all matters Trans 101. The executive director invited Branson in for a private meeting with the organization's board, where he was peppered with questions about transition-related medical procedures and asked to defend the validity of people using they/them pronouns. (Branson has not medically transitioned, and his pronouns are he/him.) Then he was "voluntold" to create and lead a workshop that would teach all the organizations' care providers about how to meet the needs of their trans clients.

"My training was in working with patients who self-harmed and families in poverty," Branson says. "I didn't think I was the right person to be leading a discussion like this."

Rather than putting procedures in place that would help an employee transition on the job more easily in the future, Branson's employer expected him to create all the knowledge and resources that he needed himself. But more than that, Branson was being used as a symbolic stand-in for all other transgender and genderqueer people's concerns as a whole. And that was where Systemic Shame asserted itself most forcefully. "After many conversations, I convinced my company to hire a consultant on transgender issues," he tells me. "And they bring in this person who goes through a long list of gender-related terminology and tells everybody to start putting their pronouns in their email signatures. And they say things like, 'Use the word *transgender*, don't use the word *transsexual*.' I know people who happily use the word *transsexual*! Our clients are poor, and mostly BIPOC people and many don't have documentation. They need help navigating doctor's appointments, navigating social service agencies. They need more from us than pronouns in our emails."

When Branson complained about these gaps, his manager told him he was being "divisive" and making progress more difficult. And when he chose not to be "out" to all of his clients or to all the external service agencies that he worked with, Branson was criticized.

"I care about people I serve, I want them to have a good experience, and making everything about me being genderqueer does not make them safe," Branson explains. "If I'm interacting with a foster care system that is discriminatory to queer parents, me being out might not make things better for my clients—in fact it can make it worse. And it sucks for me as well."

Branson's experiences mirror the ones that I've witnessed as a disability justice advocate. Because of my writing and advocacy around Autism, organizations often invite me to speak about how neurodivergent employees could be better accommodated. Before I give a talk, I do as much research as I can and then I come to the company with a whole long list of recommendations: They should offer work-from-home options to all employees as well as flex time, for example, and disability accommodations should be offered readily even to those who can't access official documentation. When it's relevant, I also like to point out some of the policy changes that Autistic people need: We need to be able to be openly disabled without risking having our legal autonomy or our child custody taken away, and our neurotype needs to stop being viewed as so socially undesirable that many of us are barred from ever immigrating to other countries. These are high-level, systems-focused solutions to the problem of ableism, and it pains me to say that many companies, universities, and nonprofits don't want to hear them.

Instead, organizational leaders ask me to fill my talk with tips that are useful only to individuals: a long list of which disability terms are offensive, and tips for what Autistic *employees* should do to better manage their workload. Some of these conversations are worth having. Yet I can't help but notice that managers' eyes glaze over when I discuss changes the *company* must make—such as beginning to cover Autism assessments on their health insurance—only to see them liven back up again the moment somebody asks if the phrase "on the spectrum" is okay to use. In one instance, when I began describing how the use of employee surveillance software (such as key-loggers and screen trackers) harms Autistic employees, a tense HR professional cut my talk off early, and then disappeared all the employee complaints about the use of such programs from the meeting's chat box. Discussing the systematic ways in which certain classes of employers were harmed became impossible. All the company wanted to hear was platitudes about how proud Autistic people were to be working there.

As a professor, I have also watched in real time as a collective push for racial justice was slowly diluted by Systemic Shame into something far smaller, weaker, and focused on personal responsibility. Many organizations have a vested interest in approaching racism through an individual lens rather than making costly, dramatic changes to how they operate. This was evidently true at my own university. Throughout 2020, a diverse coalition of Loyola students lobbied for campus security to stop working with the Chicago Police

Department. Pointing both to the Chicago PD's horrific acts of racist violence, as well as to instances where Black students had been harassed on campus, students demanded a clear-cut systemic change.

The university sent the Chicago Police to arrest student protestors[40]—then it issued public statements about its commitment to antiracism. From there, the university encouraged all its faculty and staff to attend workshops focused on assessing our own personal racial biases, where we were asked to count how many scholars of color we have listed on our class syllabi. Including more scholars of color on a syllabus is a worthwhile endeavor, to be sure. But my academic institution seemed unwilling to consider how its own treatment of Black students might have contributed to the lack of Black scholars in many fields. It's hard to thrive as a young Black academic when cops harass you for trying to attend your own school's basketball game, as one Loyola student was.[41] During this period, a Black admissions official at Loyola stepped down, citing a "toxic atmosphere of hostility . . . especially pertaining to people of color."[42]

I've worked with many academics and DEI consultants at a variety of public and private institutions, so I know that what I witnessed is far from unusual. Numerous employers responded to the protests of 2020 by encouraging individual employees to work on their racism—while taking no steps at an institutional level to pay Black employees more or grant them more leadership power, or to alter an organizational culture that is hostile to them. Sadly, when an organization does take an interest in addressing racism, research shows it is often Black and brown employees who are burdened with leading the initiatives, often for no additional pay.[43]

Black employees at both nonprofit and for-profit institutions are often asked to facilitate community dialogues on racism and field questions about racial justice from their white colleagues, regardless of whether they show any interest in doing so.[44] Data shows the same heavy emotional load is placed on Black students at predominately white schools as well.[45] Systemic Shame blames the victims for their suffering. So it's no surprise that the epidemic of organizational racism is turned into a problem Black employees and students must solve by working hard at an ever-expanding list of expectations.[46]

Of course, discussions of white defensiveness and casual racism are important to have. But just as individual consumers cannot end climate change by obsessing over our grocery store purchases, white individuals can't end systemic racism by obsessing over our own feelings.

If I really want to make Black people's lives easier, there are concrete, structural changes I can push for. I can fight for racial pay equity at my workplace and draw attention to the fact that Black faculty are far less likely than white faculty to have long-term or tenure-track contracts. I can lobby for my school to lift its standardized testing requirements for admissions, since I know those tests disadvantage Black, brown, and immigrant students.[47] I can support the adjunct and graduate student unions, because I know that increasing pay and benefits will improve the circumstances of Loyola's most marginalized workers. And of course, I stand beside students in demanding our campus stops partnering with the Chicago Police Department, which has been responsible for the pain and death of so many Black people in our city.[48] Unfortunately, under Systemic Shame, personal feelings and reactions are all we get to explore— collective organizing for larger changes is not on the table.

Evidence shows that the Systemic Shame approach to racism does not work. *Harvard Business Review* reviewed decades of diversity and inclusion research and found that at best, the positive effects of such interventions last a few days. Often, organizations that utilized antiracist workshops actually wound up getting *worse* at placing Black and brown employees into leadership positions afterward.[49] One reason for this, according to the authors, is that the mere presence of such workshops provides a legal shield against accusations of institutional racism. It's easier to shame a few racist cogs than to deconstruct an entire racist machine. Plus, it feels more psychologically satisfying to focus on small boxes that can be checked off ("Add a racial equity statement to your website!" "Add more scholars of color to your syllabus!") than to confront an unwieldy, centuries-old problem.[50]

Our laws and economic system have been busily creating racial, gender-based, and ableist disparities in wealth, education, and mortality for centuries. It will take extensive legal and economic change to even begin slowing down that machine, let alone reversing its course. Most companies don't stand to benefit from investing in that process. At the federal level, a bill to merely *research* racial reparations has languished in Congress for more than two decades.[51] The people who benefit from our current economic system lobby tirelessly to maintain the status quo—and one way that they do that is by filling individuals with persistent, overpowering shame.

Unfortunately, as the next chapter will show, shame is one of the worst ways to facilitate change. Instead, it freezes and overwhelms us, floods us with dread, and makes it difficult for us to think rationally about long-term solutions to global problems.

—◆——◆—

Before we turn our focus toward the rich research literature showing that shame does not motivate healthy change or collaboration, I thought it would be useful to take a pause to recenter our focus on the values that we do hold most dear. As I've outlined in this chapter, Systemic Shame prioritizes the values of perfectionism, individualism, consumerism, wealth, and personal responsibility. If we care more deeply about values such as cooperation, patience, generosity, growth, or grace, then adopting a Systemic Shame approach will never serve us. If we wish to build loving, supportive families and communities, or work to improve the lives of those around us who are suffering, then looking through the lens of Systemic Shame will only bring harm and drive us away from the solutions and shared healing that we need most. So let's take a moment to review a list of some potential values—and see how widely our own beliefs diverge from the damaging lessons of Systemic Shame.

WHAT DO YOU VALUE?

Systemic Shame has five core values:

- Perfectionism: Only endless, flawless work and accomplishment matters.
- Individualism: Everything that we do we do completely alone.
- Consumerism: Who we are is what we buy and own.
- Wealth: The only power that matters is economic power over others.
- Personal responsibility: Change only happens through personal willpower and strength.

However, each one of us gets to decide which values in life matter most. Here are just a few examples of other values that a person might view as important:[52]

Adventure Authenticity Art Caring Connection Courage Freedom Flexibility Forgiveness Excitement Gratitude Growth Intimacy Invention Justice Love Openness Pleasure Patience Reciprocity Respect Self-awareness Spirituality Skillfulness Trust

Choose five values that stand out to you as important (they can be from the list above, or ones that you come up with on your own) and write down what each value means to you.

Value 1:

Value 2:

Value 3:

Value 4:

Value 5:

CHAPTER 4

Why Shame Doesn't Work

"Just Say No" Isn't Enough

The first time I saw my mom order wine at a restaurant, I was five years old, and it made me unbearably distraught. As soon as the glass came to our table, I burst out crying: "Don't do drugs, Mom!" I could not believe she would do something so *wrong*.

I was a 1990s kid, and deep into the teaching of Drug Abuse Resistance Education, or D.A.R.E. In the 1980s and '90s, just as Big Tobacco's personal responsibility messaging was being adopted by other industries, D.A.R.E. was catching on across the United States, teaching children that a life free of addiction was as simple as choosing to say no.[1]

D.A.R.E. classes typically took place in the middle of the school day and were led and facilitated by police officers. D.A.R.E. officers taught children about the "street names" and effects of various substances, shared stories about what they'd seen those substances do to people (usually people they were about to arrest), and ran children through various skits to help them practice saying no to drugs. When I look back on my own time in the program, I mostly recall hearing horrific stories of drug-addled people losing touch with reality and harming themselves or others. I also vividly recall one officer scoffing as he pondered why anybody would even *want* to try anything as disgusting as a cigarette. Smoking's appeal seemed completely unfathomable to him—even as he lectured about how seductive and popular it was.

D.A.R.E. provided a straightforward and personal answer to addiction: Always make the right decisions. Resist the evil temptation. Set yourself apart from other people by deciding to do good. Thanks to D.A.R.E., I grew up viewing drug use as shameful, even evil. My parents didn't keep any alcohol in the house, so whenever I saw an adult imbibing, I felt confused and terrified. When I learned my mom's best friend, Carol, was a lifelong smoker, it disturbed me. How could my mom let me around someone who'd do something so wrong?

D.A.R.E. did not acknowledge how factors like poverty, trauma, chronic pain, or unemployment contribute to substance use, or the role pharmaceutical companies have played in getting people hooked on barbituates and, later, opioids. It did not mention how a robust support network helps addicted people find greater stability and regulate use. And aside from promoting incarceration, D.A.R.E. did not offer any societal solutions. It was an approach utterly rooted in individualistic, moralizing Systemic Shame.

My fellow '90s kids mostly already know this, but D.A.R.E. infamously did not work.[2] Research shows that at best, students who underwent the D.A.R.E. program were indistinguishable from same-aged peers who did not attend the program, in terms of their knowledge, attitudes, and behavior surrounding drugs.[3] Since D.A.R.E. spread many inaccurate myths about drug use (for example, the claim that marijuana is a "gateway drug" that leads to using harder substances), it sometimes left students *less* informed than they were before the program.[4]

At its worst, D.A.R.E. appears to have actually made some students *more likely* to try drugs, because it gave many of us the impression drugs were impossibly alluring and popular.[5] D.A.R.E. preached that being a weak-willed drug user was common and that deciding to abstain from drugs would made you an outsider. It also presented abstinence as a black-and-white moral binary: Either you had the willpower to say no to everything, all of the time, or you'd given in, opening up the gateway to dependence, arrest, and violence. D.A.R.E. also worsened social stigma for drug users: Former D.A.R.E. students are more likely to view addicts as weak and immoral and to see relapses as personal failures, when in reality they're an incredibly common stage of the recovery process.[6]

Additional data suggests that D.A.R.E. left many Black and brown students feeling alienated and stigmatized.[7] D.A.R.E. classes were taught by police officers, after all, not professional educators or addiction experts—and many of those officers harbored inaccurate, racist views about who used drugs and why.[8] I remember my school's own D.A.R.E. officer talking in racially stereotypical ways about drug-addicted "crack moms" who had their babies taken away from them by the state.[9] After that lecture, a biracial student in my grade was given the nickname "crack baby" by some classmates—it followed him around for years.

Data showed very early on that D.A.R.E. was ineffective. But throughout the 1990s, it remained the most popular anti-drug program in the United States, receiving hundreds of millions of dollars in public funding[10] and eventually being adopted in more than fifty countries.[11] Yet there isn't a single published academic study showing it having any benefits.

It never really mattered to most school administrators or lawmakers that D.A.R.E. was not evidence-based. In a world ruled by Systemic Shame, addressing the widespread social problem of addiction by pointing the finger at "addicts" made intuitive sense. It was more comfortable to target the specific people who used drugs than to discuss how society might prevent things like heart and liver disease, mass incarceration, early mortality, and the cycle of poverty. D.A.R.E. was largely inspired by the Scared Straight anti-crime education program of the 1970s, which also taught children it was their personal responsibility to resist crime and violence, and which data also revealed to be ineffective.[12] Yet like D.A.R.E., Scared Straight held massive public appeal. A documentary on Scared Straight's tactics won an Emmy and an Oscar[13] and continued to be shown in the classroom long after researchers found that children who went through Scared Straight were actually *more* likely to be arrested.[14]

The long-lasting appeal of D.A.R.E. and Scared Straight really shows just how compelling our culture finds shame to be—and how wildly counterproductive it is in either shifting individual behavior or preventing societal crises. Shame disempowers. It demotivates and isolates us. When applied to massive social issues like health epidemics or climate change, it fills us with dread. Yet we keep reaching for it. In this chapter, we will explore the psychology of shame, and look to the research that illustrates why relying on shame is not only ineffective, but self-defeating. We will also explore why Systemic Shame continues to pull us into its web, despite the mountain of evidence against it.

Shame Makes the Forbidden Seem More Alluring

At the same time as I was enrolled in D.A.R.E., my own dad was secretly smoking cigarettes behind dumpsters and in secluded parks all over town. Though he claimed to have quit when I was born, my dad secretly continued smoking for more than sixteen years. Then one day when I was in tenth grade, I cut class to go smoke in the park with my friends. There he was, standing between the trees, a pack in his hands, a deer-in-the-headlights look on his face.

My dad's entire outlook on life was ravaged by shame. He kept his cerebral palsy and seizure disorder hidden his entire life. Throughout my childhood, he told me I was lucky to not have inherited his "ugly" red hair and large nose. When he developed diabetes in middle age, he lied to our family and his doctor about his eating habits, bingeing on hidden stashes of sugary foods late in the night. He believed in keeping bank accounts that no one else knew about, having illicit trysts, and keeping other people at bay. When he slipped into a diabetic coma and died when I was eighteen, no one found his body for days because he was so socially isolated.

"Your dad liked having secrets" is how my mom explains it. I think he felt compelled to revel in his shame. When he died, my family found piles of therapists' business cards scattered all around his home, but as far as we can tell, he never called any of them. His shame kept him drawing a forceful line between the rest of the world and his lonesome, spiraling self, and that was what killed him.

In my early twenties, I'd do much the same thing, smoking in private, relishing both the thrill of getting away with something verboten, and languishing in shame over my lack of self-control. To this day I can't explain why I did it, except that I hated myself, and I felt pulled, as if by some gravitational force, to do something risky and secretive. Like my dad, I binge-ate, and I also excessively exercised. I always did it at night, long after everyone else had gone to bed. I hid my self-harm habits from other people. I hid the fact that I'd get online and meet strangers for anonymous sex, often in thrillingly risky scenarios. When my eating disorder got bad, I hid that I'd lost my period and explained away my sudden fainting spells as the effects of overwork (which, of course, I was also engaging in because of my shame). My immense self-loathing did nothing to stifle my self-destructive impulses. It only fed into them and ensured that I went about meeting my needs in the least healthy ways possible.

There is something compelling about shame. Locking certain activities behind the bars of the forbidden often makes them more attractive to us. And the intensity of shame makes it difficult for us to form reasoned decisions about how to get what we need—and so instead we enact our desires in impulsive, uncontrolled ways that leave us feeling even worse.

As the licensed dietician Michele Allison writes on her blog *The Fat Nutritionist*, teaching people to completely abstain from supposedly "bad" foods only makes them more likely to binge, or experience sensations of "food addiction."[15] As a fat person who repeatedly has been shamed for how her body looks and how she eats, Allison is well acquainted with this phenomenon in her own life.

"I used to have a bit of a fixation on sweets," Allison writes. "Since childhood, they had been a mildly forbidden food . . . I assumed that I was somewhat bad for liking them so much, and I believed that I could never really be in control with them."[16]

Allison writes that when she began dieting as an adult in an attempt to lose weight, it only worsened her belief that certain foods were "bad." The belief that sugar was evil and addictive became a self-fulfilling prophecy for her, imbuing it with a power it otherwise wouldn't have possessed. Though fearmongering about the dangers of sugar is common in mainstream media,[17] its health risks have largely been overstated,[18] and there is no empirical evidence that such a thing as "sugar addiction" really exists. In fact, a review article in the *European Journal of Nutrition* found that the only people at risk of bingeing uncontrollably on sugar are those who have been actively limiting their sugar intake.[19]

This finding is consistent with a great deal of eating disorder research showing that people are most likely to "lose control" and binge on food when they have been restricting calories severely.[20] The leading predictor of bingeing is deprivation, not addiction. The more we reprimand ourselves for wanting sugar, or cake, or french fries, the less in control we feel around those food products and the more desperate our hunger becomes.

On her blog, Allison describes how she stopped having addictive-seeming cravings when she stopped acting as though sugar was evil. Rather than taking a "just say no" D.A.R.E.-type approach to eating, she gave herself permission to enjoy whatever she wanted, and started listening nonjudgmentally to her body's cravings and hunger cues. With time, sweets lost much of their allure.

"I feel quite happy now with sweets," Allison writes.[21] "I will occasionally eat too much in one sitting and feel a little bit off afterward, and I accept that . . . I don't get caught up in the shame-spiral of judging myself. I usually end up feeling less hungry afterward for the next few meals or the next day, or I start craving a completely different type of food that seems to address the feeling of imbalance."

In Allison's work with clients, she promotes what she calls "eating normally." Eating normally has a lot in common with the method eating disorder recovery experts call "intuitive eating." Both approaches involve a person learning to trust their body to signal what it needs, and not judging any desires they might feel or "mistakes" they might make. According to intuitive eating and eating normally, there are no forbidden foods and there's no reason to try to argue with hunger—because of this, there's far less risk of the negative health effects of dieting or compulsive, disordered habits.

Systemic Shame teaches that our health is under our control—and when we make "bad" decisions, the consequences are our fault. When we take a supposed "risk" with our health, we're likely to feel ashamed and immoral. Even the fact that indulgent desserts are commonly marketed as "sinful" or even "better than sex" reveals diet culture's close relationship to Puritanical morality and its fears around sexuality and other bodily impulses. But the more you broadcast an action is compelling and bad, the harder it is for people to make judicious decisions around it. This is part of why dieting typically causes far more people to *gain* weight than to lose it.[22] Forbidden foods tend to be a major trigger of emotional upheaval and compulsive eating habits for those with eating disorders as well.[23] Associating a food with shame only distorts our relationship to it.

Conversely, people who listen to their body's hunger cues and eat intuitively tend to have better health outcomes and a more consistent weight[24] than those who suppress or restrict themselves. Our bodies are quite good at self-regulating. After several days of filling, carb-heavy meals, we tend to crave vegetables, fresh fruit, and fiber. If we go too long without enough sugar or fat, our brains hyperfixate on those nutrients until we consume what we require. But when we feel ashamed about our cravings or hunger, it throws off an otherwise very effective, nearly automatic system.

Some research shows that merely *believing* you are cutting back on calories, for instance, can stimulate production of the hunger hormone ghrelin. In an experiment by the psychologist Alia Crum and colleagues, participants who drank a shake labeled "low calorie" experienced a significant uptick in ghrelin production, and felt hungrier afterward, whereas participants who drank a shake labeled "high calorie" experienced a drop in the hormone.[25] The two shakes were identical. So even just *thinking* you've been restricting can make your hunger ramp up. In this way, obsessing over the evils of sugar and the need to resist it might actually predispose a person to eating more of it, in a shame-fueled rush, and feeling horrible afterward.

The same is true of other behaviors associated with shame in our culture, like unprotected sex. While typically these behaviors are completely morally neutral on their own, our fear of "losing control" and enjoying them too much becomes a self-fulfilling prophecy. Shame only makes it more challenging to communicate honestly about what we are going through and which needs we are trying to fulfill. Below is an exercise to get you thinking a bit about which needs and hungers in your life you tend to suppress because you're afraid that giving in to them will make you "lose control."

LOSING CONTROL:
Which Needs Do You Fear?

Write down your responses to the following questions.

1. Are there any foods, substances, sexual experiences, or other exciting activities (such as shopping, gambling, or even self-harm) that make you feel "out of control"? What are they?

2. What does going "out of control" look like for you?

3. How does it feel in your body when you compulsively eat/gamble/ use substances/etc.?

4. What's on your mind when you are in the middle of "losing control"?

5. Many people report "losing control" over their willpower when certain feelings are triggered in them. Below is a brief list of some potential triggers. Check off any that resonate with you:

6. I am mostly likely to "lose control" when I am:

____ Feeling stressed

____ Feeling disconnected from my body

____ Exhausted

____ Hungry

____ Lonely

____ Lacking in stimulation or excitement

____ Feel that I have nothing to look forward to

____ Upset with myself

____ Reliving memories of past traumas

____ Want to assert my freedom

____ Want to get back at someone else

____ Angry

____ Other:

7. One of the leading predictors of compulsive behavior are feelings of deprivation. What do you feel deprived of? Check off any of the following that apply:

____ Food

____ Pleasure

____ Attention

____ Money/resources

____ Comfort

____ Excitement

____ Appreciation

____ Privacy

____ Control over your own body

____ Self-expression

____ Physical contact

____ Affection/warmth

____ Other:

table continued

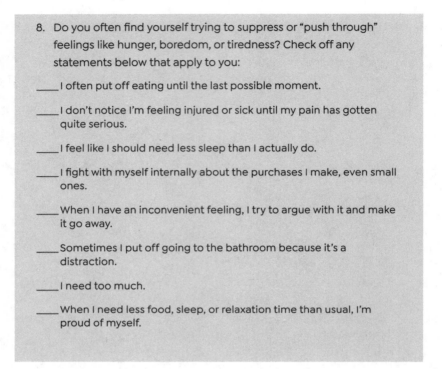

8. Do you often find yourself trying to suppress or "push through" feelings like hunger, boredom, or tiredness? Check off any statements below that apply to you:

_____ I often put off eating until the last possible moment.

_____ I don't notice I'm feeling injured or sick until my pain has gotten quite serious.

_____ I feel like I should need less sleep than I actually do.

_____ I fight with myself internally about the purchases I make, even small ones.

_____ When I have an inconvenient feeling, I try to argue with it and make it go away.

_____ Sometimes I put off going to the bathroom because it's a distraction.

_____ I need too much.

_____ When I need less food, sleep, or relaxation time than usual, I'm proud of myself.

Systemic Shame leads many of us to believe that we must earn the right to be alive through tireless hard work and by forever making the correct, most "virtuous" possible decisions. This Puritanical approach makes it very hard to be honest with ourselves about what our bodies need and can easily make us ashamed of even basic bodily functions and cravings. On Instagram a few years ago, I even saw a post created by a therapist reminding her followers that it's okay to "take a break" at work and go pee. The post was very well-intentioned, but by framing urination as a pleasurable act of "self-care" rather than a fundamental human need that is impossible to argue with, it just further revealed our culture's absurd belief that bodily functions are distractions we should be able to power through. That's how deeply Systemic Shame has divorced us from our own bodies and needs. We see the mere act of feeding ourselves as "sinful," and peeing as a lavish indulgence.

Shame Prevents Self-Care

A great deal of research shows that when people feel shame, they become less likely to take care of themselves. Shame reduces self-efficacy, a person's trust in their ability to get things done.[26] Shame-ridden people have less energy and motivation to advocate for their own well-being—and less trust that doing so would have any benefit in the long run. It's yet another absurd paradox of Systemic Shame: By holding people morally responsible for the tough situations that they're in, we actually make them less able to do the "right" things, like schedule doctor's appointments, exercise, seek help controlling their drinking, or wear a condom.

Shame also leads people to think they don't *deserve* to treat their bodies with kindness and consideration. When diabetes patients feel shame about their disease or eating habits, they stop monitoring their blood sugar as closely[27] and show less interest in attending educational programs about managing the condition.[28] When people with drug addictions are ashamed of themselves, they're less likely to carry medications that might save them from an overdose.[29] Depressed people who experience a high degree of mental health stigma have a far lower likelihood of speaking to anyone about their symptoms, and a far higher risk of instead committing suicide, for the same reasons.[30] It's hard to imagine how shaming people for engaging in "unhealthy" or "bad" behaviors might ever be beneficial when we look at how consistently it blocks help-seeking and proactive, preventative care.

It's no coincidence the very same Ohio public school system that pushed me through D.A.R.E. as a child also pressured me to sign a virginity pledge when I was sixteen. A college-aged Christian performing arts troupe came to my school and extolled the virtues of abstinence and the evils of sex. Performers passed around a red Solo cup, asking every boy in the room to spit into it. The performers made everyone look into the cup at the bubbly, cloudy morass of saliva inside. This is what being a promiscuous woman does to you, they said. And gay sex? Anal was a repulsive, violent act that could never lead to love. As the actors spoke to us, their faces screwed up with disgust. Many of my straight classmates laughed and jeered. When one of my friends attempted to pass out educational resources on safer sex and queer sexuality in protest, the principal forced him to stop.

Those abstinence-only educators must have believed they were waging a righteous war on teen pregnancy, sexually transmitted infections, and "sin" by shaming us for our sexualities. But because they trained us to fear our desires, many of us couldn't plan to have sex safely by carrying condoms or taking birth control. We couldn't explore our bodies and identities to figure out who we were and what we liked. Instead, many of us had impulsive, shame-fueled fumblings with people who didn't respect us. We hooked up with adults we met at our jobs or had anonymous sex in closets and around campfires with people we'd met on the internet. Some of my peers got pregnant very young or found themselves in marriages with older men who mistreated them. But no matter what harm came to any of us, Systemic Shame preached that it was just punishment for our bad behavior.

A great deal of research affirms these experiences. Religious, shame-based approaches to sex education have been repeatedly shown to be counterproductive; they make teens less likely to practice safe sex, on average[31] because they create a black-and-white binary between virtuous abstinence and risky, "sinful" sex. When queer people feel ashamed of their identities, they find it too threatening to have open conversations about sexually transmitted infections and preventative measures such as condoms and PrEP (pre-exposure prophylaxis, which helps prevent HIV infection). A study on the sexual health habits and attitudes of Black queer men conducted by Jerilyn Radcliffe and colleagues found that the more HIV stigma men experienced, the more likely they were to impulsively have condom- and PrEP-free sex while intoxicated or high.[32] After suppressing their desires out of sheer self-hatred, these queer men needed the release of substances to allow them to "lose control" and enjoy the activities they longed for. When PrEP was first rolled out in Canada in the early 2010s, researchers found that many gay men were ashamed to use it, and felt they had to hide that they were taking the drug from others.[33] Instead of empowering us to look after our well-being, shame jams up our decision-making process and fills us with inner turmoil over basic acts of preventative care.

In the table below, you'll find some questions designed to get you thinking about desires and habits you might feel ashamed of in your own life. Try to consider your fantasies, fears, and behaviors from a nonjudgmental place, or at least to notice self-judgment as it arises. Pay particular attention to the sense that you can't *let yourself* feel or want something. If something you crave doing feels unspeakable, that's a surefire sign shame is at work. We might only feel free to voice our most forbidden desires when we're extremely tired, intoxicated, or in an unfamiliar setting where nobody will remember what we've done or said. Answering these questions may help you tap into the yearnings that you don't normally allow yourself to voice.

"DESIRES YOU'RE ASHAMED OF" EXERCISE

Shame often makes it difficult for us to admit to ourselves or others what we really want out of life. Our minds put up strong defenses against our impulses and fantasies, because we find facing them too embarrassing or threatening. Use the following questions to reflect on the desires you block yourself from experiencing.

Do you ever find yourself trying to push certain thoughts and desires from your mind? When these thoughts come to you, how do you feel?

Complete the following sentences:

"It's wrong for me to want _____."

"If I admitted that I wanted _____,

it would make me _____ [weird/creepy/

pathetic/gross/other]."

"If I were free to do whatever I wanted for a day, and nobody in my

regular life would ever find out about it, I would _____

_____

_____

_____."

"I wish someone could just *know* that I need _____

_____

_____

_____

without me having to ask."

In my case, I know that when I'm ashamed of how I'm feeling, I will only admit the truth to myself in moments of profound exhaustion, or when I think there won't be any lasting consequences. For example, I once confessed a deeply suppressed sexual fantasy to a random acquaintance, on the patio of a bar where he and I had been drinking all night. I'd never shared the fantasy out loud to anyone before, only Googled porn featuring that fantasy late when no one was around, and then hated myself for it. But then this guy, a near stranger, started telling me drunkenly about his love for older women, as if it were some terrible, salacious secret he'd never been able to indulge.

I was tipsy and tired, and this random man's confession put me at ease. It seemed so silly for him to be ashamed of thinking women in their forties and fifties were attractive. It made me think that perhaps some of my own desires weren't all that terrible either. So I explained my own fantasy aloud to him, for the first time in my life. Once I'd found the words for what I desired, I could finally imagine myself bringing it up to sexual partners and trusted friends. Within a year, I was actually engaging in some of the kinks I'd been hiding away inside of myself for over twenty years.

I have also noticed that after repressing my true feelings or longings all day long, they often hit me like a ton of bricks when I'm lying down in bed. And usually the desire I'm so terribly ashamed of is a completely neutral or even positive thing to want, such as yearning to be cuddled, or spoken to kindly and taken care of. Under Systemic Shame, wanting to be coddled in any way feels immoral, and actually asking for what we desire may be so terrifying that it halts us in our tracks.

Shame Freezes Us

There are deeply wired biological reasons that shame makes it hard for us to take care of ourselves or to behave in supposedly "responsible" ways. It all comes down to the type of emotion shame is, and the likely role shame played early in humans' evolutionary history.

In cognitive and social psychology, we sometimes discuss emotions in terms of which are *approach-based* and which are *avoidance-based*.[34] Approach-based emotions (like hope, love, curiosity, and even anger and mild sadness) encourage you to move *toward* others and to engage with reality in an active way. When you experience approach-based emotions, your pupils dilate, your sense of smell improves, and time seems to slow down. All of this makes it easier to do things like fight off an enemy, reach out for a hug, or locate resources. Approach-based emotions cause us to experience an uptick in production of the hormone oxytocin, which can encourage prosocial behavior, empathy,[35] bonding, and even cuddling,[36] though it also makes people more biased in favor of their own in-group and more prejudiced toward out-groups.[37]

In essence, oxytocin and the approach-based emotions that come with it seemed to have helped early humans find affiliation and belonging, as well as defend themselves from outsiders they perceived as threats. When you're in approach-based-emotion mode, you want to defend your community and build up your existing relationships, as well as seek help, and you feel empowered and motivated enough to do so.

In contrast, avoidance-based emotions (such as disgust, apathy, and despair) close the body off and move us to separate from other people.[38] Our pupils shrink and our energy levels plummet. Oxytocin drops.[39] Aggression lowers. So does our sense of connectedness and belonging. The drive to reach out for help—and the belief that doing so will do any good—all but disappears. There are a variety of explanations for *why* avoidance-based emotions function this way, but one of the leading theories is that they help preserve energy and provide protection when a situation looks hopeless.[40] If you feel you're past the point where crying out for aid or trying to ward off an attacker will do any good, your body may slip into a withdrawing, low-energy state in order to help you hide and survive until conditions improve.[41]

Here is a table summarizing which emotions are approach-based and which are avoidance-based, and some behaviors and coping strategies that come with them.

APPROACH- AND AVOIDANCE-BASED EMOTIONS		
Emotion Type	Example Emotions	Example Behaviors[42]
Approach	Anger Happiness Mild sadness Pride Curiosity	• Confronting an attacker • Sharing good news with a friend • Crying visibly and requesting a hug • Showing off an accomplishment • Learning about a new hobby or skill
Avoidance	Despair Fear Apathy Disgust Shame	• No longer following an upsetting topic or issue • Withdrawing from a stressful social situation • Losing interest in a hobby or pursuit • Not trying new foods or visiting unfamiliar spaces • Lying or hiding sensitive information from family and friends

One really harrowing example of how avoidance-motivated emotions function can be found in the Still Face experiment by the developmental psychologist Edward Tronick. In the Still Face experiment, a parent is instructed to stare blankly and emotionlessly at their infant child, and remain totally unresponsive for several minutes, no matter what their child does to get their attention. At first, infants in the Still Face experiment make all kinds of approach-motivated gestures to get a rise out of their nonreactive parents. They point to objects in the room to try to draw their parent's attention toward it. They laugh and smile and reach out for comfort. When these efforts fail, many infants flail around, cry, and show distress— anger and sadness both being more desperate approach-motivated emotions than happiness is. Finally, as their parent continues to stare blankly at them, not reacting, infants in the Still Face experiment eventually become listless and emotionally "blank" themselves. After all attempts at approach fail, babies slip into avoidance mode and give up. Watching a young child's desperate desire to connect give way to apathetic dejection is crushing to witness.[43] It's a feeling of hopeless detachment that shame-sufferers know all too well.

Shame is a powerful avoidance-based emotion. People experiencing shame pull away, physically and emotionally.[44] They also become more passive and adopt more submissive postures.[45] They bow inward, protect their necks with their hands, and can't marshal up the courage to look anyone in the face. Because their oxytocin levels drop, ashamed people feel more overwhelmed and have a harder time focusing and processing new information. Some research suggests that when people experience shame, they are also less attuned to their bodies and emotions, and more prone to repressing how they truly feel.[46]

Early in human history, looking visibly ashamed might have reduced conflict—think of a dog tucking its tail between its legs and slinking off after a fight. But when people no longer live communally and interdependently, shame doesn't work quite so well. Withdrawing from other people becomes isolating, not pacifying. The emotions researcher June Tangney has repeatedly found that shame renders people less likely to make amends with those they've wronged, and more prone to deny their past actions, or try to escape.[47] This brings us to the next reason that shame does not lead to meaningful change: It encourages us to detach, and it tears supportive communities apart. We'll explore that negative effect of shame in the next section.

Since shame is such a visceral emotion, it has many effects throughout our bodies. The following exercise will get you thinking about how shame feels in your body, which may help you recognize when it's affecting you so that you can take more proactive steps to circumvent it in the future.

HOW DOES SHAME FEEL IN YOUR BODY?

Think about a time when you felt profoundly ashamed, or a factor in your life that you currently feel shame about. Pay close attention to any bodily signals of discomfort that shame creates in you.

Check off the body sensations and behaviors that you notice when you're experiencing shame. Add as many of your own sensations to the list as you'd like.

_____ Mental "fog" or trouble focusing

_____ Frequent blinking, or eyes that can't blink pivoting around the room

_____ Downward-looking eyes, or more difficulty looking at others than usual

_____ Furrowed eyebrows

_____ Tension in the temples, or headaches

table continued

____A hot or blushing face

____Tightness in the jaw and neck

____Covering your face or looking away/turning from others

____Difficulty speaking or finding words

____Crying

____Staring off into space

____Exhaustion and needing to lie down / zone out

____Hunched shoulders

____Crossed arms

____A sour stomach or an uneasy digestive tract

____Butterflies in the stomach

____Racing heart

____Tightness in the chest

____Rapid breathing

____Jitteriness or the need to fidget

____A desire to tear or break items apart, or to grip onto something strongly

____Curling your legs up against your body or crossing your legs

____Curling of the toes, or tension in the feet

____Sitting or standing in a compressed, curled-up way that makes your body "smaller"

____Physical agitation, or the desire to physically "get away"

____Slowness in reacting or responding to outside stimuli

____Trouble initiating activity; feeling stuck or frozen

____Other:

As you can see from just looking at this list, the physiological effects of shame can be quite paradoxical. Shame fills us with nervous energy, but it also tends to make us feel demotivated, and slow to react to our surroundings. Shame causes bodily tension, but never provides us a comfortable release. When we recall that shame is similar to experiencing a fight-or-flight response, and when we consider how infants react at the end of the Still Face experiment, however, these many reactions add up in a way that makes sense. Shame floods us with distress, but also signals to us that there's no point in trying to resolve it. Pushing through that sensation of hopelessness and claiming the support we need is vital, and brings us both personal and shared healing. But when we are ashamed, every instinct inside us screams to do the complete opposite.

Shame Isolates Us

In early 2020, the philosophy and culture YouTuber Natalie Wynn released the viral video essay "Shame," in which she came out as a lesbian. In the video, Wynn describes how she spent years forcing herself to date men. She wasn't attracted to them, but having a conventionally hot straight man on her arm proved to everyone around her that she was a desirable woman. Conversely, thinking of herself as a lesbian made Wynn feel predatory and disgusting. For years the prospect of coming out struck her as unthinkable.

Wynn says she was experiencing something called "compulsory heterosexuality," or "comphet."[48] Many lesbian women describe going through comphet, forcing themselves to develop crushes on fictional men or unavailable older male figures while privately fantasizing about female friends and acquaintances. Comphet suffers push themselves to have "straight" sex they don't actually desire, hiding their sexual identities from everyone, and denying pleasure to themselves.[49]

Comphet appears to be especially prevalent among lesbians for a couple of reasons. First, women are generally taught in our culture to prioritize the attention of men, and to define themselves by their relationships to them. Taking on a man's last name and having children with him are presented in our culture as some of the most life-defining moments of a woman's existence, and when a woman has no desire to take part, she may struggle to understand where she fits in the world. Furthermore, women's sexual pleasure is severely undervalued in our culture, so many queer women don't get to explore their identities through porn, masturbation, and fantasy the way many straight people and young men do. Then there's the way lesbians have traditionally been portrayed on screen: lesbian characters are often violent, controlling, jealous, and unbearably "creepy" to the straight women around them.[50] All of these factors help explain why lesbians, on average, come out of the closet at a far later age than gay men do,[51] and frequently report anxiety and inhibition in approaching other women and asking them on dates.

In Wynn's case, the shame of comphet was further complicated by the fact she's a transgender woman, an identity she also felt immense shame about.[52]

"There's two problems that kind of multiply together," Wynn says. "One, I'm ashamed of being trans. Two, I'm ashamed of being a lesbian. And whatever one times two is, I'm really ashamed of being a trans lesbian. Ew . . . It does make me feel like a monster sometimes. Like a mutant that has no place in society."[53]

Trans women have been villainized in the media for decades. Typically, when trans women are shown on screen, they are not even correctly identified as women, but rather labeled as delusional or dishonest "men" masquerading as women for their own benefit. An early cinematic example of this is Norman Bates in Alfred Hitchcock's *Psycho*, who wears his mother's clothing and adopts her personality before embarking on murderous rampages. Perhaps the most infamous example of such transmisogyny (hatred of trans women) on screen is the character of Jame Gumb in the film *Silence of the Lambs*.[54] Though Gumb identifies as transgender and has sought out gender-reassignment surgery, the writing and dialogue of the film only paints Gumb as a depraved "man." Gumb kidnaps and murders young women in the film, in order to craft a wearable woman suit out of their skin. The character basically represents every negative media stereotype of trans women all rolled into one: She's not really a woman, she's delusional, she's dangerous and violent, and her close relationships with other women aren't genuine, they're just a twisted attempt to steal what supposedly "real" women have.

Once you become aware of tropes like these, you'll find them everywhere. A murderous trans woman who "tricks" straight men is the main villain of *Ace Ventura: Pet Detective*. The villain orchestrating everything behind the scenes in *Mr. Robot* is a nefarious trans woman who's desperate to shake off her old male persona. The television shows *Friends*, *Two and a Half Men*, *Law & Order: SVU*, *Family Guy*, *Futurama*, and even, bafflingly, *Cake Boss* all feature a shocking "reveal" that a trans woman is "actually a man" setting out to deceive people.[55]

Decades of media demonization has taken a significant toll on trans women. They experience depression, substance use, self-harm, eating disorders, and social anxiety at elevated rates.[56] Trans women (especially Black and brown ones) also experience extremely high rates of sexual assault, battery, abuse, and even murder. Society's systemic, pervasive hatred of trans women infects how other people view them and treat them—and it erodes how trans women perceive and feel about themselves.

In her videos, Natalie Wynn says she regularly reads forums run by transphobes such as 4chan and Kiwifarms, where users relentlessly tear down the appearance, mannerisms, and identities of trans people (particularly trans women) and fantasize about enacting violence against them. Wynn internalizes these hurtful observations and applies them to the other trans women around her. She judges trans women for their body shapes, their faces, their voices, and how they dress. Internally, she can't stop critiquing their mannerisms, interests, and how hard they appear to be trying (or not trying) to "pass" as respectable, feminine cisgender women.

Wynn doesn't like that she's doing this, and she's clear in her videos she doesn't think these reactions are right. But she can't seem to stop herself from dwelling on negative thoughts about her own community. Wynn's personal Systemic Shame has radiated outward, creating damaging interpersonal shame that attacks the very women who understand her suffering most. Instead of finding community among other trans women and working together to heal their shared trauma and push for greater acceptance in society, Wynn finds herself spiraling downward into further withdrawal. In more recent videos, she's open about finding it incredibly difficult to date or make friends with people in the trans community in her city.

I relate to Wynn's conflicted feelings and loneliness so much it hurts. Before I transitioned into a male identity, I felt myself pulled toward queer masculinity, yet repelled by my own interest. When I first met a swishy, effeminate gay man in real life, at an Italian restaurant in Cleveland when I was a young child, the world around him seemed to suddenly light up. I could not take my eyes off his perfectly gelled hair and delicate, soft-wristed gestures. I had long admired gay characters in film (Harvey Fierstein's character in *Mrs. Doubtfire* and Jeremy Irons's Scar in *The Lion King* were early favorites), but until that moment in the restaurant, I hadn't been sure if gay men were "real." The fact that gay men actually existed filled me with hope, though I didn't yet realize I could also be one.

I often found myself identifying with gay, feminine male characters in movies and video games. In my teens and early twenties, I routinely developed crushes on gay men. I knew in my heart that I was one of them—but social conditioning told me there was no way I could be *both* gay and trans. That was doubly immoral, and doubly freakish.

For decades I insisted to myself that I was just a confused straight girl, a pathetic "fag hag" who mistook her friendships with gay men for love. To steel myself against rejection, I lashed out at the gay male friends whom I secretly adored. When I started meeting other trans men, I found my brain rattling through a long list of their supposed flaws—always qualities I considered wrong and unacceptably "womanly" in myself. I also would compulsively check hate sites like Kiwifarms, poring over the ruthlessly vile things members of that forum had to say about trans people in the public eye, including me and other people I knew in real life.[57]

Back in Chapter 1, we explored how internalized shame kept Ellen from being able to connect with her daughter, Jenna. By verbally punishing herself and beating herself up with overwork every time that she caught Jenna self-harming, Ellen unwittingly communicated to her daughter that she was directly hurting her mom. This only motivated Jenna to hide her true feelings and self-harming habits from Ellen even further. Shame drove a wedge between them, even though they were both already coping poorly with isolation and depression. And it took a very long time for Ellen to find a less self-defeating way to address both their issues together.

Here's a reflection tool to get you thinking about the negative beliefs you might harbor about yourself—and how those beliefs might affect you internally *and* be externalized toward other people.

INTERNALIZED / EXTERNALIZED SHAME EXERCISE

Complete this exercise by answering the questions below.

1. Name a marginalized, vulnerable, or unfairly stereotyped group that you belong to. This could be an identity group such as "women," "queer people," "Black men," or "intersex people," or it might reflect a particular experience, such as "abuse survivors," "people who didn't go to college," "first-generation immigrants," or "wheelchair users."

2. List some common stereotypes applied to members of your group. Try to come up with five to ten examples.

3. Look over the list of stereotypes above, and circle the ones you find the most painful or embarrassing to think about.

4. Underline the stereotypes that you often worry about other people seeing in you.

5. Do you ever find yourself feeling embarrassed or annoyed by other members of your identity group? Which kinds of behaviors elicit this kind of reaction in you?

6. What does it mean to be a "respectable" member of your group, in society's eyes? How are you "supposed" to look, carry yourself, dress, and behave?

7. Do you hold members of your group to a higher standard than other people? In what ways?

Systemic Shame can cut us off from our own communities, languishing in self-hatred while lashing out and punishing anyone who reminds us of ourselves. Unfortunately, the impact of Systemic Shame can cut still deeper than this. Beyond eroding our self-concept and fraying the bonds we share with others, Systemic Shame can also destroy our outlook toward the world and to humanity as a whole, filling us with such immense existential dread that we find imagining a better future impossible.

Shame and Dread in a Greenwashed World

In her book *Is Shame Necessary?*, the environmental studies professor Jennifer Jacquet describes being haunted as a child by photos of dolphins choking to death in tuna-fishing nets.

"I needed to do something," she writes. "At nine years old, I had already learned what the 1980s taught as the new rite of passage: to alleviate my guilt as a consumer. I insisted that our family stopped buying canned tuna, and I wasn't alone."[58]

Faced with a torrent of public criticism, companies like Heinz began marketing "dolphin-safe" tuna around this time. Decades later, in March 2021, National Geographic reported that the three largest tuna companies in the world were facing a class-action lawsuit for having misleadingly labeled their products as dolphin-safe for years.[59] This was just the latest instance of corporations utilizing greenwashing, presenting a product as environmentally sound to appeal to consumers' Systemic Shame, and to obscure blame regarding their own acts of destruction.

In the late 1980s and early 1990s, greenwashing took hold of the consumer economy. Products were increasingly marketed with terms like *organic, sustainable, recyclable,* and *ethically sourced.*[60] In most cases, these terms were unregulated falsehoods, or vague technicalities. The triangular recycling symbol, for example, appears on thousands of products that we currently lack the technology to recycle in any sustainable way.[61] But from a marketing perspective, all the label really needed to do was offer consumers a brief respite from shame. And for decades, that tactic worked beautifully. As research into the negative footprint effect has demonstrated, many conscientious consumers are desperate to find some small step to take (or some small purchase to make) that can offload the immense guilt they feel for consuming too many items, burning off too many fossil fuels, and having an active hand in what often feels like the end of the world.

Like Jacquet, many of us were aspiring environmentalists in childhood, reminding our parents to turn off the spigot while they brushed their teeth and demanding we buy rainforest-friendly chocolate. Yet after repeated instances of greenwashing, we learn that no matter how many soda rings we cut up or how much water we conserve, it never winds up being enough. It's no surprise that even highly committed environmentalists feel increasingly hopeless and demotivated in recent years.[62]

Systemic Shame hinders the fight for climate justice (and against many other global issues, such as global pandemics and natural disasters) in two key ways:

1. It fills individuals with despair over our own inability to make a difference,[63] and
2. It causes us to believe it's too late to save the world.

The former manifests in us obsessing over our individual habits, and setting out desperately to "cancel out" acts of ecological destruction by purchasing the right things. The latter is more of a collective, global manifestation of shame. It is echoed in claims that "human beings are the real virus" or that we deserve to die out. Systemic Shame teaches us that our suffering is our fault. But when it is applied to an issue as existentially threatening as climate change, it takes a downright apocalyptic turn.

In 2004, the oil company British Petroleum (BP) introduce the term "carbon footprint" to the public and created and promoted a personal carbon footprint calculator. The company did so in order to distract from the role they played in rising carbon dioxide levels and disasters such as oil spills.[64] And it worked. Today, we are offered carbon-tracking applications that help individual people calculate how much damage their daily commute or online shopping habit is doing to the environment.[65] Sixty-five percent of consumers express a desire to shop sustainably—though only about 26 percent say they've been able to do so.[66] Our best intentions, it turns out, don't matter nearly as much as the elaborate network of obligations and economic incentives that surround and entrap us.

When I was in graduate school, "ecoguilt" was becoming a hot topic in the social psychological literature. Ecoguilt is the uneasy feeling of recognizing that your actions don't really line up with your own moral standards for pro-environmental behavior.[67] Social psychologists have tested whether feeling ecoguilt might motivate people to recycle more, to increase donations to green organizations, to compost, to conserve water, to take public transit, to carry reusable tote bags, and more.[68] And what they find, generally speaking, is that when people experience ecoguilt, they express a *desire* to do more for the environment in the future. They are also more likely to buy into the negative footprint effect and try to counteract "bad" actions with "good" purchases.[69] Researchers have analyzed the content of thousands of online posts about ecoguilt, finding that many people use quasi-religious language to describe it.[70] Posters write about the environment in terms of personal "sin," and effects like climate change and natural disasters as forms of cosmic punishment.

Interestingly, although ecoguilt has been extensively studied for well over a decade, not one single study has found that feelings of ecoguilt actually lead to individuals taking more environmentally-friendly behavior. Instead, research finds that eco-guilty individuals state that they *want* to do more for the environment (they have what psychologists call a behavioral intention), but they don't actually have any means of doing so. One 2016 study conducted by Bissing-Olson, Fielding, and Iyer, for example, found that guilt over past environmentally-unfriendly decisions didn't make participants any more likely to behave in green ways in the future. The only thing that promoted eco-friendly action in the future was having been able to recycle, compost, or otherwise help the environment in the *past*, and feeling empowered and happy about that fact. Now, almost a decade after the boom in ecoguilt studies, leading voices in the field such as Ganga Shreedar point out that experiencing ecoguilt can cause people to emotionally check out of an issue—exactly as fat-shamed and sex-shamed patients do regarding their health.[71] The researcher Elisa Aaltola even calls feelings of ecoguilt a form of "morally destructive shame."

As Rebecca Solnit recently wrote in *The Guardian*, "Some of what I could tout as personal virtue is only possible because of collective action . . . I do some of my errands by bicycle because the San Francisco Bicycle Coalition worked for decades to put bicycle paths across the city and otherwise make it safer to get about on two wheels."[72] In a city without bike lanes, sustainable electricity, or a robust recycling system, most people can't decide to do the "right" thing even if they want to.

When we consider that the bulk of environmental damage is done by large corporations and governments, it's easy to make the case that the entire ecoguilt literature has misplaced its focus by worrying about personal behavioral intentions in the first place. Even if every person who could afford to do so suddenly decided to go vegan tomorrow, we would still live in a world where the beef industry is subsidized to the tune of nearly forty billion dollars per year,[73] and where the supply chain for fresh produce is incredibly wasteful and ecologically destructive.[74] If I always sorted and recycled my garbage for the rest of my life, that would not alter the fact that the vast majority of recycled items ultimately end up in a landfill (after undergoing extra rounds of shipping and sorting, consuming even more fuel).[75] Systemic initiatives like the Green New Deal (which aims to reduce US carbon emissions annually, reaching zero net emissions by 2050) are quite popular among the American public, but politically, they have proven incredibly difficult to move forward[76]—because they would come at a severe cost to corporations.

For many years, Systemic Shame has sold us a vision of environmental salvation rooted in individual behavior. Only you can prevent forest fires. Reduce, reuse, recycle. And all that vision has left us with is persistent fears about the future of our planet, combined with maddening powerlessness.

It very well may be that the powerlessness Systemic Shame creates in us is entirely by design. As the political theorist Mark Fisher wrote in his book *Capitalist Realism*, forever growth of the economy is impossible, and so believing that the world is on the verge of collapse can actually seem easier than imagining an end to exploitation and capitalism.[77] Fisher and other theorists such as David Graeber and Frederic Jameson have argued that believing the world is ending can actually help take the pressure off corporations and governments that refuse to change. There's no point in cutting back on emissions, ending child slavery in sweatshops, or imagining new ways of living if we're all about to die anyway and we think we deserve it.

But humanity doesn't have to consign itself to the ash heap like this, no matter how ashamed, terrified, and doomed we often feel. If we wish to address problems like climate change, public health crises, economic injustices, and white supremacy effectively, we need to find ways to forgive ourselves, restore our faith in other people, and build communities that fight for structural change. Despite the relentless cultural training that says shame is the answer, life does not have to be like this.

We've devoted a lot of pages to the many ways in which Systemic Shame harms us and tears us all apart. But now it's time to move out of the bleakness and toward solutions and healing. For the latter half of this book, I have interviewed therapists, public health researchers, authors, and activists about what a shame-free approach to human healing looks like. I've also sat down with marginalized and vulnerable people of a wide array of identities and asked them about what steps they take to unpack and process shame. From all this, I've developed a framework for understanding what the opposite of Systemic Shame is. The opposite of blaming individuals for systemic problems is recognizing that all people are harmed by a wide network of structural forces beyond our control, and that rather than judging people for their human foibles, we need to radically accept others as they are, as well as embrace our true, imperfect selves. This is a multilayered, dynamic approach to personal and community healing that I like to call "expansive recognition," and we'll explore what it is and how to cultivate it in the next chapter.

Part Two

Expansive Recognition

CHAPTER 5

Understanding Expansive Recognition

After years of being stuck, Ellen finally decided to approach her and her daughter's shame in a completely new way. One afternoon, she begged Jenna to skip cheerleading practice (like her mother, Jenna had begun coping with depression via hyper-productivity, in her case in the form of numerous extracurriculars and volunteer work). The two women went out to a park they'd visited back when Jenna was young. Ellen sat next to her daughter on a bench and confessed her fear that she'd being doing everything as a parent completely wrong.

"I blame myself for you cutting, and I know it all started when I asked your dad for a divorce," Ellen remembers saying to her. "I don't expect you to forgive me. But I have to tell you how sorry I am."

Her daughter blinked and turned toward her, surprised.

"Mom, that isn't it," she recalls Jenna telling her. "It wasn't anything to do with the divorce. I was relieved. I wanted both of you to be happy. It was school. I started hurting myself when I couldn't handle all the stress at school."

That possibility hadn't ever occurred to her, Ellen tells me.

"[Jenna] was at that age where standardized testing was getting really serious, and she had expected herself to get into a really good

school," Ellen tells me. "I completely missed what was going on because I was too afraid to ask."

Finally unburdened of her fear that she was an inexcusably horrible parent, Ellen began a series of frank conversations with her
daughter about the steps they could both take to manage their stress.
Ellen had to stop working so much—that was clear right away. She
left the nonprofit she'd been pouring all her waking hours into for
years, and began writing grants as a consultant. It paid a lot better
and consumed a lot less time. She quit the volunteer position that
ate into her evenings and weekends. Then she and Jenna made the
decision to have Jenna complete high school at home.

"Unschooling has been a godsend for our family," she tells me.

Unschooling is an approach to education that allows a student to
guide their own learning and decide for themselves how to spend
their days.[1] Everyone unschools a bit differently, but at its core, it's
a child-driven, autonomous practice in which parents and teachers
don't aim to force a student to learn or achieve in a particular way,
but instead set out to help students find the resources, social opportunities, and activities that line up with their goals. Ellen says
that by working far less, easing up on the external pressures, and
focusing on unschooling her daughter, her family has finally been
able to thrive.

"When Jenna had no control over her life, she self-harmed.
When she has control over her life and body, she does not need to
do that so much."

Through unschooling, Jenna has learned that she's passionate
about caring for animals. She supplements her studying with raising
chickens in a small coop in the backyard. She wants to find a way to
donate excess eggs to a local food pantry, and her mom's helping her
figure out whether that's possible, given food safety laws. She's cut
back on most of her volunteering and extracurriculars, aside from a

dog-walking gig that she does because she enjoys it, not because it will pad out a college application.

For Ellen's part, the change has also been freeing. She used to believe her life's calling was to save as many self-harming children as she possibly could, to make up for the role she thought she played in the suffering of her daughter. But it's only been by living at a slower pace and pulling back from the hustle of nonprofit fundraising that she's actually been able to make a difference where it matters most.

Ellen tells me that she and her daughter aren't entirely past all the trauma they've been through. But at last, it isn't getting any worse. She tells me they're finally growing together, rather than apart.

—————

What is the opposite of Systemic Shame? How do we learn to stop hating ourselves and judging other people, while despairing about the future of the world? The rest of this book is all about answering those questions and exploring new ways of relating to others and to ourselves. Finding alternatives to Systemic Shame is a process that might prove to be lifelong for most of us, but it can be nourishing and worthwhile every step of the way.

Systemic Shame has many layers, and its messaging is everywhere we turn. So, the challenge we face isn't to find some way of shucking it all off at once, leaving behind a bold, unabashed version of ourselves who never harbors doubts or allows guilt to seep in. Instead, healing from Systemic Shame is all about developing resilience in the face of society's numerous shaming messages and developing more productive strategies of coping when we're feeling ashamed.

Moving beyond Systemic Shame also means working to build

vulnerable relationships with other people, witnessing firsthand the restorative effects of being fully seen and recognizing that even in its imperfections, humanity can be loved and trusted. Healing from Systemic Shame involves developing a sense of purpose and perspective in life, which will allow us to discern for ourselves what is best for us, even in the face of external judgment. Soothing our Systemic Shame doesn't mean becoming immune to it; rather, it involves learning how to dodge and weave away from the constant psychological blows our culture deals us, and finding safe people to run toward and embrace when it feels like we can't stay in the fight.

The antithesis to Systemic Shame is something that I've taken to calling expansive recognition, an awareness and acceptance of one's position in the larger social world. Expansive recognition is the reassuring and grounding sense that you are unbreakably connected to the rest of humanity, and that all sides of you, including your flaws, are part of what keeps you bonded to everybody else. Expansive recognition is also the ability to find common ground within the struggles of another person, even when your outlooks and lived experiences differ significantly. Where Systemic Shame judges, expansive recognition respects. When Systemic Shame doles out obligations and expectations, expansive recognition acknowledges how much difficulty each of us has been facing. And while Systemic Shame attempts to cleave us apart from one another with mistrust and fear, expansive recognition affirms that there are always ties that bind us together, especially in our lowest moments.

Systemic Shame is rooted in a variety of really damaging, contradictory values: an emphasis placed on individual morality, a tendency to blame victims for the suffering, the sense that a person's "worst" or most difficult qualities must always be hidden away, and a belief that society has no responsibility to look after other people. Expansive recognition, in contrast, holds that people are indelibly linked to one another, and that the only way for us to make it through times of danger and oppression is by holding space together. In the list below you'll find some of Systemic Shame's core values, and expansive recognition's alternative values, which exist to counter them.

Systemic Shame Value	Expansive Recognition Value
Perfectionism	Acceptance
Individualism	Vulnerability
Consumerism	Coalition-building
Wealth	Compassion
Personal responsibility	Humility

Just like Systemic Shame, expansive recognition is both a feeling and a point of view. As an emotion, expansive recognition is the sensation of being witnessed and fully understood when you least expected it. If you've ever revealed a closely held, shameful secret to a stranger only to discover they have been through the exact same experience as you, you're familiar with how expansive recognition feels. Or when a trait you've always felt self-conscious about is celebrated or lovingly joked about by friends. It's an incredibly warm, affirming feeling to discover that the parts of yourself you're the most frightened of are part of what makes you so lovable.

Expansive recognition declares that our battles are only won when we realize they are shared. It encourages us to open ourselves up and reveal our pain, and to name when we are overwhelmed, so we can seek out the support we deserve. Expansive recognition tells us that even our feelings of crushing loneliness and self-disgust unite us, and that no matter who we are or what limitations we are facing, we can build a life that's guided by our passions and our beliefs in what's right.

I chose the name *expansive recognition* for a couple of reasons. First, I looked to the origins of the word *shame,* and the history linking shame to hiding or turning oneself away. When we are ashamed, we often go to extreme measures to avoid being seen. When society shames marginalized groups and oppresses them in a systematic way, it often does so by robbing them of control over how they are seen. Marginalized groups are thrown away in prisons and mental institutions, forced to cover their bodies or wear badges marking them as other, or are not given the freedom to declare their genders or names. Under Systemic Shame, the challenges that oppressed people face are often silenced or tone-policed; the mere naming of an unfair reality is seen as excessive complaining, "reverse racism," or "letting your disability hold you back." *Recognition*, then, is one of the remedies to Systemic Shame, because it offers us the opportunity to be seen fully, on our own terms, and to have our humanity and our struggles be openly acknowledged.

Recognition, I should point out, is not the same thing as mere visibility. In fact, Systemic Shame often presents "visibility" or even media "representation" as the hallmark of progress for marginalized groups. But visibility is a false, individualistic kind of freedom that often renders oppressed groups even more vulnerable to attack. Increased visibility without increased social protection and support is nothing but a liability—and it places immense pressure on the handful of marginalized individuals who do get the spotlight turned upon them. If a Black woman becomes the vice president, Systemic Shame praises her for the personal accomplishment rather than asking *why* Black women were excluded from leadership for centuries. When a character who is Deaf, bipolar, or HIV positive is depicted on screen in a humanizing light, Systemic Shame encourages us to see this as a win for "disability representation" rather than criticizing how these groups have been excluded from the stories that get told for decades.

Visibility is limited in its usefulness and comes with real drawbacks. For example, as the identities and concerns of trans people have become more publicly "visible" in recent years, members of the trans community have increasingly found ourselves under legal attack—and we've experienced far more hate crimes and assaults.[2] Now that the average person has some idea what trans people can look like and what some of the signs are that a person might be trans, it's easier to target us. And as the number of out and proud trans individuals rises, so does the anxiety of transphobic people, who now think they're waging battle against the "trans trend" and protecting the next generation of trans youth from a lifetime of "irreversible damage."

For decades trans women have been more "visible" in media than trans men like myself have, but nearly all those depictions have been graphically violent and dehumanizing, as we've discussed earlier in this book.[3] It's no coincidence that in light of this, trans women face domestic violence, sexual assault, and murder at far higher rates than trans masculine people like me. Though in the present culture queer people are often encouraged to view coming out and being visible as a freeing act, unchecked visibility puts a target on our backs.[4]

For many disabled people, abuse survivors, and people with addictions, the downsides of visibility similarly hold true: The second a stigmatized side of you becomes public, your coworkers, bosses, and random acquaintances will begin scanning your actions for signs that you're broken or cannot be trusted. One disabled two-spirit person I spoke to for this book, Lilac, told me that because of their disabilities they are constantly under the surveillance of doctors, government disability offices, and the prying, judgmental eyes of non-disabled people. To receive benefits and accommodations, Lilac must constantly prove that their body works the way they say it does, and that their medical needs are what they say they are. No matter how much pain they push through every day, they keep having to prove to others that they're really "trying their best."

Lilac's hypervisibility does not protect them. It restricts them and robs them of control over their own life. Recognition, then, can be nothing like surveillance, with its constant intrusions, evaluations, and threats. To fully *recognize* someone's situation is to believe the barriers and limitations they are facing are legitimate, and to trust them as the expert on their own life. Expansive recognition places a person within their life's context—with their overly long workdays and frustrating commutes, the persistent pain in their knee that makes getting around difficult, the demands of the aging parent they're caring for, the traumas of racism they regularly endure, and the decades-long nicotine addiction that takes a toll on their wallet and their health—and it accepts these realities as they are rather than trying to assign any moral value to them or arguing a person must change them.

This brings me to what makes expansive recognition *expansive*—it sees a person as forever connected to other people, their environment, their history, and their larger social condition. This places the motivation behind a person's actions within a broader context and helps us better see life's greater meaning. The psychologist Arthur Aron theorized that nearly all people have a strong motivation toward *self-expansion*:[5] We want to grow our skills and knowledge and become more than we currently are. We yearn to leave a mark on the planet that outlasts our own lives. We also want to belong to something bigger than our individual bodies. We do this by cultivating friendships, caring for our families, creating works of art, inventing new tools, and building communities that are united by shared goals and beliefs.

Similarly, the physician Robert Lifton has observed that when medical patients are facing their own deaths, identifying some form of symbolic immortality helps to bring them comfort.[6] Symbolic immortality comes in many forms: It can be the children we have raised, the music we've composed, the garden we've grown, the church we've helped build, the students we've mentored, or any other lasting social contribution we've made. We can also find symbolic immortality through sharing a culture, religious practice, belief system, craft, history, or legacy with others. By *expanding* our sense of self beyond our individual lives, we give our existence a long arc of significance. This is an excellent remedy for Systemic Shame's message that what we accomplish on our own is all that matters, and that there's no "excuse" for fumbling or falling behind.

Where Systemic Shame cleaves a person off from the rest of humanity and judges their actions in a vacuum, expansive recognition sees that we cannot understand someone's actions in isolation: We always have to look to the incentives and punishments around them that shape what their options are and how attractive each one might be. It's a very humbling approach to understanding ourselves. Neither our best accomplishments nor worst decisions are entirely our own. And the story of our lives does not end when we do. We're just one small, beautiful part.

In developing the concept of expansive recognition, I was partially inspired by dialectical behavioral therapy, or DBT. DBT was created by Dr. Marsha Linehan, a psychologist who specialized in treating people with Borderline Personality Disorder, many of whom report having overpowering urges to lash out at others or engage in self-harm. Dr. Linehan herself was diagnosed with this disorder as a young woman; she suffered from a violent self-injury habit and suicide ideation beginning in her teens. During her own process of recovery, Linehan discovered she had to learn to hold two principles in balance: First, she had to learn to radically accept her reality as it was, including when it was unpleasant and painful, and second, she had to develop the inner resilience and coping strategies to deal with that reality. These two forces—acceptance and change—are forever held in tension with one another under DBT. The need to face reality as it is and the need to find better ways of working with that reality are forever in dialogue (hence the term *dialectic* in DBT).

Here's a quick example to illustrate how the dialectic between acceptance and change can play out in DBT: Let's say a depressed patient struggles with a compulsive shopping habit. Instead of beating themselves up over the money they've spent and the resources they've consumed, the patient might benefit from *accepting* that they suffer from chronic depression and that shopping helps them cope. Their shopping serves a purpose in their life, even if it's just helping them ignore how miserable they constantly feel. A DBT therapist might encourage the patient to *accept* the experience of their depression and sit with the potentially very frightening reality that they could suffer from low mood for the entire rest of their life.

If a lifetime with depression is the reality the patient is facing, then going on Amazon binges is just one of many strategies for coping with it that they could employ. It's probably not the ideal one, but this isn't an ideal reality. Shopping has obviously "worked" for them in some way. Maybe waiting for a package to arrive kept them going when thoughts of suicide were especially pronounced. Perhaps heading to the outlet mall gave them a reason to push through depressive fatigue and get out of the house. Choosing to go shopping, under this framework, is neither inherently good nor bad: It's a decision that has a logic behind it, and that comes with benefits as well as costs. As a therapeutic technique, DBT opposes perfectionism: No coping strategy is inherently *bad*. It makes sense in certain situations, and it might increase or decrease the odds of a person's life getting better. We can choose to change if a coping mechanism no longer works, but we don't have to in order to become morally redeemed people.

This concept of holding acceptance and change in dialogue with one another is very useful when it comes to combatting Systemic Shame. Systemic Shame operates under an unforgivingly black-and-white logic. But rather than demanding perfection of ourselves, we can evaluate each decision as a dance between acceptance and change, an ever-evolving negotiation with reality.

The truth is, I don't *want* to throw my hands up and conclude that fighting to save the planet is pointless because corporations pollute far more than I do. That doesn't feel any better than fixating for hours on whether I'm composting correctly. I want to feel less shame about being just one small, flawed person—but I also want to take action that I believe matters in this world. Under expansive recognition, we can both come to terms with our individual smallness *and* challenge the idea that our every effort is meaningless. When we see our small efforts as interconnected to the work and support of others, we become a lot more powerful (and our lives more meaningful) than individualism ever allowed us to be.

In coming up with expansive recognition, I was also inspired by the writer James Baldwin's observation that suffering is a bridge.[7] Systemic Shame teaches us to see our deepest pains as entirely personal and mandates that we suffer alone. But as Baldwin observes, our worst wounds actually offer a meaningful through line to other people—connecting us across disparate groups, as well as throughout time. In his writings, Baldwin often emphasized the violence of being rendered invisible to society because he was a queer Black man. Not only was his well-being overlooked, but people refused to recognize him as human. Recognition of his full, complex humanity and his suffering was the answer to his pain—but it could only be on his own terms, and under circumstances in which being seen would be safe. Reflecting upon the work of Baldwin, the philosopher Olúfẹ́mi O. Táíwò writes that he is connected to all other people on the planet through the mutual recognition of our shared vulnerability.[8] Building solidarity, he writes, is not a question of who has suffered the most, or who ought to bow to whom. Instead, solidarity is a question of how best we can join forces. Each one of us has a role to play in such efforts. We all have our bridge. None of us is disconnected from the human experience.

The Levels of Expansive Recognition

Just as Systemic Shame consists of three levels (the personal, the interpersonal, and the global), expansive recognition does too:

1. *Radical self-acceptance:* Being able to sit with the knowledge of our strengths, as well as our flaws and mistakes.

   How it affects us: Radical self-acceptance makes it possible for us to face our desires and needs without allowing self-judgment or fear to block us.

2. *Vulnerable connection:* Trusting there are people in the world who can accept all of who we are, and accepting other people's full, messy selves in turn.

   How it affects us: Vulnerable connection makes it possible for us to get the help we require. When we receive love from others and recognize that other people need just as much aid as we do, we stop seeing the outside world as a menacing place.

3. *Hope for humanity:* Cultivating communities where we can find belonging and identifying activities that help us experience life as meaningful.

  How it affects us: Community support allows us to relax into ourselves and let go of the anxious obsession that we are not ever doing "enough." Belonging gives us an internal sense of safety and peace, and the clarity to identify where we belong and where our energy is best placed. Instead of scrambling to fix everything, or giving up all hope of doing anything worthwhile, we can feel grateful to have been planted exactly where we are.

These three levels fit together in a growing "snowball," just as was the case with Systemic Shame:

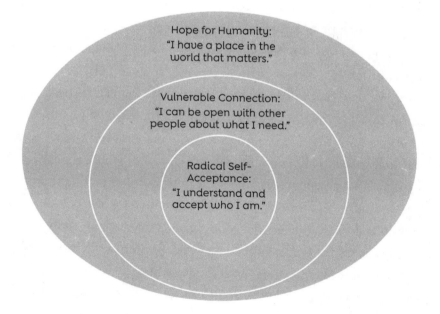

Nearly everyone that I interviewed for this book told me that they were only able to heal from shame through their relationships to others. Given that shame is inextricably tied to social rejection, I think it's safe to conclude that social acceptance is a necessary component of healing. However, in order for us to connect to people vulnerably, we must challenge the self-protective behaviors that keep us isolated. When we begin opening up, we start to find social acceptance, which relaxes our worst assumptions and self-protections, allowing us to reach out and expand ourselves even more.

Let's take a deeper look at how a person might experience expansive recognition in their own life, one layer at a time:

Level 1: Radical Self-Acceptance

Experiencing personal Systemic Shame nearly always involves some degree of retreating from the self. There are elements of who we are, how we behave, or even what we desire that embarrass us, and to cope we attempt to bury them away or to pretend they don't exist. Learning to cope with personal Systemic Shame, then, requires that we confront the sides to ourselves we might not otherwise want to face. We don't have to love these aspects, and we can't expect ourselves to act as though a lifetime of stigma didn't happen—but each of us can come to know who we really are, and to recognize that even our least-liked qualities are fundamental parts of who we are. Practicing radical acceptance is one of the best routes to getting there.

Radical acceptance involves fully listening to our bodies and minds, and cultivating slower, gentler habits that are guided by what really matters to us and lights us up with passion, as well as by our genuine limits. It encourages us to notice when we feel stuck, or as if we've been aspiring to do the impossible. Acknowledging that we've been doing too much allows us to let go of unfulfilling pursuits and obligations.

In August 2015, a prominent makeup and gaming YouTuber

named Stef Sanjati came out publicly as a transgender woman.[9] Up until that point, Sanjati had mostly made fun, conversational videos about her favorite beauty products and what she'd been up to in *World of Warcraft*, with the occasional discussion of her personal life and viewpoints. But after coming out as trans, the focus and emotional tenor of Sanjati's videos changed radically.

Sanjati started creating educational content that explained trans identities to her cisgender viewers. She put together a whole tool kit of advice for trans women on how to feminize their voices and soften their appearance with cosmetics. She created a full documentary on the harrowing abuse she'd endured as a visibly queer child in a conservative rural Canadian town. As her medical transition progressed, Sanjati released videos about surgeries she had undergone, broadcasting her healing wounds and tear-filled recovery process to the world. She also regularly participated in panels and gave talks at colleges and universities about trans issues and her experiences.

I followed Sanjati's YouTube channel actively through all of this. I loved her bubbly, sweet personality and her ethereal fashion sense. I was contemplating a gender transition of my own back then, and watching Sanjati's new life unfold comforted me. I was impressed by how much time Sanjati devoted to educating others. She seemed to me like the perfect portrait of the respectable trans person: endlessly educational, unfailingly patient, never offended, and willing to bear her entire life (and her body) on camera for all the world to see.

Eventually, though, Sanjati's public persona took a turn. Once a nerdy, cozy homebody, Sanjati started talking about going out drinking and partying a lot. She became addicted to laxatives and released emotionally raw videos in which she cried while discussing sexual assault experiences and her parents' divorce. In more casual vlogs, Sanjati seemed less genuine, more flippant and superficial. She seemed at war with herself, releasing fluffy, surface-level videos about fashion and facial injections one day, then long, dreary discussions of body dysmorphia and suicide ideation the next. Fans began criticizing her for no longer being the warm, cuddly "bread mom" that she used to be. After numerous fits and starts and sudden shifts in content, Sanjati's YouTube channel fell silent.

After spending a year off of the platform, Stef Sanjati released one final video announcing that she was quitting YouTube and all trans activist work.[10] Sitting at her gaming PC wearing a baggy hoodie and glasses, she explained how the pressure of being a public symbol of transness was too much for her to bear. It was a role she never wanted—just something that, as a well-known transitioning woman, she'd been expected to do.

"Unfortunately, because I was a trans person talking about my experiences, I was essentially branded an activist without ever having been asked if that's what I wanted," Sanjati says. "I was never an activist. I was just a trans person. I tried to do the role for many years, and it was not good for me. I was not prepared for the level of responsibility, scrutiny, weight on my shoulders, or critical self-reflection required for a role like that."

When she first started her YouTube channel, Sanjati was just nineteen years old. By age twenty-six, she knew she wanted out of the influencer/activist game. After quitting YouTube, Sanjati began livestreaming herself playing video games on Twitch. She's back to reveling in being a cuddly, cute nerd now, enjoying titles like *Sea of Thieves* and *World of Warcraft*, and working as a narrative designer at a gaming company. On screen Sanjati comes across as relaxed and happy. When a game that she's streaming touches on difficult themes such as self-harm or gender dysphoria, she sometimes excuses herself to stop the broadcast early or take a break.

Stef Sanjati spent many years trying to live up to other people's expectations—impossible, Systemic Shame–fueled expectations that preach trans women must be flawlessly attractive, entertaining, and self-sacrificing. Systemic Shame had turned her into a symbol of her entire community without her prior consent. It was too much for a vulnerable teenager to be expected to shoulder. But once she accepted that she was not suited to YouTube activism or to beauty influencing, Sanjati was able to get back in touch with her sensitive, nerdy self.

Systemic Shame will never stop demanding more of us. Instead, we must let go of society's punishing expectations, allowing ourselves to settle into an easier, more humble existence informed by our real passions and our needs.

Lilac, the physically disabled two-spirit trans person I mentioned earlier in this chapter, told me they have often struggled with the shame of not meeting expectations as well.

"Both my parents were Mexican American immigrants," they say. "You know, they have had to pull themselves up by their bootstraps in many ways. And being somebody who is disabled and not able to do that for myself, you know, there is a lot of shame. Not meeting the expectations. Not being worth your parents' sacrifice."

Lilac tells me that overcoming shame has meant radically accepting their disabilities and the barriers that come with them, and rejecting mainstream society's demands.

"I was always a square peg being put into a round hole, and I will never fit that. I will only end up misshapen," they say. "I feel very strongly about doing my best, and then that's it, you know. I may not be the most productive, but I'd rather have my well-being than my productivity."

Lilac says that in their work, they are very meticulous and intentional, but quite slow. They can take pride in the quality of the writing they do, and how carefully they lead support groups for people like themselves. They might not get a huge volume of work done.

But they never set out to do more than their methodical, committed best.

In the next chapter, we'll review a great deal of research about radical acceptance and go through a variety of exercises designed to help a person heal from personal Systemic Shame using it. But for now, here are a few radical acceptance affirmations, adapted from the work of DBT therapists, for you to contemplate and try applying to yourself.

RADICAL SELF-ACCEPTANCE AFFIRMATIONS[11]

Read each statement, and consider how these sentiments differ from how you currently think about and speak to yourself. The next time you experience a shameful moment, try to redirect your thoughts to statements like these.

Changing our internal self-talk is a long process, and having negative knee-jerk attitudes toward yourself is completely fine, and quite common. However, no matter what your internal dialogue sounds like, you can make a practice of dwelling on more accepting, neutral statements like these.

1. My present moment is the only one I have any control over.

2. Fighting this emotion won't help. It's just something I'm experiencing right now.

3. The reality I'm facing is a fact I will have to deal with, even if I don't like it.

4. I wish things were different, but I cannot change what happened in the past.

5. I can't control everything that will happen.

6. A million variables outside of my control have led to this moment.

7. The thoughts I'm currently having will not hurt me.

8. I struggle with certain things more than other people do, and that might not ever change.

Once we've started to work on knowing and accepting our genuine selves, we can begin revealing that self to others and start trusting in our own ability to be loved as we are.

Level 2: Vulnerable Connection

Interpersonal Systemic Shame motivates us to hide away from others—because it teaches us that no one else could ever find our worst aspects lovable, and that most people's true selves aren't reliable or worthy, either. The counter to Interpersonal Systemic Shame, then, is to learn to become vulnerable among safe others, and to embrace the deeper connections that such openness permits.

Recently, following a two-week medical leave, Lilac had to come to terms with the fact they now need daily help with bathing. At first, requiring the aid of others was difficult for them to accept.

"A woman's role in the world is often to serve others and make others comfortable," they say. "But here I am, needing to be comforted. It's really hard to sit back and just let this nurse give me a sponge bath, and it does feel dehumanizing in some ways."

Since Lilac is so practiced in rethinking shame, they were able to reframe this experience. They came to see the new way their body functions as yet another means of connecting with another person.

"It is very human to ask for help and it's very human to be interdependent," they say. "No one can actually make it through alone. Knowing that helps me to feel like, *Okay, I can accept this help. I might not be used to it, but I can do it.* When you're sick, you already have so much shit to deal with. You don't want to deal with shame on top of that."

As Lilac's words acknowledge, all humans are deeply reliant on others. Other people brought us into the world, changed and fed us, taught us, and kept a watchful eye over us as we grew. Every single day of our lives is made possible through the support of hundreds of other human beings. Other people harvested the beans in the coffee I make, and prepared, packaged, and shipped the oat milk that I drink it with. Human beings constructed the door to my bathroom, sanded and painted it and installed it in my apartment. A specific human being whom I've met and gotten to know fixed my venetian blinds when they broke last week. People wrote the books that I read, mixed the music I'm playing, and stocked the toothpaste I'm browsing for on the store shelves. There is so much to feel grateful for that my mind staggers thinking of it.

Systemic Shame moves us to ignore just how connected we all are, and always will be—and it convinces us needing assistance is shameful. But a life free of social support is impossible and would not be worth living. The impact of others is everywhere. We can't run away from their gifts. And why would we want to?

Think of the difference between shamefully tolerating a sponge bath compared to gratefully accepting it and feeling thankful to the person providing it. If Lilac were to turn away from their caregiver and stew in shame every time they were cleaned, they would only continue to feel disconnected. Their nurse would pick up on their discomfort and feel awkward, too. But if both parties instead choose to be present and open with one another, the experience has the potential to be rewarding or even beautiful, at least some of the time.

Instead of living under Systemic Shame's myth of flawless individualism, we can accept what's true whether we like it or not: We need other people, and others show up for us dozens of times every day. Psychological research shows that *perceived social support* is a huge predictor of both mental and physical health. When people with mental illnesses such as depression and bipolar disorder believe that others love them and will show up for them, their mood symptoms are less severe, and they're more likely to recover from acute episodes.[12] Patients with multiple sclerosis are less likely to develop depression and anxiety related to their disability if they recognize they are highly connected to and supported by others.[13] For decades, medical research has consistently found that loneliness puts a person at risk of poorer physical health,[14] more chronic conditions,[15] and increased mortality,[16] and the flip side is also true: When people have supportive relationships that they cherish, they're more likely to thrive.

When we lean into the support of other people, we become more adaptable and resilient. People with a high perceived social support experienced less depression and fewer sleep disturbances early into the Covid-19 pandemic.[17] They also had an easier time complying with lockdown requirements,[18] proving yet again that the main predictor of a person doing "the right thing" is not their willpower, it's whether they have help. A study of patients with chronic obstructive pulmonary disease (COPD) and heart failure found perceived social support helped predict whether patients could effectively manage their conditions.[19] Systemic Shame makes us believe that being a good and strong person is what's needed for meaningful change to happen, but the data shows that what's necessary is social support.

Crucially, all these empirical findings examine the effects of *perceived* social support, how cared for and connected a person *feels* that they are. Social scientists and physicians have frequently attempted to quantify social support and found it's quite hard to pin down. It's not the number of friends a person has that matters, or how many resources or social connections they have. What predicts positive outcomes is a person recognizing that they are bonded to others and appreciating those connections.

Many of us genuinely do have the potential for caring connections, but we do not realize it—because Systemic Shame prevents us from ever admitting to other people that we could use a hand. But once we open up about both what's missing in our lives and what we have to offer, our needs and others' capacities can begin weaving into one another, building a complex social web that catches us both.

Carole, a middle-aged woman with ADHD, tells me that before moving in with her girlfriend, Denise, she regularly missed meals. Carole's an analytical thinker with a real need to be of service to others in a practical way. Working in tech support, her attention usually got swept up by customer problems that seemed more important and interesting than figuring out her own meals. This changed the moment Denise moved in and Carole had to begin thinking about her partner's numerous dietary restrictions and allergies.

"Making sure Denise had good things to eat suddenly was a *problem* I could develop a *system* to solve," Carole says. "When Denise isn't here, I don't care about feeding myself and I eat a lot of junk. But with Denise I have a reason to care, and I can do the creating a grocery list, the chopping veggies, the practical aspect."

If we took a purely individualistic view of this relationship, we'd conclude that Denise is too reliant and Carole's too codependent. Systemic Shame would argue that both women should have the willpower to eat and meal plan for themselves, because doing things on your own is morally *better* than benefiting from the presence of somebody else. But in reality, each woman's needs fits perfectly into the other's. Carole takes better care of herself when she has Denise to care for. Carole's no-nonsense approach to meal planning helps Denise feel loved as she is. Each woman's sense of well-being has expanded into the other's.

One leading measure of perceived social support is the Duke Social Support Index.[20] In the table below are some items from the index, which I have adapted and left open-ended, so that you can ponder the state of your social connections. If you struggle with Interpersonal Systemic Shame, you might not yet realize the supportive potential of your existing relationships. You might also be hesitant to offer aid to others, particularly to those who you don't think really "deserve" it and might not ever pay back your efforts. Or you might know you need help but have no clue of where to begin in getting it. Reflecting on these gaps and challenges in your relationships may help you learn to open up and connect more often.

ASSESSING YOUR CAPACITY FOR CONNECTION:
Adapted from the Duke Social Support Index[21]

Read and respond to each of the questions listed below, in as much detail as you like.

1. Do you feel that you have a definite role in your family/friend group?

2. Are there people close to you who seem to really understand you?

3. Do you feel appreciated by your loved ones?

4. When you talk to your loved ones, do you feel listened to?

5. Who is someone that you can talk to about your deepest problems?

table continued

6. During the past week, how often did you spend quality time with loved ones?

7. Are there people in your local area who you feel you can depend on? List their names.

8. Does anything feel missing in your relationships? If so, what?

Vulnerable connection is the remedy to interpersonal shame. In Chapter 7, we will take a deeper dive into how to cultivate it. And after we learn that we don't have to hide ourselves away from other people, and begin reaping the benefits of such genuine connections, we can finally begin targeting the broader social problems that have left all of us so hopeless and ashamed.

Level 3: Hope for Humanity

Global Systemic Shame is the existentially bleak feeling that humanity is doomed, and it's often combined with the moral belief that ultimately, we're all so lazy and selfish that we pretty much deserve it. In order to counter this terrible outlook, we must learn to foster hope for humanity—as well as hope that our own lives can have a meaningful impact, however small. Once we stop thinking of ourselves solely as individual actors and realize that our efforts expand beyond us and combine with the work of countless others, our small sparks of hope can grow into a more brilliant, enduring blaze.

In the summer of 2022, when the Supreme Court overturned *Roe v. Wade*, I was bereft. I knew that abortion would swiftly be banned in Ohio, where I'd been born; it was quickly joined by fifteen other conservative-leaning states.[22] How could I continue living in a country where each year, hundreds of thousands of people would be forced to be breeding vessels for what Justice Samuel Alito called "the domestic supply of infants"?[23] No amount of political organizing had made the federal courts care about the body autonomy of myself or anyone else who could get pregnant. I felt powerless.

I had to unplug from the internet that day. Instagram and Twitter were awash with posts warning that things were "about to get very bad" in America and that people needed to be "paying attention"—as if the present situation were not already horrible and our eyes weren't already glued to our screens. *They'll try to ban abortion on the federal level, too,* one close friend warned. *The Supreme Court will come for gay marriage next,* said a journalist I followed. *We can't look away from this,* an acquaintance admonished. I couldn't see what good bearing witness to all this suffering was doing. I was already deeply aware of the devastation that lay ahead. The chiding that we needed to stay attentive and afraid seemed like yet another confusion in focus: as if the media we passively, anxiously consumed was an expression of our beliefs that had an impact on the world on its own. Clearly, it hadn't. I just wanted to crawl under a rock and look away.

That was when a friend introduced me online to "auntie networks." These anonymous communities provide abortion access to people in need across the globe. Aunties who live in areas where abortion procedures remain legal offer up their homes to pregnant people and provide assistance with travel and doctor's appointments. They also compile resources on how to safely access emergency contraception pills and abortion pills. The groups I checked out were trans-affirming and carefully moderated to prevent anti-abortion activists from infiltrating them.

"BC Auntie posting again after today's news," one user wrote. "Beautiful Vancouver, British Columbia, is a wonderful vacation spot for people who need medical assistance. Spare room, cat, car, and empathetic ear."

"Abortion clinics in the Netherlands also help foreigners," stated another. "It is pretty affordable to book a ticket and get oneself here."

Scrolling through auntie network posts, a hopeful sense of purpose began coursing through me. I couldn't undo the fact that getting an abortion was now illegal in many places—but I could take concrete steps to help abortion-seekers get around the law and find the care they needed. I could help pay for a young, distressed Texan's flight to a state where abortion remained legal. I could walk a newly pregnant person through the process of removing all data from their period-tracker app so that their information could not be legally used against them. I also found solace in the existence of groups like the Chicago Abortion Fund, and Midwest Access, both of which provide travel and financial support to abortion-seekers around the country.

A few days later, a lifelong friend texted me, asking how I was holding up in light of the news. In her state, abortion was now illegal—but she had begun thinking about contingency plans, and what she could do to aid others. Her partner owned a coworking space, and together they had decided to use some of the facility to store Plan B and Plan C pills for distribution to people in need. I offered to help my friend by researching additional steps and putting her in contact with another activist who was also providing underground abortion access in that state. I was so incredibly impressed by my friend's efforts, and the bravery and generosity she and her partner were showing to others. Her efforts made me feel less alone, and immediately I wanted to do everything I could to support them.

The overturning of *Roe* was a horrifying reality that at first I wanted to run away from. But pretty quickly, I was able to accept it was our new normal, and that the democratic process would not be saving us anytime soon. From there, I had to ponder what I was willing and capable of changing. The problem of statewide abortion bans was too enormous for me to handle. But the question of what I could personally do to make one other person's life easier? That I could manage.

As legal attacks on trans healthcare also began exploding across the country, I took solace in the fact that so many members of my community were creating alternate ways for trans people to access hormones and other medications necessary to our well-being. I know trans liberation activists who have developed private websites that allow trans people throughout the United States to share their extra hormone doses with one another, and a pair of trans women I'm acquainted with prepare and distribute doses of hormone replacement therapy to homeless trans people at encampments in the California desert. Online, trans people exchange medical knowledge and DIY recipes for hormone supplements with one another, often building a rich literature on trans healthcare that does not exist for us yet within conventional medical avenues. I've done all that I can to bolster these efforts, throwing money toward these initiatives, passing on spare doses, and spreading the information to my many gender-variant siblings in need.

Historically, the only way that trans people were able to liberate our bodies was through such underground methods. My friend Mardi is in her sixties, and she began taking estrogen back in 1979 by asking fellow trans sex workers on the streets where they got their doses. If trans people in the United States are left with no other options, we can take care of one another in these same ways again.

Instead of asking how we as individuals can personally *solve* massive structural problems, as Systemic Shame does, expansive recognition has us identify a single step that we can take that contributes to something more meaningful. When I recognize that I am part of a vast network of human goodness that expands far beyond my own choices and efforts, I can take comfort in whatever difference I make no matter how small. There is no more asking whether I am doing "enough" (a question for which there is no objective answer), only pondering what I am in the position to do.

As we've already discussed, one of the reasons people find Systemic Shame so appealing is because it makes abstract issues more practical and concrete. The average person wants to take actions that matter. They want poverty, systemic racism, gun violence, healthcare disparities, and other seemingly insurmountable problems to become surmountable. This is a wonderful, practical desire. It only becomes a problem when we assign individual people the full moral burden of fixing these issues on their own, without the support of anyone else.

In order to foster hope for humanity and create our own sense of meaning in this world, we have to stop thinking in terms of obligation and focus instead on *opportunity*. Each of us has been planted in a completely different spot in the world. We all have a unique combination of skills, vulnerabilities, experiences, needs, and passions. All these factors will influence what making a difference looks like for each of us. We cannot all be held to identical moral standards. We each have to decide what we feel called to do.

Steven is a research assistant at a university, and up until a few years ago, he resented the younger, less reliable undergraduates assigned to work on his team. Steven viewed the twenty-somethings he managed as lazy and flighty. Whenever he failed to meet a dead-line or had to pull an all-nighter to cover up the slack a student had left behind, Steven fumed. Then one day, Steven vented about his frustrations during his department's Christmas party—and realized, far too late, that the person he was complaining to about his "lazy, unreliable students" was an undergraduate herself.

"This young woman looked me in the eye and very somberly said to me, 'No offense, but I think you're mad at the wrong person. It sounds like you're taking on too much work. Maybe you should take things easier and then you wouldn't be so mad.'"

"I hadn't ever thought of it that way," Steven says. "I grew up with the idea that whatever work you are handed, that's what you have to do, and you work as hard as you have to, and if anybody isn't going at that pace, they should be in trouble."

But the next time a student missed a shift because they were cramming for an exam, Steven didn't rat them out to their supervisor—instead he just moved that student's project down on the priority list. When another student complained that the data-entry task he'd been assigned was too large for him to handle, Steven paused to consider whether that might actually be true.

"When I stopped seeing the kids I was managing as my enemies, I started seeing how I actually had been the person who was doing too much," Steven explains. Once he let go of unreasonable expecta-tions, he began finding all kinds of opportunities to release the pres-sure his lab and his students had been facing.

"I'm on a committee now that's looking into giving paid mater-nity leave and retirement benefits to our student workers," Steven says, as proof of how much his outlook's changed. "Old me would have said these kids don't deserve handouts. Now I'm like, no, we *all* deserve more."

To help get you thinking about what opportunities for change to exist in your life, complete the following exercise. Some of your answers to questions in this exercise will be helpful when we get to Chapter 8, which will explore how to foster hope and find purpose in more detail.

OPPORTUNITIES FOR HOPE
Growing Into Where You Are Planted

Answer the following questions in the space provided. You can return to this exercise whenever you find yourself feeling hopeless about a social issue or personal crisis.

1. Think of a problem that causes significant stress in your life. It may be personal (for example, "I don't know how I'm going to pay down my student loan debt") or it may be a broad societal issue (for example, "I'm worried about the rising cost of food for everyone"). Name and briefly describe the problem here.

2. If you wanted to talk to someone who is also concerned about this problem, where could you go? You can list specific people in your life who are good to talk to, or look up support groups, online forums, meetup groups, events, and other public spaces.

3. List any steps you have taken in the past that have helped you feel more in control of this problem, no matter how small.

4. What are some strategies for coping with this problem that have *not* been helpful in the past?

5. Do you know anyone who shares this problem or concern with you? If you were to reach out for support, what might you say?

6. Are there any groups or organizations in your area that do work to address the problem, or problems like it? If you're not sure, take a moment to do some online research. Are you curious or interested in anything that you've found?

The goal of the exercise above is not to flood your nervous system with even more obligations that you'll then go and beat yourself up for not fulfilling. Rather, I encourage you to take a step back and take stock of the resources that are available to you, as well as your vulnerabilities. Both what you have and what you need will help direct you to where you belong. As in dialectical behavioral therapy, remember that the goal here is not to make everything better, but rather to take stock of the unpleasant reality you are in, and what some alternate ways of coping with it could be.

You don't have to respond to the stress of your own student loan debt by committing to become a debt forgiveness activist, for example. But you *might* find it helpful to join a support group for people who are experiencing shame related to their own debts. In the process of talking through your own anxieties, you will bring solace to other people coping with that same kind of shame. Asking for help itself is an act of aid to others. It helps people feel needed and makes them recognize they're not alone. Maybe some lasting political change will emerge from the time you spend together, or maybe it won't. Either way, you'll have helped exploited people feel less to blame for their suffering. That matters, and it's something you deserve to take pride in.

Now that we've taken a moment to get acquainted with what expansive recognition is and how it operates, we'll embark on the process of using it to combat Systemic Shame, one layer at a time. The first stage, of course, is to work on what's within—finding ways to heal from the many damaging external messages that tell us we need to hate ourselves and hide from the rest of the world.

CHAPTER 6

Radical Self-Acceptance

My friend Eric Boyd is an award-winning fiction writer who carries within him the shame and trauma of being incarcerated for a felony when he was young. Before his time in prison, Eric was an artistic, sensitive, gender-bending teen; he listened to the Cure a lot and wore skirts and pleather. Prison forced all that to change. To protect himself from violence, Eric drew his emotions inward and projected a tough-guy image. Once he got out of jail, the stigma of being a felon made matters even worse. Finding a job was extremely difficult. The few places that would hire him paid poorly and treated their workers inhumanely. Even once Eric found an okay gig working at an escape room, Systemic Shame kept looming over his head.

"A girl I was working with asked me, 'Why don't you get a better job?'" Eric says. "And I said to her, 'Did nobody tell you? I'm a felon.' And this girl was nice, I felt I was close enough I could tell her. But then she gave me that *look*. That look that's half disbelief, and then half horror . . . That look sucks."

Eric has received that *look* a lot. The shocked beholding of shame. He's had to perfect a tight two-minute explanation of why he went to prison that he can deliver when anybody gives him that look. But there's nothing he can do to prevent that look from coming. Formerly incarcerated people can be legally discriminated against in employment and in education. Often they can't vote, serve on juries, own firearms, or work in schools or in healthcare. Felons can lose custody of their children and be denied driver's licenses and passports. The massive societal stigma of incarceration is baked into how every major public institution functions—and it seeps in the private thoughts and reactions of every person a survivor of imprisonment meets. There is no escaping it. It is a wound the world constantly reopens.

In recent years, Eric has started trying to uncover his latent sensitive side. He goes to therapy. He keeps a journal. He collects fragrances and rides railway cars; he writes poetry and has bright tangerine-colored hair. Whenever we speak, he teases me knowingly, to show his affection.

"You went, what, over a year without telling your boyfriend you'd started hormones?" he asked me when I interviewed him for this book, a twinkle in his eye. "You know that's pretty messed up, right?"

"Well, I don't think that it was!" I said back defiantly, before listing my many justifications. Eric and I both have carefully practiced narratives that can help explain our shame to others. But as friends, each of us can see right through it—and roast each other for it.

"You know, in your teen years you pretty much figure out what you are about," Eric tells me. "And then you spend your twenties pushing back against that, thinking you need to be a serious adult person. And then you hit your thirties and you're like, *Oh, fuck, I just wasted the last decade, I should go back to listening to the Cure and wearing skirts.*"

Eric's twenties were a lot more tumultuous than many other people's. Before he got arrested, he'd already been dealing with housing insecurity and a whole lot of stress. The circumstances that led to his arrest were themselves very traumatic. Then there was the long, slow path back to normal life following incarceration itself.

Ultimately, healing for Eric has meant returning to where he started, and learning to love the sensitive, artistic side of himself that thrived as a teen.

I think that working to soothe Systemic Shame usually does require revisiting the parts of ourselves we've been convinced we have to hide away. There is no undoing our past traumas, of course, and no getting rid of the society-wide *looks* that tell us our most vulnerable selves are best kept hidden. But I do believe there is healing to be found in making a kind of spiritual return, bringing our older, wiser, stigma-scarred selves back to the tender selves of our pasts, and finding ways to unite them.

The first level of expansive recognition is the personal. Self-loathing and isolation are the core, interior experiences on which Systemic Shame runs; it is impossible for us to fully connect with others and thrive if we still behave as though we must hide ourselves away at all costs. By making a first gesture toward self-acceptance and trust, we can start to accept the deeper growth and healing that can only occur in community with others.

Each of us needs help as we fight forces like systemic racism, income inequality, gun violence, ecological devastation, and global pandemics. Many studies have observed that when people feel deeply connected to (and supported by) others, they are more likely to behave generously, giving money to those in need,[1] supporting pro-environmental policies,[2] actively listening to people who are struggling,[3] and enacting their values more in their daily lives.[4] Conversely, when people feel unsupported and ashamed, they disconnect, and are forced to either become more self-sufficient or perish.

If we wish to escape from Systemic Shame, we have to practice building up relationships with other people again. But to get there, we first have to tackle some of the internalized hatred we've absorbed and directed at ourselves, so that it stops presenting such a massive barrier to help-seeking. So how do we get there? Broadly speaking, the scholarship on healing personal feelings of shame come down to a few overarching tips:

- Opening up to other people about the qualities we're ashamed of
- Getting vulnerable about our shame itself (also known as "speaking shame")
- Practicing self-compassion regarding our flaws and mistakes
- Radically accepting ourselves and our present situation, even if we don't like it
- Being driven by our pleasure and joy rather than by fear

In this chapter, we'll examine how to put each of these tips into practice, taking a look at therapeutic techniques that assist people in accepting themselves, learning from marginalized individuals who have begun working on their Systemic Shame, and reflecting on social movements that have effectively aided vulnerable groups in moving away from shame and toward acceptance and mutual support.

Opening Up

In her book *Hiding from Humanity*, the philosopher and legal scholar Martha Nussbaum explores shame as it has become embedded into our laws.[5] An example of this are "ugly laws," which made it illegal to be disfigured, disabled, or mentally ill in public. These laws lasted longer than you might think: Chicago didn't repeal its ugly law until 1974.[6] These ordinances blamed "unsightly" individuals for social crises such as homelessness and disease, and their legacy is still very much with us.

The city of Los Angeles banned homeless encampments in July 2021,[7] transforming an economic crisis impacting sixty-six thousand Los Angelinos per year into a personal crime punishable with jailtime.[8] It's like city governments banning jaywalking rather than building safer streets for pedestrians all over again. Historically, the police harassed and arrested gay men for similar reasons: They were seen as the root of "ugly" problems like the HIV epidemic. When we ban incarcerated people from living in certain neighborhoods or working in fields that are supposedly too "pure" for them, we are also enacting shame via legislation, deeming individual humans as "ugly" rather than the problems that haunt them.

Shame is a hiding of one's face. Sometimes that hiding is literal, and socially enforced. Part of the solution, then, is finding safe forms of *revealment*: openly baring what society has forced us to obscure so that others can accept us. Expansive recognition is only possible when we are acknowledged in the fullness of our identities and social positions—including the supports we are desperately lacking.

One group that helps tackle Systemic Shame through acts of openness and revealment is Reclaim UGLY (Uplift, Glorify, and Love Yourself), which was created by the Black femme writer and activist Vanessa Rochelle Lewis.[9] A Los Angeles–based organization led by Black and brown queer people, Reclaim UGLY offers regular programming both in person and online, designed to help a variety of marginalized people whom society has "uglified" to build meaningful connections and warmly reveal themselves to one another.

When Vanessa Rochelle Lewis was fifteen, a teacher publicly embarrassed her by remarking, "Wow, Vanessa, you may not look like Beyoncé, but you sure can write a moving poem."[10] Years later, a Los Angeles–based party promoter created a meme viciously mocking Lewis's body and appearance. It spread widely; for a while, Lewis's photo was the second image to pop up in Google searches for "ugly black woman."

Rather than retreat from all the hatred and disgust directed her way, Lewis responded by creating the first-ever Ugly Conference in 2019. Dozens of transgender, gay, disabled, disfigured, Black, brown, and fat individuals attended. In workshops, attendees paired off and opened up about traumatic experiences of having been insulted or excluded based on how they looked. People took to the mic to share art about their experiences, or just to messily, openly explore how shame had cleaved them off from society. Whenever an attendee's courage faltered, Lewis and the rest of the crowd cheered them on, encouraging them to claim space. The success of the conference led Lewis to launch the Reclaim UGLY organization.

Since the group's leadership is disabled and most are in poverty as well, Reclaim UGLY deliberately moves at a slower pace than your standard service organization. It's not a federally registered nonprofit, which means it's less reliant on grant funding and less beholden to the heavy paperwork and evaluation requirements that come with it. Lilac (whom I quoted in the last chapter) does regular work with Reclaim UGLY, and they told me that everyone within its ranks is encouraged to move at the speed of their own body and their own body alone. As someone who has witnessed even the best intentioned of nonprofits overwork its members and exploit their passions, seeing Reclaim UGLY operate in a more radically accepting, horizontal fashion was absolutely lovely.

One participant at the first Reclaim UGLY conference, Rebecca Brill, reported that she had always found affirmations that "everyone is beautiful" to ring hollow. It felt condescending and divorced from her actual reality. People treated her like she was ugly! It was better to confront her uglification with an indifferent "Yeah, so?" than pretend it didn't exist. That's part of the magic of Reclaim UGLY's ethos: It doesn't attempt to cover up shame with empty positivity or by denying society's prejudices. It accepts and affirms what has long been forcibly obscured.

Rebecca Brill's experience is consistent with psychological research showing that repeating uplifting, positive statements (such as "I am beautiful" and "People like me") can sometimes backfire and worsen a person's self-esteem. Repressing unwanted thoughts or feelings leads to something called *ironic rebound*, wherein all the negativity a person has been holding back resurges more powerfully as soon as they run out of energy.[11] Just as we cannot deny our humanity by repressing our hunger, our emotional needs, or our sexual desires, we cannot repress our wounds into healing.

Accepting and sitting with unwanted realities can help us make peace with them. That can mean confronting feelings of ugliness rather than hiding them away. Brill says that hearing a diverse array of people speak about the ways they've been rendered "ugly" was a whole lot more useful to her than pretending everyone was beautiful.[12] "We're all ugly," she writes, quoting an essay by Mary Gaitskill. Giving up on the pursuit of beauty is far more liberating than claiming everyone can and should aspire to it.

Psychological research shows that there are many benefits to openness and revealment. When sexual assault victims choose to disclose their status with safe people, it helps them feel in control of their past experiences, offloads shame, and helps them identify others who can understand what they went through.[13] The more often a transgender teen is able to safely share their identity with others, the lower their risk of depression and the better their health outcomes.[14] When HIV positive people self-disclose their status, they are more likely to adhere to medication regimes and feel pride in themselves and trust for others.[15] These findings don't just apply to people with shame-riddled identities; they also hold true for people who believe that they have done something truly "wrong" in the past, such as former members of violent extremist groups.[16]

Open self-disclosure also improves the depth and quality of friendships.[17] When a therapist chooses to reveal vulnerable details about themselves in an appropriate way, it can help "de-shame" a shy patient and build their trust.[18] Naming our shame helps to bring us together. It releases the tension of holding unwanted feelings and realities back.

How do we begin opening up about what we're ashamed of? A crucial first step is taking stock of which experiences we have never given voice to before. The truths that are desperate to burst out of us are often revealed by our private writings, worst fears, deepest fantasies, and the secrets we only let slip to strangers or in anonymous online communities.[19] Here are a few questions to get you pondering what you need to practice revealing—and how you might start cultivating more openness in your relationships.

1. Some aspects of myself that I still really dislike are

   _____

   _____

2. A choice from the past that I still feel really guilty about is

   _____

   _____

3. A painful personal secret that I have never told anyone out loud is that I

   _____

   _____

4. A difficult feeling or experience that I'd like to talk to others about is

   _____

   _____

5. Below are some ways a person might practice disclosing shameful feelings and experiences, in order from least risky and exposing to most risky and exposing. As you read through this list, see if you can find a way to practice self-disclosure that might be challenging but possible for you.

    a. Setting aside time to think privately about the topic.

    b. Writing about the topic in a private journal.

    c. Speaking to myself privately about the shame-inducing subject.

    d. Posting about the subject in an anonymous blog online.

    e. Posting about the subject in an anonymous online group.

    f. Speaking about the subject in a private support group.

    g. Writing an email or letter to a trusted friend about the subject.

    h. Talking in person about the subject with a stranger I won't see again.

    i. Talking in person about the subject with a close friend.

    j. Speaking publicly about the subject in front of multiple people I know.

6. Using some of the tools above, make a brief self-disclosure plan. Choose a difficult subject that you'd like to practice self-disclosing about, and a relatively safe-feeling yet challenging method for doing it. Finally, choose a time-line for making this disclosure. Some self-disclosure methods (such as speaking to a support group) might

require additional research and preparation time, so make sure to build that into your plan.

I would like to practice self-disclosure related to this subject:

_____

One way that I could practice self-disclosure is by _____

_____

I plan to try making this self-disclosure by this date:

_____

In order to make this self-disclosure, I need these resources or supports: _____.

After I practice this self-disclosure, I anticipate feeling this way: _____.

If I feel triggered or ashamed afterward, here is how I'll cope:

_____.

Each time that we reveal ourselves to others and nothing terrible happens, our distress levels can begin to wane a bit. Our old expectations shift as new data updates them. Openness can turn shameful truths into neutral facts about ourselves that we have the power to work with rather than aim to correct. And later in this chapter, we'll talk a lot more about what working to accept such facts feels like. But first, let's discuss another core part of opening up to others: being vulnerable and honest about the experience of shame itself.

Speaking Shame

In the essay collection *You Are Your Best Thing: Vulnerability, Shame Resilience, and the Black Experience*, the therapist Deran Young describes the day her young son came up to her and declared that he wished he was white.[20] This revelation initially sent Young down a turbulent shame spiral.

"How did this happen?" she remembers thinking. "What did I miss? . . . I'm the founder of Black Therapists Rock, for goodness' sake! I've really messed up somewhere along the way if my own kid wants to be white."

At first, Young was certain she'd failed as both a counselor and a mother, because she'd "allowed" her child to internalize racism. Of course, all the maternal love in the universe could not shield a young Black boy from enduring racism in America. A white kid at school had told Young's son that brown children were not as fun to play with. That single comment opened up an entire wellspring of pain in her kid's heart—pain that reached all the way back to the beginning of enslavement. After a moment of sitting in her grief, Young discovered she felt grateful that her son was able share such deep feelings.

"I realized that what mattered most was that he was able to give words to his sadness," Young writes. His vulnerability—and Young's open acceptance of it—allowed them both to sit down together and discuss the white supremacy that had shaped both their lives. Young and her son were not immune to feelings of shame, but they could speak openly about where that shame came from, acknowledge its external source, and work to combat it together.

The psychologist Brené Brown has spent decades studying how people can develop greater shame resilience. Shame resilience helps a person to create mental distance between their self-image and what society has taught them is ugly or shameful about who they are or how they behave.

Research shows that people high in shame resilience still encounter triggering messages and experience shame sometimes, but they feel far less distress when they do. In her work, Brown found that two crucial ways that people build shame resilience both involve openness: first, sharing the feelings and experiences others might judge, as we've already discussed, and second by *speaking shame*—acknowledging the experience of shame *itself*.[21]

Shame often functions as something that psychologists call a meta-emotion—a feeling we have *about our other feelings*.[22] If I am angry at a friend but I believe it's "wrong" or "abusive" for me to feel anger, shame may overwhelm me, making it difficult to even recognize my underlying mood. When we name our shame for what it is, we get the chance to lift up the lid it has placed upon our primary emotions, and see what's really been lurking underneath.

How might this look when resisting Systemic Shame? It might involve opening up about the impossible standards we are holding ourselves to, and naming some of the small behaviors and basic human needs we still feel shame about. Let's take the example of the Covid-19 pandemic, a systemic problem that individuals were repeatedly blamed for. Though spikes in Covid-19 cases were nearly always linked to government policy changes, such as a return to indoor dining, the reopening of schools, or loosened mask requirements, government officials repeatedly claimed that case numbers were rising because individual people had failed to "do the right thing," by not masking or social distancing enough.[23]

At times, I found strict Covid-19 lockdown protocols very challenging to follow. In 2020 I was stuck living in a tiny apartment with my straight male partner, feeling more than ever the gulf between my identity as a gay man and his rapidly diminishing romantic interest in me. Every time I reached out for a hug or a tender touch and he twitched his body away from me, it crushed my spirit. As the months and then years wore on, all I could think about was getting out of the house and being near people who might actually want me and see me as the man I was. But even voicing my basic human requirement for physical contact felt morally unacceptable at that time. Most of my friends were very conscientious about Covid and took social distancing super seriously. Anyone who lapsed in their mask-wearing or quarantining was swiftly cut from the social roster, no questions asked. During that first year, I could barely find anyone who was willing to spend time with me outdoors, let alone partake in anything more intimate. For over a year I went to bed every night sobbing while fantasizing about being held.

Around this time, I began medically detransitioning. I stopped taking hormones, and broke lockdown to attend laser hair removal sessions at a spa every six weeks. I wore dresses occasionally and learned how to do makeup. Though my body had changed back to a more feminine appearance, my partner continued to freeze me out. He still had no interest in me, and I was lonelier than ever. So, I gave up on trying to win his affection, and threw myself headfirst into the gay world. Whenever I had the house to myself, I broadcasted myself nude on the livestreaming porn platform Chaturbate, reveling in the thrill of random men masturbating to me. I downloaded the gay hookup app Grindr and messaged with random men late into the night, some of them mere feet away from me in my apartment complex. A few times, I set up anonymous hookups in random guys' hotel rooms and wine cellars.

I was ashamed of my actions. Though I knew Covid's rampant spread was caused in large part by systemic failures, I did feel like a bad person for lacking the willpower to always isolate. A colleague of mine had posted online that if anybody left the house for unnecessary socializing, they should feel his grandmother's death on their conscience! The fact I'd slinked off to have anonymous sex made me feel complicit in a murder. I was also deeply ashamed of myself for staying in a romantic relationship with a man who no longer wanted me, and that I'd even risked intense gender dysphoria to get him back. I'd gotten myself into a pathetic situation, I thought, and the way I'd dealt with it was even worse.

I only began to recover from this immense shame when I finally started letting other people in on how I was feeling. In the winter of 2020, I told my friend Rick that I desperately needed socializing. We'd been in each other's lives for over a decade, through all kinds of difficult periods, and I was certain he would not dispose of me. We found relatively low-risk ways to hang out: sitting on his porch or eating sandwiches together in the abandoned "business center" of my apartment building with the windows open. After hanging out with Rick, it felt silly that I'd been terrified to share that I was suffering. Of course I was! He was suffering, too! Being around someone who cared for me was the most human thing I could possibly do.

After I got vaccinated, I met up with my friend Melanie and confessed to her that my relationship was falling apart. We sat on her bed and I cried sloppily, Melanie cradling me in her arms. In the months that followed, she cheered me on as I left my relationship and began dating queer people who actually found my masculine body desirable. For years I'd hidden from her just how awful my relationship had gotten, erecting a distance between us. Allowing her to know my inner world again helped to enrich our bond. In months following, many close friendships have deepened.

Though I had tried to hide my pain for a very long time, I eventually wound up doing what Brown's work recommends. I trusted the right people with my needs and found ways to meet those needs more healthfully. I revealed I'd been carrying around shame and had become unable to find comfort. And when it came to addressing systemic problems like transphobia and Covid-19, I learned that perfection was not possible. I had to take some measured risks in order to lead a life worth keeping.

Here are some questions to help you start unpacking the hard feelings that shame might be covering up in you:

- Why does it feel like I'm never allowed to want?
- Are there any emotions (such as anger, resentment, jealousy, desire, or sadness) that I try to keep myself from having?
- When I do experience one of these forbidden emotions, what other feelings come rushing in to cover them up? (For example, do I try to stifle my anger by becoming apologetic?)
- What feelings and needs would I express if I knew I wouldn't be judged for them?

A study published in early 2021 found that learning to speak openly about shame helped anorectal disease patients take better care of their health, feel more supported by other people, and develop a greater sense of agency in managing their own care.[24] Developing shame resilience has also been shown to help women in drug addiction treatment,[25] patients with severe depression,[26] and even burnt-out medical students who were ashamed of being exhausted.[27] Speaking shame has massive health benefits in everyone from HIV positive patients to eating disorder sufferers, to queer people, to people with highly stigmatized mental illnesses. When we're honest about what we need and how badly we've been made to feel about those needs, we can make supported decisions that reduce harm.[28]

After we have acknowledged the powerful role shame has been playing in our lives and the ways it's been blocking us from experiencing our full humanity, we don't have to believe in its toxic messages anymore. We can separate our cultural conditioning from what we truly believe—and show the alienated selves inside us a hell of a lot more compassion.

Develop Self-Compassion

Like a lot of people who care about social justice, I've spent many years rethinking my upbringing and all my old media tastes. *Kill Bill* meant a lot to me as a teenager, but was it okay to still love that film now, knowing that Quentin Tarantino endangered Uma Thurman on set?[29] Am I transmisogynist for having loved *Silence of the Lambs*? Over the last several years, I've had countless conversations with friends about the guilt we feel regarding the musicians that we like or the television programs that helped raise us.

This is all of a piece with how Systemic Shame operates—individual people are taught our goodness is defined by what we purchase and consume, and that with our media choices, we are essentially voting in favor of sexism, racism, and homophobia. The brands we support become an extension of our moral identities, and so when those brands prove to be tainted, we feel the scourge on ourselves. And at times, people who consume flawed media genuinely are blamed and shamed for it. Recently, at an activist meeting I was attending, an older woman lamented that she can't visit Disney World with her family anymore because she can no longer afford it.

"This is a wake-up call for you to stop supporting homophobic, patriarchal corporations," another woman at the meeting told her snidely. "You're lucky to be given this opportunity to rethink what you've been supporting."

Considering that nearly all the media properties that defined our childhoods were chock-full of bigotry, shaming random people for having been exposed to them (and for then forming an attachment to them) doesn't really make sense. Yet Systemic Shame's individualistic lens makes it hard for us to draw a distinction between pointing out a piece of media's flaws and lambasting anyone that ever was influenced by that piece of media.

It is not a personal failing to be a product of the society that one is living in. In fact, that is inevitable. I grew up on transphobic movies like *Ace Ventura*, and fatphobic ones like *Shallow Hal*. On daytime television, queer people were freaks to be interrogated and impoverished, addicted, or homeless people were the subjects of disgust. All of this impacted me in ways I morally reject, but this doesn't mean they did not happen. And amid all this media poison, there were tastes of something sweeter: the flighty sashaying of Nathan Lane in *The Birdcage*, the soft, pretty intonations of Savage Garden's Darren Hayes. In these imperfect flashes of queerness, I first recognized myself. Unfortunately, to be able to see myself reflected in these places, I also had to witness daytime TV audiences gawking at "the pregnant man" and see trans women portrayed as murderous villains.

The entire media landscape I was raised on had been polluted with bigotry, and nearly all of it was created by powerful people who were insulated from the consequences of hurting others. Some of that media means a great deal to me and always will. This past has shaped me, as it has all of us, so it's beneficial to be conscious of it. I cannot purify myself by removing all negative associations from my past, or from my present. But I can seek to understand it, and practice self-compassion for all the ways in which my upbringing has harmed (and benefited) me.

The writer and fat liberation activist Aubrey Gordon says she has a conflicted fascination with all things true crime.[30] As a white queer woman who sometimes suffers from anxiety, Gordon says the stories of real-life murders and rapes give her an outlet for all her worst fears—fears that white women in America are particularly conditioned to hold. "True crime offers a steam valve to the pressure cooker of my turbulent internal life," she explains. "It nurtures my anxiety, grows it, then offers a controlled path for that anxiety to escape."

True crime is a multibillion-dollar business and an explosive cultural phenomenon.[31] The leading creators and consumers of most true crime properties are white women, usually ones from middle-class and higher backgrounds. And as Gordon writes, that is not a coincidence. White women are taught in our culture that their lives are precious and vulnerable, and that dangerous attackers are lurking just about everywhere. This fear doesn't line up with the statistical facts.[32] Generally speaking, white women are at a very low risk of being victimized by violent criminals (particularly if they are wealthy), facing far less danger than either men and women of color or white men. When white women are preyed upon, it is typically by someone they already know and trust, such as a romantic partner, a close friend, a boss, a church leader, or a parent.[33] Yet the majority of true crime shows, books, and movies spotlight acts of random violence enacted against white female victims.

Research shows that exposure to true crime media distorts people's understandings of the real risk factors that predict violence.[34] True crime viewers tend to think that crime rates are higher than they actually are, and believe that most violent crimes are committed by strangers, when in reality most are committed by people the victim knows well.[35] Frequent consumers of crime media are more afraid of their neighbors, and isolate themselves from their communities more.[36]

For all these reasons, Gordon writes that she feels uncomfortable with her own interest in true crime. Gordon is an antiracist and is suspicious of true crime media for usually portraying the police in an overly favorable light. Even many progressive true crime fans celebrate the arrests and incarcerations of their "favorite" killers, with scarcely a mention of how many more people of color wind up incarcerated each year for nonviolent offenses. Gordon wants to challenge the popularity of such properties, and to interrogate how they have impacted the national psyche—but she wants to go about it in an intentional way that's not driven by shame.

"I have not stopped watching or listening to true crime," Gordon writes. But says she can feel her interest in the medium waning the more she educates herself. She says she consumes at least one piece of media about prison abolition and racism in the justice system for every single true crime program she enjoys. She pledges regular financial support to groups like the Innocence Project, and when her friends bring up their latest true crime binge watches, Gordon challenges herself to redirect the conversation toward real-world issues.

Gordon isn't berating herself for having absorbed toxic cultural messages, and she isn't equating her consumption habits with her morality, either. But she is acknowledging her mixed feelings, and honestly confronting the toll that true crime media has taken on her and her world. That seems a whole lot healthier and more effective than shame.

When I feel uncomfortable with the flaws in my favorite works of media, I find it helps to practice compassionate curiosity. I can acknowledge the emotional benefits that I've gotten from a work of art that I love, which helps me understand why I was also so receptive to its more toxic or ignorant elements. I also like to ponder whether or not someone is harmed by my ongoing consumption of a flawed creative work. I don't want to enrich an outspokenly "trans critical" author like J. K. Rowling by purchasing any *Harry Potter* merchandise, for example. But when Quentin Tarantino released a film exploring (and to some extent justifying) the pervasiveness of sexist abuse in Hollywood, I found a way to watch the film that would not line his pockets. I wanted to see how Tarantino would rationalize his own complicity in the mistreatment of women, because I knew that the messages in his film would have an impact on millions of other people beyond myself. I live in a world that has long celebrated Tarantino and handsomely rewarded him for the work that he's made. As an avid *Kill Bill* lover, I've contributed in a tiny way to his massive success. Rather than turning away from that reality, I decided I wanted to confront it, and seek to understand why his messages have enchanted so many people (myself included). Making sense of these tensions is an ongoing navigation for me.

One way that we can make peace with the more "problematic" preferences and media messages that we've internalized is by practicing a little self-compassion. Having self-compassion requires recognizing that we make the choices we do for a reason, and that most people would have a difficult time meeting their needs "perfectly" and virtuously under the same circumstances. Self-compassionate people tend to be resilient in the face of setbacks.[37] They tend to be less wounded by their own mistakes, suffer fewer negative mental health symptoms,[38] and are less fearful of rejection.[39] Whereas shame dampens motivation, self-compassion facilitates healthy change.[40] The social psychologist Kristin Neff developed a psychometric measure of self-compassion back in 2003,[41] and it remains very widely used today. In developing the scale and examining how people utilize self-compassion, Neff found that highly self-compassionate individuals tend to exhibit six key skills:

1. **Self-Kindness:** They extend the same gentleness and patience to themselves that they would grant to someone they love.

2. **Non-Judgment:** They accept themselves as they are, rather than judging their "flaws."

3. **Common Humanity:** They recognize that their imperfections help bond them to all of humanity.

4. **Avoiding Isolation:** They embrace connection and reject the urge to withdraw and hide.

5. **Mindfulness:** They observe and reflect on their situation with curiosity.

6. **Avoiding Over-Identification:** They recognize that their feelings, thoughts, and mistakes do not define who they are.

To examine how these skills look when put into practice, let's return to the example of my conflicted feelings and actions during lockdown. Instead of feeling ashamed of myself for requiring human connection, I could have walked myself through Neff's six skills, telling myself the following:

1. **Self-Kindness:** I am living through an international crisis, and my closest relationship is falling apart. It makes sense that I need a lot more social contact than what I'm getting right now.

2. **Non-Judgment:** My feelings are what they are. My emotions and thoughts are completely morally neutral. I can just let them be without beating myself up.

3. **Common Humanity:** I bet lots of other people are finding strict lockdown protocols hard to follow right now. I also can't be the only person going through a painful breakup during this time. None of this is unspeakable.

4. **Avoiding Isolation:** If I found safe people to confide in, I'd probably realize I am a lot less alone than I think. I'm

going to schedule some online hangouts with my queer friends and find some safe ways to see a few people in person and talk about what I'm going through.

5. **Mindfulness:** I should pay close attention to my feelings, including the urges and fantasies I'm a little ashamed of—those emotions are trying to tell me something important about what matters to me, who I am, and how my current life is out of step.

6. **Avoiding Over-Identification:** I am stuck in a difficult situation and doing my best to make it through. The actions I'm taking right now in order to survive do not define me as a person. My "worst" impulses or most shameful feelings don't define me either.

Baseline levels of self-compassion vary from person to person. However, studies have shown these skills can be learned. And since boosting self-compassion appears to not only improve well-being, but to also facilitate greater growth and connection to others,[42] it's a great way to begin breaking free of Systemic Shame.

Of course, there are some feelings that may be challenging to ever see in a positive or compassionate light. And there are situations in life that are so difficult and unfair we can scarcely make peace with them. For situations like these, when a gentle and self-loving approach feels impossible, it is time to harness the potential of radical, completely neutral acceptance.

Radical Acceptance

Self-compassion is a warm and reassuring feeling that tells us our actions and feelings are understandable. It's easiest to experience self-compassion when we believe we did the absolute best we could with the resources that we had at the time. But no one does their best all the time. Sometimes, we make decisions we just can't be proud of from any angle. When we can't endorse reality as good, we can still strive to accept it—and therein lies healing, even if it isn't pretty.

In August 2017, the journalist Freddie deBoer falsely accused his colleague Malcolm Harris of sexual assault.[43] DeBoer was experiencing a psychotic break related to untreated bipolar disorder at the time. After being hospitalized and medicated, deBoer regained touch with reality, realized he had been lying about Harris, and issued a swift, unequivocal apology.

This incident cost deBoer many professional opportunities. Once regularly published in outlets like *The New York Times, Vox,* and the *Daily Beast,* deBoer says many of his former editors stopped speaking to him. To this day, friendly colleagues will suddenly drop off the map and stop contacting him, leaving deBoer wondering what they've been told about him, or whether they've been pressured to cease correspondence. He's taken full responsibility for his actions, and Harris has been publicly gracious about deBoer's actions, but that hasn't changed the immense damage that has been done.

In the world of mental health self-advocacy, deBoer is a complicated figure. He supports many of the same economic policies that most of us push for, such as guaranteed basic income and universal healthcare.[44] He believes all people should be able to lead reasonably comfortable and dignified lives, no matter what their abilities are or how they have behaved. But unlike most of us who do disability activism, deBoer does *not* believe that society should view mental illnesses and disabilities as a neutral source of human diversity, deserving of acceptance rather than a cure. He believes in involuntary treatment for noncompliant patients.[45] He's no fan of Autism acceptance, "mad pride," or the concept of neurodiversity. And part of that is because Freddie deBoer says he *hates* his mental illness, is ashamed of it, and resents the massive toll it's taken on his life.

"Though I long to be free of both, my mental illness and the medications I take to treat it have been two of the most dominant influences on my entire life," he says.[46]

If you are disabled, systemic ableism will negatively impact your life regardless of whether you're proud of your disability or if you hate it. But despite this, many disability advocates think that it's necessary for us to embrace all our conditions, with no strings attached. People who express shame over their disabilities or long to be cured are often silenced or regarded as betraying the movement. Multiple times, my friend Charity has been sent death threats and been forced to delete her anonymous Tumblr blog because she's written that she wishes she wasn't Autistic. Charity is nonverbal and identifies as low intelligence, and she truly hates what her status as a disabled person has done to her life. Yet whenever she expresses this grief and shame, fellow disabled people treat her as a threat to their broader societal acceptance. I've found it endlessly frustrating to witness.

In anti-fatphobic activism, there's a similar conflict at play between the people who think we should all be fighting to create more feelings of fat *positivity,* and those who think it's more important to push for the social and political changes that would grant all fat people *justice.*[47] Books, workshops, and social media accounts about fat positivity or the far vaguer *body positivity* are wildly popular; people of all sizes are enchanted by the idea that the pain of fatphobia can be healed when individuals *choose* to have a sunnier attitude about how they are shaped.

But as a variety of fat writers from Roxane Gay[48] to the previously mentioned Aubrey Gordon[49] point out, public exclusion cannot be fixed with personal pride. If there are no seats on the bus that can comfortably fit you, and no prescription medications were ever tested on a person of your size, body positivity isn't fixing your problems. Even if you do feel fat pride, you will still be oppressed—and so will every other fat person around you who lacks your Teflon confidence.

It is for this reason that many fat liberation activists push instead for body *neutrality*, as well as economic and legal policies that will directly improve fat people's lives. Body neutrality is a way of accepting reality—no longer trying to force one's body into a smaller, more socially approved state, but not pushing oneself to feel desirable all the time either. Fighting for fat liberation means protesting to ensure fat patients are studied in medical research, for instance, and pointing out how evil it is that many countries ban fat people from immigrating to them entirely.[50] Fixing these glaring systemic issues would improve the lives of all fat people, the proud and the self-loathing alike.

The same exact principle holds true of the mental health advocacy movement. We don't all have to feel positively about our neurotypes, and it's actually quite understandable that some of us wish our disabilities would go away. Those internal feelings have absolute zero bearing on whether or not we should fight for access to benefits and expanded legal protections. A person with severe manic episodes like Freddie deBoer doesn't have to love his mental illness—and neither do people like my friend Charity. Even when we are still marked with social stigma and self-hatred, we can choose to stand up for ourselves and others and lobby to end predatory conservatorships, expand federal disability payments, and improve access for disabled students at schools and universities, among other interventions. By tackling the external sources of our shame rather than our shame itself, we can prevent future generations of mentally ill and disabled people from hating themselves so much.

The pressure to hide the scars of Systemic Shame behind a mask of personal pride doesn't affect just disabled people or fat liberation activists. It can also appear, in a much stealthier way, when women are told that they can become empowered by apologizing less, quieting their self-doubts, and carrying themselves with a slightly masculine swagger. For decades now, professional women of all backgrounds have been advised to cure themselves of "imposter syndrome" by broadcasting endless self-confidence—but these tips personalize a problem that, yet again, is structural. No amount of pitching one's voice down or power-posing can change the fact that women are disadvantaged compared to men, in virtually every industry in existence. What we mistakenly write off as "imposter syndrome" in women is, in fact, accurate pattern recognition: Women notice that their contributions are recognized less than men's are;[51] that they are less likely to be promoted but if they are, they are more likely to be punished for institutional failures;[52] that they earn less than their male colleagues; and that when they have families, they are penalized for it whereas men are rewarded.[53] To seem deeply insecure in the face of an insecure reality is not absurd. It is rational. And so, rather than making women even more self-conscious about revealing how uncomfortable and uncertain systemic sexism has made them feel, we ought to radically embrace those tough feelings as sensible, and as an indictment of *society's* failures, not the individual woman's.

Rather than trying to force ourselves to love the sides of ourselves society has taught us to hate, it's possible to merely accept our lives and the pain still lurking within us. Freddie deBoer has done that by taking full public accountability for falsely accusing Malcolm Harris, and by committing to watching over his mental health so that he doesn't ever hurt anyone in that way again. He's also "spoken shame" about his mental illness, writing numerous essays and producing videos about how to go on with life after taking actions you regret. These writings have brought solace to countless bipolar people. And he keeps advocating for social welfare and affordable housing expansions that would help all disabled people, whether they have "mad pride" or not.

Dialectical behavioral therapists often work to help patients accept difficult feelings and realities. Suppressing unwanted facts and troublesome feelings behind shame is tiring—it can lead us to drink, use drugs, beat ourselves up, overwork ourselves, isolate, and then explode in rage and tears. Sitting with the unpleasant realities of a situation allows us to adopt a more solutions-focused point of view. We can be grounded in the present rather than obsessed with the unchangeable past.

Here is a resource that dialectical behavioral therapists use to help clients accept themselves and hard realities:

REALITY ACCEPTANCE EXERCISE[54]

Below, list three unpleasant truths you have resisted accepting. This may be past experiences you wish had not happened, facts about yourself you wish were not true, elements of a relationship you have been trying to deny, or losses you have not allowed yourself to grieve.

1. _____

2. _____

3. _____

What are some steps you take when you are trying to fight reality? These may include things like distracting yourself with overwork or video games, numbing your emotions with substances, judging yourself for how you feel, or attempting to control other people's actions.

Ways I distract myself: _____

Ways I try to numb my feelings: _____

Hurtful things I tell myself: _____

Ways I try to control other people: _____

Unfair facts I keep obsessing over: _____

Other ways I "fight" reality: _____

What does trying to fight reality cost you? For example, it might drain your energy or frustrate others, or the methods you use might require a lot of money and time:

From "should" to "wish":[55] One way we can work to accept reality is by shifting from the insistence that things "should" have gone differently, and instead allow ourselves to wish we'd experienced something else.

*Should*s resist reality, but wishes allow us to grieve. Try reframing three of your persistent "shoulds" using the prompts below.

Damaging "Should"

I "should" be able to _____ on my own.

"I Wish" Reframe:

I wish I could _____, but I can't.

Damaging "Should"

This event should have never happened: _____,

"I Wish" Reframe:

I wish _____, didn't happen, but it did.

Damaging "Should"

I shouldn't feel this way: _____,

"I Wish" Reframe:

I wish I didn't feel _____, but I do.

Systemic Shame is obsessed with the power of the individual, but the unfortunate fact is that there are many circumstances individuals cannot mend on our own. It's okay in these situations to let ourselves sink into sadness—and to grieve that we don't live in a better world. Sorrow is not as bottomless as it might initially feel. When we try to push reality away, we lock ourselves in a losing struggle with our emotions that seems like it will never end. Paradoxically, it is only when we give up the fight and allow ourselves to feel unpleasant emotions that the suffering comes to its natural and eventual end.

"Whatever the experience is, it's already there," the DBT therapist Sheri van Dijk writes about emotional repression. "Just let it come to your awareness."[56] Thankfully, greater awareness of reality means taking notice of positive sensations too, such as joy and pleasure. These emotions can guide our actions far more effectively than shame.

Listening to Pleasure and Joy

We can practice expansive recognition by learning to listen to what feels pleasurable, or lights us up with joy. Pleasure and joy are effective shame-busters because they help retrain us to trust our bodies and emotions again. Systemic Shame makes us suspicious of what feels good, as well as what we need—but expansive recognition encourages us to expand our awareness of our bodies and honor what feels "right."

Pleasure is a great motivator because it's an emotion that drives us to satisfy our physical and emotional needs in a pretty immediate way: Eating gives us pleasure because it satisfies our hunger and nourishes us; sex is pleasurable because it satisfies our libidos and our desires to bond (or to have our senses stimulated). Joy is empowering in a slightly more abstract way—we feel joy when we are excited about what lies ahead of us and feel connected to a purpose or a community larger than ourselves.[57] Both emotions are transcendent and expansive: Pleasure takes us outside of our preoccupied heads and into our bodies and environment; joy connects us to other people and the future. Together, both emotions can lead us to take far better care of ourselves and be less ruled by shame.

As we've already discussed, shaming people for how they eat, which drugs they use, or their sexual habits doesn't motivate positive change, and instead isolates people and overwhelms them with decision fatigue. The Health at Every Size Movement, in contrast, encourages people of all sizes and health statuses to exercise in ways that feel pleasurable, and to prioritize physical activities that challenge and reward them to create joy.[58]

Research has found that when people exercise because it feels good, or to explore what their body is capable of instead of trying to lose weight, their exercise habits and health improve.[59] Treating exercise as a source of pleasure also benefits elderly people (who often feel shame about the loss of physical abilities)[60] and eating disorder patients (who are accustomed to using exercise to punish themselves).[61] "Joyful movement" programs have repeatedly been found to be more effective than shaming or lecturing.[62] And of course, lifting a person's mood and helping them feel more at home in their body is a net good unto itself.

Similarly, intuitive eating helps people heal a shame-fueled relationship to food, by encouraging them to trust their hunger and cravings rather than seeing these basic bodily cues as suspect.[63]

If you don't feel much shame around eating, you might still be able to apply these ideas to your life. Simply identify a basic need that you often deny yourself or that you feel some shame about, and think of how you might go about honoring that need more fully. If you feel shame about resting, you might offer yourself a nap every afternoon for example, lying down for a few moments in the dark with a soothing meditation music on. Or if you suffer from the pressure to overwork, you could tell a favorite coworker that you want to end the culture of "busy bragging," because hearing about how tired and overworked everyone is only makes it harder for you to set limits and take care of yourself. You can learn to adopt a more intuitive and accepting relationship to just about any need you've persistently suppressed.

Another way to unlock the power of pleasure is to really let yourself revel in how good certain activities feel. Because of moral Puritanism and Systemic Shame, a lot of us are too embarrassed to freely appreciate a good orgasm, a tasty meal, a walk in the park, or a languid, weed-smoking weekend cuddled up in a hammock. Simple, harmless pleasure so often feels *wrong* to us. In her book *Overthinking About You*, Allison Raskin, a mental health advocate, describes how she started encouraging herself to make loud, delighted sounds while eating. It can feel silly at first to sigh and say *mmmm* or excitedly wiggle in our seats when we are experiencing pleasure—but there is nothing wrong with feeling good.

When I was still closeted, I was highly suspicious of everything that made me feel good and right in my body. Since I was a teenager, I'd noticed that when I watched gay porn or imagined myself as a man having sex with men, I felt a level of pleasure "straight" sex couldn't provide me. Gay porn and fanfiction had a magnetic pull on my attention. For a few moments of rapture they made all my worries about the outside world drop away. But I ignored the meaning of these feelings for years, telling myself I was a creepy straight girl who was fetishizing gay men. In my late twenties, I finally began to consider that my pleasure was valuable. In fact, it might even reveal some essential truth about who I was meant to be.

Around that time, I also started experimenting with my gender expression. The first time I wore a men's button-down shirt with my chest bound flat, I felt an airy joy immediately upon gazing in the mirror. I couldn't imagine a future for myself as a woman. I could barely see and understand myself in the present. But when I imagined living and dressing as a man, forming relationships as one, even growing old as one, it was like a series of soft, warm streetlights had illuminated a path before me that had been blocked by darkness.[64]

Like pleasure, joy is an approach-based emotion. It often signals to us that we are on the correct path and doing something positive for ourselves that will pay off in the long run. And public health researchers have found it's far more effective to present healthy behaviors such as getting vaccinated, using a condom, or getting screened for a disease in terms of their benefits,[65] or how good they will feel to do,[66] rather than scaring and shaming people by playing up the danger of not "doing the right thing."

Joy can also motivate productive social change. Some of the most effective labor and activist movements of the recent past have relied on loud music, dancing, shared celebration, and joy to keep its members moving. Even at the worst of the HIV epidemic, LGBTQ organizers made sure to infuse art, self-expression, and playfulness into their demonstrations. And when Amazon warehouse workers were beginning to unionize in New York in 2020, rage was not the focus—instead, organizers like Chris Smalls made certain that events were filled with delicious free barbecue, weed, conversation, and champagne.[67]

Here are some questions for you to reflect on, to help you feel a bit more guided by pleasure and joy and less motivated by shame or fear:

- What activities help me feel relaxed and at ease in my body?
- Which sensations do I find pleasurable?

- When I feel good, how can I express that pleasure more openly?
- How can I incorporate more pleasurable tastes, smells, textures, or physical sensations into my daily life?
- Which activities help me feel like I'm doing something nourishing and beneficial for myself?
- When do I feel most accomplished and proud of myself?
- If I try to imagine the brightest, happiest possible future for myself, what do I see?

Practicing expansive recognition on a personal level is not about erasing the pain of our pasts, nor is it about purging ourselves of every single negative feeling and thought we have about ourselves. Neither is possible. Instead, it's about carefully observing the ways in which shame has shaped our lives and continues to shape it, and then consciously making the choice to follow what feels enriching and connective instead.

Eric might always feel the shame that comes with being a felon in a country of mass incarceration. Without the advocacy of other felons and their allies, Eric can do very little to combat the legal structures that keep him and over a hundred million other Americans with criminal records oppressed.[68] But Eric *can* grant himself the joy of wearing Robert Smith haircuts and pleather pants again. He can fill his home with books on trains and soft stuffed dolls he's won from crane games and build a cozy writing nook in his closet. He can reveal his status to people who are deserving of his trust, cry openly when he needs to, and slowly abandon the serious, tough-guy façade that only worsened his shame. Being more honest with himself won't fix all of Eric's problems, but it does make genuine connection to others possible, and that's absolutely essential to moving beyond shame.

CHAPTER 7

Vulnerable Connection

My friend Kelly, the fat liberationist parent I quoted in Chapter 1, has frequently found it difficult to connect to other parents. In the Chicago suburb where they live, Kelly is one of the only out trans or nonbinary adults around. They're also one of the few parents not actively trying to lose weight, and not interested in talking about diets, exercise regimes, or bodily self-loathing.

It's alienating. For the sake of their kids' friendships, Kelly's often had to choose between not rocking the boat with moms who often want to talk body shame and dieting and challenging other parents on their triggering remarks.

"This one mom whose kid was friends with my kid, she was so wrapped up in shame about her own body, and so die-hard about exercise and dieting," Kelly says. After a year of sitting through agonizing playdates pretending to find all the weight-loss talk interesting, Kelly finally decided to push back.

"I was like, *Can you not talk about diets around me?* And she was like, *No, fuck you, that's my entire life.*" The mother stopped letting her child have playdates with Kelly's kid after that. All too often, that was the cost of Kelly being openly themselves. Simply being a fat queer person with boundaries got them and their children excluded.

The shame of it was heavy. And the isolation hurt. Kelly found their neighbors and fellow parents increasingly difficult to trust.

When they signed on to become Girl Scout troop leader, though, Kelly found an unexpected opportunity to build a more genuine, respectful relationship—this time with their co-leader Autumn, a mom Kelly didn't know very well.

"I wrote Autumn an email saying, *Listen, I'm trans and nonbinary, I use they/them pronouns, if we are going to work together for a year as co-leaders, you need to know this about me. How do you want to handle this*," Kelly says.

Later on, Autumn revealed to Kelly that she'd never met a transgender person before—at least not as far as she knew. When she first read Kelly's email, she was taken aback and wasn't sure what to do. But because the Girl Scouts was a trans-affirming organization and both parents were committed to being the best co-leaders they could be for their kids, Autumn put real time into educating herself. She learned how to use Kelly's pronouns. The Girl Scouts organized a workshop on respecting pronouns and gender identity. With the organization and Autumn's support, Kelly came out to all the other parents. Over the months, the two of them became close.

"It became a real friendship, and it was really healing," Kelly says. "Months later, Autumn came to me and told me that her workplace had just started having people add pronouns to their email signatures, and because of me, she was able to explain pronouns to people. I was like, *Good job!*" Kelly hadn't needed to teach Autumn about trans identity much; all they'd done was come out and express how important being accurately recognized was to them. Autumn had taken the lead on her own growth from there. Kelly wasn't used to people showing up for them like that.

"You know, that was a really good exercise in letting go of shame, in terms of showing up as myself," Kelly tells me. "And letting other people do their own work about it, off-screen."

From all their negative past experiences, Kelly could have concluded that vulnerability was more trouble than it was worth. Fatphobia and transphobia had forced them to withdraw from many unsafe spaces in the past. They could have continued to withdraw, assuming quite logically that the abuse they'd endured would only ever continue. Instead, Kelly was able to keep making the choice to be honest about themselves and their boundaries. And when it finally paid off by cultivating a positive dynamic with Autumn, Kelly walked away feeling more empowered to stand up for themselves in the future.

After we begin healing our inner Systemic Shame, it becomes time for us to look outward, and contemplate how we relate to other people. Systemic Shame makes us both pull away from people and cast a judgmental eye toward them, evaluating their every action for signs of failure or suspiciousness. We have to learn to build trust again and find ways of seeing the potential in those we've been conditioned to fear. Working on this layer of expansive recognition is behavioral, and interpersonal. It's not just inner work. Even when we still feel deeply ashamed of ourselves or fear getting close to other people, we can begin taking practical steps that, in time, bridge social rifts.

In this chapter, we will examine how a person might begin to practice expansive recognition in their relationships using the following techniques:

- Unlearning dysfunctional attachment patterns
- Showing compassion toward others

- Learning to understand the context behind people's actions
- Taking pride in your history and the struggles you share with others
- Building community one relationship at a time

Recovering from Interpersonal Systemic Shame is not linear. We all carry many emotional wounds and behavioral defenses inside ourselves that will continue emerging as we keep expanding ourselves outward and take the risk of being fully recognized by others. But every single time we choose to turn toward other people instead of turning away, we are giving ourselves an opportunity at connectedness—and that is essential to healing from Systemic Shame in the long run. Individuals cannot solve or recover from systemic injustices on our own. We need one another.

Healing Doesn't Happen Alone

Shame is a social emotion, tied to our fears of rejection and the belief abandonment is all we deserve or should expect. A life less ruled by shame therefore requires positive social support. When we experience open, nourishing relationships, we can start to reset our social expectations, and retrain ourselves to be more communicative and capable of trust.

One piece of research literature that can be very helpful in understanding all of this is the data on healing from insecure attachment. A person's attachment style is the set of expectations they bring to their relationships and the interpersonal tools they reach for when they experience uncertainty and threat in those relationships.[1] When a person experiences secure attachment to another person, they respond to difficulty by sharing what they're going through. They might ask a close friend for help moving instead of making passive-aggressive comments about the stress of the move and hoping someone offers up support, for example. They'll also be willing to tell a friend or romantic partner if something they've done has disappointed them, trusting that improvement and repair is possible. Secure attachment in many ways resembles an "approach-based" emotional frame: When we are secure, we feel empowered, communicate our needs capably, and trust in ourselves and others to get those needs met. In securely attached relationships, both parties can move toward conflict and see it as necessary, instead of shutting down out of fear or avoiding difficult conversations.

Insecure attachment, in contrast, reflects the belief that a person cannot trust others to show up for them. When a person experiences insecure attachment, they may seem to require constant reassurance, yet never really feel supported or soothed (this is usually called anxious attachment); or they may fail to voice their needs at all and completely pull away from open emotion (this is usually referred to as avoidant attachment). Some insecurely attached people use a mix of anxious and avoidant attachment patterns, for example criticizing a partner for ignoring them (which is typically seen as an anxious behavior), and then disappearing into a locked room to sit in their sadness (an avoidant behavior) rather than accepting the quality time they said they wanted.

Decades ago, psychologists used to believe that every person had one single, enduring attachment style, which got locked in during their childhood. Today, most relationship researchers instead hold that every single close relationship in our lives can have its own unique attachment style, reflecting the particular nature of that dynamic. Beyond our individual relationship pairings, we can have attachment patterns for our friend groups, families, neighborhoods, communities, and even our environment. These many different relationship patterns stack inside one another, in what some relationship psychologists call the nested attachment model.[2] These attachments all have the potential to influence one another.

The parallels between being insecurely attached and experiencing Systemic Shame are numerous. Generally speaking, when people do not feel securely attached, they experience a great deal more internal feelings of shame.[3] They're more likely to experience all the hallmarks of Interpersonal Systemic Shame, too: They're more prone to isolate, and less likely to advocate for themselves effectively—either pushing and demanding too much or failing to be emotionally present at all. Anyone who has experienced abuse, neglect, or other adverse experiences early in life is at risk of insecure attachment.[4] Research also reveals that marginalized people are far more likely to show signs of insecure attachment as well; this includes queer people,[5] people with intellectual disabilities,[6] and Autistics like me.[7]

In one study, the authors Eileen Cooley and Amber Garcia observed that Black women were far more likely to report insecure attachment patterns than their white counterparts.[8] However, the authors noted that for Black women living in America, a pattern of not trusting other people and choosing to keep one's emotional distance makes *sense*. Black women are unfairly regarded as hostile and morally suspect nearly everywhere they go in America, and their actions are more harshly judged than others'. It is highly protective for Black women to keep their walls up, as much as it also costs them.

A similar phenomenon touches the literature on attachment security among Autistics: We can't usually trust that other people will sympathize with us when we are in need. When we were young, neurotypical adults probably did not take our sensory sensitivities or need for structure seriously. So it's no wonder that as adults, many of us refrain from sharing that our work clothes overheat us or that it stresses us out when a loved one's schedule undergoes unexpected changes. In her book *Polysecure*, the psychotherapist Jessica Fern writes that some of her patients have attachment insecurity because they faced a lot of financial instability as children, or grew up in houses infested with pests, or even because they fear for the future of the environment. Developing an insecure attachment related to any of these challenges also makes sense. It's hard to feel safe and interconnected when your world has always been unpredictable, and shows no signs of becoming any less menacing.

Most people afflicted with Systemic Shame have reasons for hiding. A lifetime of negative, shaming experiences has taught us that we cannot count on society to look after us. But no matter how understandable it might be, insecure attachment is psychologically and physiologically damaging. There is research linking insecure attachment with a variety of negative health outcomes and earlier mortality.[9] Beyond these really strong, negative correlations, there is the simple fact that insecurely attached behavior reinforces a person's isolation. It is very hard to receive love if you constantly behave as though you will never get it.

Let's take a moment to gauge how we go about relating to others. Below are selected items from the Experiences in Close Relationships Scale and the Adult Attachment Scale, two of the leading measures of attachment style in the psychological literature.[10] Read through each of set of statements (which reflect secure, anxious, and avoidant attachment patterns) and determine which ones are most generally relatable to you. Since we all have a variety of attachment patterns in our various relationships, certain statements may remind you of particular relationships in your life. Take note of any patterns that emerge there, too. I have also added example behaviors reflective of each of the three attachment styles, as I find these can some-times be a lot easier to recognize ourselves in.

ATTACHMENT STYLE SELF-ASSESSMENT TOOL
Adapted from the Experiences in Close Relationships Scale and the Adult Attachment Scale

Below are three sets of statements, grouped by attachment style: secure, anxious, and avoidant. Read through each statement and check off the ones that resonate with you.

Secure

- I turn to my loved ones for many things, including comfort and reassurance. ___

- I don't worry about being abandoned. ___

- I usually discuss my problems and concerns with people close to me. ___

- It helps to turn to my loved ones in times of need. ___

Signs of a Secure Attachment Style:

- Brings up concerns quickly after they arise

- Seeks out quality time with loved ones and enjoys time alone

- Approaches relationship conflict in a collaborative, compromise-seeking way

- Requests and accepts comfort in times of need

Relationships in your life that show a secure pattern:

table continued

Anxious

- I need a lot of reassurance that I am loved. ___
- I find that friends and potential partners don't want to get as close as I would like. ___
- I want to completely merge with another person. ___
- I get distressed if a loved one is not available when I need them. ___

Signs of an Anxious Attachment Style

- Brings up concerns repeatedly, but never feels they have been addressed or resolved
- Rarely feels they have received enough attention, affirmation, and quality time to be comfortable and secure
- Approaches relationship conflict with panic and fear of abandonment
- Seeks comfort during times of need, but is not able to feel comforted

Relationships in your life that show an anxious pattern:

Avoidant

- I want to get close to people, but I keep pulling back. ___
- I try to avoid getting too close to partners or friends. ___
- I find it difficult to rely on others. ___
- I'm not sure I can depend on others when I need them. ___

Signs of an Avoidant Attachment Style

- Rarely or never brings up concerns
- Seeks a great deal of alone time and does not often initial social contact

- Reacts to relationship conflict by trying to minimize it or resolve it as quickly as possible

- Seeks distance during times of need and shuts down at attempts to be comforted

Relationships in your life that show an avoidant pattern:

Some relationships in your life may exhibit a mix of secure, anxious, and avoidant attachment patterns, depending on the circumstances. Take a moment to try to think about the situations where your relationships look secure, as well as the situations that predict insecurity.

Situations where I behave in a more securely attached way:

Situations where I behave in a more anxiously attached way:

Situations where I behave in a more avoidantly attached way:

In order to feel secure, I need:

As you read through these items, keep in mind that a person's attachment style is a reflection of their past experiences, their current relationship dynamics, *and* the social and relational skills they've been allowed to develop in the past. Having anxious or avoidant attachment patterns is incredibly common, with anywhere from 30 to 65 percent of the population exhibiting some form of insecure attachment, depending on the study.[11] Since we live in a highly individualist culture that shames people for having limitations and needs, feeling a lack of support and security is incredibly common.

Since attachment patterns are interpersonal and nested, rather than fixed, here are a few questions to get you thinking about how you relate to others on a multitude of levels:

- Do I feel secure in my relationship with my romantic partner(s)?
- Do I feel securely attached to my closest friends?
- Do I feel securely attached to my family?
- When I am hurting, what's my first instinct?
- In my neighborhood, do I feel safe and as if I "belong"?
- Do I feel that I have a meaningful place in a larger community?
- When there is a fight going on within my friend group, family, or larger community, how do I handle it?
- Do I feel connected to nature, or the earth?
- Am I part of something larger than myself?

Even if you have a securely attached family relationship or belong to a wonderful, supportive friend group, you might feel detached on at least one level of the nested attachment model. Hopefully, the questions above have highlighted the kinds of relationships you still have room to work on—and some behaviors that might be keeping you separate from others.

We know from psychological research that one of the primary means of healing an insecure attachment pattern is by developing secure relationships. Historically, many psychologists claimed that the only way for an insecurely attached person to have secure relationships was through forming a serious romantic bond with someone who already had a secure attachment style. These two broad categories of attachment types—secure and insecure—were treated as static traits that defined who a person was. Insecurely attached people were viewed as broken and in need of a secure person's all-healing love.

More recent research shows this is not the case. A romantic bond with a securely attached person is not necessary to undo the trauma of insecure attachment; in fact, there are many ways to recalibrate how we relate to others. We now know that a person's attachment style is not a frozen personality trait[12] so much as an array of learned *behaviors* they can change.[13] What's more, we don't need to feel secure in order to change how we relate to others—we can begin by acting in ways that foster secure attachment, and allow warm, reliable relationships to germinate.

The research by the psychologist Philip J. Flores and colleagues has found that adults with insecure attachment patterns can form and experience secure bonds in support groups,[14] including support groups filled with other insecurely attached people. This is especially true when the support group weathers healthy conflict together, and if members teach one another how to express themselves more effectively.[15] Sometimes, getting more secure in one's attachments is as simple as starting to voice how one feels—and noticing that there are people in the world who actually care, and will listen.

One group therapist who works with insecurely attached patients, Aaron Black, published an excellent case study in 2019 that illustrates this principle in action.[16] One man in Black's support group, a patient he calls "John" was initially very withdrawn during sessions. John was always very angry at himself and neglected his own emotions. He also kept his fellow group members at bay, refusing to answer their questions about his life because he believed he wasn't "interesting enough" for them. John self-sabotaged by showing up to appointments late and ignoring other patients' requests for sympathy. Over the course of eighteen months, though, other group members continued making overtures, asking John why he wasn't initiating contact with them, and were encouraging when he did share a bit about the childhood neglect that had left him so guarded.

Black writes that one day, John finally relaxed a bit and vented frustration in front of the group for the first time. John complained that Black had not been coordinating with his couples' counselor, and that it was causing himself and his wife problems. Several other patients in the session spoke up, too, with their own complaints. Sometimes Black was slow in responding to their calls and messages. He deferred to the most vocal members of the support group too often, instead of prompting quieter folks to speak up. Instead of challenging his patients' critiques, Black listened, taking it all in and asking them clarifying questions.

Black recognized that for the first time in eighteen months, John felt that he and the other group therapy patients were on the same team. They were all united in finding Black to be an imperfect therapist who frustrated them at times. By listening respectfully and validating their grievances, Black let John and the other patients see that for all his faults, he was on their team, too. He wasn't going to abandon them for having issues with the way he'd done his job. He cared about them, and about doing his job right.

"John was clearly shocked that not only had he not damaged his valued relationship with me . . . but that he received support and outright admiration from the group for using words to express his anger effectively," Black writes.

This experience impressed on John that his concerns mattered to people, and sharing what was going on inside of him was not useless. It completely changed how he conducted himself in group therapy sessions, and later on, in his work relationships and marriage. Black writes that after this moment, John became more forthright and willing to claim space. Instead of retreating the second he went through a difficult emotion, he could express what he wanted and stand a fair chance of actually getting it. John's healing from shame did not happen internally—it occurred because *other people* welcomed him once he finally took the rare risk of revealing how he felt. Of course, no one could force John to open up before he was ready— but they could accept that openness instead of punishing it the way others in John's life had.

John's insecure attachment and shame was caused by a lonesome upbringing, being raised by workaholic parents who didn't emotionally tend to him. But research shows that developing secure attachments can help people struggling with the stigma and shame of marginalization, too. A study published by Shayne Sanscartier and colleagues in 2019 found that among queer people, insecure attachment and internalized heterosexism were intimately linked.[17] Internalized heterosexism is basically the Systemic Shame of being gay in a world built by and for straight people. People high in internalized heterosexism agree with statements such as "I wish I were straight" and "We [gay people] need to stop shoving our lifestyle down other people's throats."

Sanscartier and colleagues found that gay people who endorse statements like these feel disconnected from the queer community at large, and uncomfortable forming trusting, intimate relationships with their partners. In the nested attachment model, they are both insecurely attached on the relationship and the community-wide level. Being thrust out into the queer community wasn't enough to help these gay men recover from their internalized shame. According to Sanscartier and many other therapists who work with marginalized groups (including queer people and people of color), oppressed individuals need to develop the interpersonal tools to forge genuine bonds.[18]

In the table below are some behaviors that we commonly see within securely attached relationships, as well as some scripts for how you might practice them in your own life.

PRACTICING SECURE ATTACHMENT
Example Behaviors and Scripts

Communicate Distress

Share your discomfort and concerns with people.

Example language:

- "I'm worried that this move will change our relationship."

- "I'm really anxious from work and I can't think straight."

- "I feel really horrible, and I need help calming down."

- "Wow, it hurt to hear your mom say that to me."

Seek Comfort

Ask for emotional support or validation when you need it.

Example language:

- "Can I complain to you about what happened?"

- "Can we cuddle on the couch?"

- "I'm still really pissed, but it helps to have someone listen."

- "Have you noticed this problem, too? Do you understand why I feel this way?"

Express Delight and Interest

Take an active, joyful interest in another person's life.

Example Language:

- "I'm so glad you're home! Tell me about your trip!"

- "Would you like to go to the museum with me?"

- "Did you finish that show you were telling me about? How did it end?"

- "I love watching you draw. It's incredible what you can make."

Approach Healthy Conflict

Turn attention toward difficulties and differences rather than minimizing or looking away.

Example language:

- "I know you need time with your friends, but I'm feeling overlooked."

- "I'd like to spend more time with the family, but the way we've been handling holidays is not working."

- "I don't feel comfortable at these events. Here are some changes that would make a positive difference for me."

- "I'm still feeling a little wounded, but I can live with the compromise we arrived at together."

Include and Engage

Create regular ways of staying in contact and invite a person into your life.

Example language:

- "Check out this boss I'm about to fight in this game—I need moral support!"

- "The LGBTQ center is having a clothing swap this weekend. Do you want to come with me?"

- "I'd love to go watch one of your boxing matches."

- "Let's run a few errands that we've been dreading together."

When we're knee-deep in the messaging of Systemic Shame, we tend to push others away without even realizing we're doing it. We don't trust others to care about how we are feeling, and so we sit on our resentments, allowing them to grow until they explode into a knock-down, drag-out fight that's far harder to repair. Or we keep all our deepest dreams and longings close to our chest, never allowing others to appreciate that tender, hopeful side of us. When other people do attempt to build closeness, we may reject them, focusing solely on their imperfections and not viewing them as someone we could share a community with. In the next section, we'll look at one particularly aggressive way that people suffering from Interpersonal Systemic Shame tend to reject others: a phenomenon some activists call "trashing the bathroom."

Don't Trash the Bathroom (and Forgive Those Who Do)

Chuck McKeever is a teacher, hiker, and labor organizer currently living in the Midwest, but for many years he did activist work with the American Federation of Teachers (AFT) and the Democratic Socialists of America (DSA) in Seattle. In the DSA, Chuck led a Medicare for All working group and spent a lot of time on community service, mutual aid, and political education projects.

Chuck tells me around the time that Trump was elected, scores of new activists came rushing into the DSA, desperate to make an immediate difference—and their panic and inexperience caused quite disastrous results.

"After Trump was elected, DSA meetings jumped from having around thirty people present to regularly like a hundred and fifty or two hundred," he says. "A lot of people were having the moral clarity of realizing our existing political systems are wrong, but lacking the framework to know what to do about it in a productive way."

The new members who flooded the DSA were righteously angry about a great number of things: President Trump's restrictions on immigration, his withdrawal of legal protections for transgender students, his comments about sexual assault, and much more. They were terrified about the future and felt an urgent need to take immediate action. Thanks to Systemic Shame, many of them viewed Trump's policies as a problem *they* had to solve by heroically "taking a stand" and saving the day. And they often seemed to believe that other individuals, including very seasoned DSA members, had not been doing "enough" to fight for change all this time. These new members voted out much of DSA's existing leadership and dismantled some initiatives, such as a nationwide Medicare for All push, which had been a long time in the making. Small disputes over differing opinions and priorities spiraled into infighting, side-taking, and personal attacks.

In one instance numerous new DSA members publicly denounced Chuck and accused him of promoting white supremacist, capitalist standards of productivity—because he suggested the chapter put a strategic plan for the year in writing. Chuck was used to there being passionate disagreements in the DSA, but he'd never been written off as a person due to a small difference of opinion before. It took over a year for him to really process how betrayed it made him feel.

"When people feel powerless, they lash out," Chuck explains. "They search for something to make them feel powerful, even if it's over just one other person. They trash the bathroom."

When Chuck says the inexperienced activists had trashed the bathroom, he is referencing an analogy first made on Twitter by user @RootsWorks.[19] In a thread originally published in 2017, RootsWorks describes his experience cleaning bathrooms at a local community center for homeless people. As part of his volunteer training, Roots was taught to expect to see the bathrooms absolutely obliterated within moments of having cleaned them.

"It's not because [homeless people at the shelter] disrespect your work or don't value having access to clean bathrooms or whatever, but because of control," RootsWorks wrote. Most homeless shelters are quite controlling institutions. In return for providing unhoused people with food and a bed, shelters typically require adherence to a curfew, no drug or alcohol use, daily check-ins with staff, and in religiously affiliated shelters, regular church attendance. People living in homeless shelters are restricted in where they can go and when, the number and types of items they can keep in their possession, what they eat, and even how they dress.

"When you feel like you have no control over your life or your environment, your brain is going to want to assert control however it can, which results in trashed bathrooms," RootsWorks explained.

RootsWorks said that he often sees marginalized and shame-ridden people attacking one another for the same reasons. Queer teens question their friends for creating art that has mildly problematic elements; individuals who are unfamiliar with the latest social justice language get publicly dragged by thousands of strangers, even if their ignorance was benign. Chuck believes this is exactly what happened in the Seattle DSA: scared, ashamed, and powerless-feeling new activists claimed control over their reality in the only way they could—but in the process, they alienated more experienced DSA members, who could have served as their mentors and friends. Often these same passionate, overwhelmed newbies would commit to far more activist projects than they had the energy to keep up with, and then disappear from the DSA entirely a few months later after they'd burned out. They held both themselves and others to unrealistic standards of perfection—and everyone paid the price.

In recent years, a lot has been written about how left-leaning communities tend to "eat our own." In my decades of activist work, I have certainly witnessed that dynamic. Vulnerable people get aggressively attacked based on unsubstantiated rumors (particularly if they are Black, trans, or disabled), and then lose all connection to their communities. A moment of ignorance gets punished with a degree of shaming and ostracism that is in no way proportionate to the original offense. These dynamics often get referred to as "cancel culture," or "call-out culture," but they existed long before social media. I've been doing activist work since I was sixteen years old and I have always witnessed these kinds of rifts. I think the analogy of "trashing the bathroom" is a lot more compassionate toward those that take part in it. We all lash out in our powerlessness at times. And each of us has been repeatedly conditioned to pick apart the most minuscule of flaws in our allies, and in ourselves.

Systemic Shame has taught each of us to tightly monitor our own behavior, and to judge and police the actions of everybody else. If this twisted moral Puritanism is all that you've ever known, it makes sense you'd attack other individuals for disappointing you or disagreeing with you rather than trusting them enough to collaborate.

Chuck tells me that over the years, he's learned not to take the bathroom-trashings personally. For many, it's a painful yet unavoidable stage of political development. This is an idea that several other longtime activists shared with me, those who have worked everywhere from the Center for Reproductive Rights to Food Not Bombs. Baby activists are scared and desperate to make a difference, they told me. And individual effort is the only route to change they know. They want to feel triumphant and in control. So they trash bathrooms.

Chuck knows there's only so much he can do to combat it. So, he's cut back on doing leadership work, and watches his own burn-out levels carefully. When an individual member vigorously opposes his point of view and won't respect his perspective, Chuck takes some space. When a person is open to a reasoned discussion, he puts in more effort. Chuck spends a lot of time in nature, with trusted friends who share his values but are not a part of the DSA. Their outside view gives him a healthy sense of perspective. And these days, Chuck sees educating other activists as his main calling—it's the perfect marriage of his skills as a teacher and his years of on-the-ground experience.

"It sounds corny, but every time I attend socialist night school I feel like I learned something, not just from the readings, but also hearing from different people with different perspectives," he says. "It helps me feel a little saner, and like I don't have to be attending every single event or showing up to every single project."

Chuck and RootsWorks's perspectives show that it is possible for us to be compassionate toward the frustrated, stuck-feeling people who "trash the bathroom," while simultaneously training that impulse out of ourselves. Each of us can choose to stop shaming others—and we can do that without judging those who still think shame is the answer. We can't force others to change. But we can keep cleaning the bathrooms. And we can take every effort to understand why others might still keep trashing the spaces we've cleaned, rather than taking their lashings-out personally. In the next section, we'll take a closer look at precisely how to do that.

Understand a Person's Context

"The elder women of the Black Baptist and Pentecostal churches I grew up in . . . were too often the secret keepers," writes Tracey

Michae'l Lewis-Giggetts in her essay "Love Lifted Me." "But by being vaults, they often unwittingly became the arbiters of shame."

During Lewis-Giggetts's childhood, the older Black women who attended her church tried to protect girls in their communities from the shame of sexual assault—but they did this by chastising girls for how they dressed and moved and covering up incidents of abuse when they occurred. Many of these women had themselves been abused when they were children and had been taught it was vital to preserve their dignity and the dignity of their families by never coming forward about what had happened. But these defensive, shame-motivated strategies only made it *more* unspeakable to be a survivor of misogynistic or anti-Black violence.

Victims of Systemic Shame often learn to spread its dangerous messaging to others. Fat parents pass internalized fatphobia onto their children, forcing them to diet or instructing them to dress "flatteringly." Mothers who have endured relentless sexism upbraid their daughters for not sitting with their legs crossed. LGBTQ professionals instruct the next generation of queer adults to behave "respectably," correcting us when we are too flamboyant or openly sexual. Instead of banding together to combat unfair societal standards, marginalized people promote those standards among ourselves. Often these traumatic lessons are spread with the best of intentions.

"What does one do when the shame is wrapped in love?" Lewis-Giggetts wonders. I think a lot of people in her position would be angry at their elders, for perpetuating the myth that assault is a mark of dishonor that you deserve if you dress and act "fast."[20] But Lewis-Giggetts doesn't see it that way. She recognizes that a long thread of pain connects her to her grandmothers and aunts and holds them together. Unless Nana gets free, she writes, her daughter and granddaughter won't be able to get free either. Unlearning and healing is a community act.

But how do we actually get vulnerable and heal together, especially when the people we are in community with are the very same ones who've worsened our shame? In his book *Healing Resistance*, the activist and restorative justice trainer Kazu Haga says it all comes down to a few key principles:[21]

1. Remember that people are never the enemy—injustice is.
2. Attack the forces and systems of evil, not the persons doing evil.
3. Seek to *hold people in community* rather than hold them accountable.

In her essay, Lewis-Giggetts makes it clear that she has already applied those first two points to her situation. She recognizes that the Black elders who have covered up abuse are not the root of the problem. Telling your granddaughter that she must never speak of her rape *is* an evil act, as Haga would put it. But it was done for a variety of well-intentioned reasons—often related to the unique, systemic risks that young Black women and girls face when they come forward about what has happened to them.

When Black girls report being victimized within their own communities, they are forced to contend with the violence that cops will then direct toward their own people—violence that white rapists and abusers rarely face when they are accused. They also risk being taken away from their families and placed within foster homes that do not understand them or respect their home cultures. Famously, when Maya Angelou reported her own sexual assault as a child, her attacker was brutally murdered and she was forced to leave her mother's home and move in with a grandmother hundreds of miles away.[22] From this experience, Angelou took the lesson that honesty has the power to kill—and she stayed completely mute for several years afterward. Lewis-Giggetts's elders grew up learning such lessons. And so, some went on to silence their daughters and granddaughters, just as they'd been silenced themselves.

Preventing future incidents like these requires we combat systemic racism, the oppression of children, and sexual violence. Blaming the individual women who grew up surrounded by these forces (and who developed flawed strategies for surviving it) will not work. Lewis-Giggetts is acutely aware that the women who shamed her were themselves victims and were preyed upon and had their sexuality policed when they were young, too. They require healing, though they also owe their children a profound apology for their actions. This leads us to Haga's third point: holding people *in community*, before we hold them accountable. A person must truly feel accepted as a whole person, and be expansively seen and recognized as the product of their culture and circumstance, if they are to own up to the harm they've done and the reasons why they've done it.

"When we feel we have nothing we need to defend, when we can own all of our actions without an ounce of defensiveness, that is when we are at our most authentic, our most powerful," Haga writes.

Psychological research demonstrates that when people feel profound shame, they find it harder to confront the fact their actions have hurt somebody.[23] In order for the women in Lewis-Giggetts's church to honestly make amends to the girls they have hurt, they'd have to be understood and loved as assault survivors who had been traumatized themselves. Expansive recognition requires that we see a person not as an individual actor, but as a single thread located within a complex tapestry of motivations, traumas, and teachings. Only when we are fully embraced within that rich context can the reasons for our actions be appreciated and our missteps be accurately understood, made up for, and prevented in the future.

I don't know anything about what it's like to be a Black woman living in a world beset with misogynoir. What I do understand is how it feels to resent people who have hurt me but are themselves victims.

For years, I blamed my mother for marrying my emotionally explosive, verbally abusive dad. I hated that I shared half of my genetic material with someone who was so erratic and cruel. When I disowned my father at age sixteen and changed my last name, I assumed my mom had to be ashamed of my actions. I was spitting in the face of the family she'd made. I lacked the patience to endure the things she had quietly tolerated for years—and I resented my parents staying in such a miserable marriage for so long. I had inherited my father's compulsive negative thinking and bent toward self-destruction, and at times I cursed my mother for having chosen him as a co-parent and having forced me to exist in the world as I was.

But a few years ago, over cocktails, my mom confessed to me that she had never been prouder of me than she was on the day I chose to disown my father. All those decades ago, she had completely understood how much loving my father hurt, because she had been stuck living with him, too. My actions had not embarrassed her; she was glad I'd escaped the way that I did. My bitterness melted away the moment she told me that. I found gratitude and relief in its place.

We don't have to forgive every person who has ever hurt us. And understanding a person's broader context does not necessarily excuse their actions or mean that we endorse them. But when we reflect on the roots of a person's actions, we can attain a deeper understanding of them and identify new ways to combat the systems that encouraged such damaging behaviors. When I find myself feeling judgmental or resentful of others (which is quite often!) I try to reflect on questions like these:

1. What incentives or rewards might have led the person to take these actions?

2. What unmet needs are this person's actions attempting to fulfill?

3. How else might this person get their needs met, if there were better support systems in place?

4. What life experiences might have taught this person they had to act this way?

5. Are there ways I can relate to this person that do feel safe and worthwhile, and if so, what are they?

When I ask myself these questions, I can see that my mom stayed in a miserable marriage for a lot of understandable reasons. She was a lonesome and depressed person throughout my childhood, and suffered from a debilitating case of scoliosis that limited her work options. She'd grown up in a family where emotions weren't talked about, and never learned how to open up. Even today, she can't verbally discuss upsetting topics. She has to share her thoughts via text. Yet by having children with a man who was far more expressive (and explosive) than she ever was, my mom was able to create people who exercised agency in ways she never could. My sister and I are both candid and assertive. We're more patient than our unruly father was, but far less passive than our mother is. Instead of being ashamed of my mom's passivity or my dad's aggression, I can be proud of myself for harnessing both their best qualities and breaking the cycles they were each caught in.

I still carry a lot of resentment and hurt inside me about a great many things. But as I continue to repair how I relate to others, I've been able to start taking pride in who I am as a person. Sometimes I am even thankful that I exist as I am. I'm also increasingly proud of all the communities I'm in, including the marginalized groups I was once ashamed to be part of. This brings us to the next step of expansive recognition: locating ourselves within broader communities and shared histories.

Find Purpose and Continuity Within Your Communities

The history of the LGBTQ rights movement and particularly the work of AIDs activists in the 1980s and 1990s offer us an absolute masterclass on how to replace individual fault and shame with community support and solidarity. Throughout the course of queer history, we can see the forces of individualism and connection butting heads with one another, as the rights of LGBTQ people are claimed, then stripped away, then defiantly retaken. Across the decades and throughout numerous countries where queer people have demanded their freedom, it's only when queer people of a variety of identities and experiences join forces with one another that any of us truly get to prevail.

In America in the mid-twentieth century, gay bars and sex clubs were frequently multiracial, multiclass, and gender-diverse spaces, where working-class butch lesbians and trans people of color rubbed shoulders with wealthy white gay men and bisexual actresses and models.[24] Gender transitions were nearly unheard of and queer sex was a crime, but together in clubs and taverns, LGBTQ people found safety in numbers, and covert moments to live as themselves. As the queer culture writers Tom Fitzgerald and Lorenzo Marquez write in their book *Legendary Children*, the history-altering Stonewall Riots were participated in by a diverse coalition of queer people of all identities, predominately ones of color—as well as homeless people and sex workers who joined in the fight from the street.[25]

The strength and success of the Stonewall Riots had a great deal to do with the number and diversity of people present at the bar when police raided it. A truly rich and expansive queer community was beginning to form, after decades of rifts across class, race, and identity lines. In the years before Stonewall, several gay awareness rallies (which back then were called Annual Reminder events) had been organized across the country, predominately by white, upper-class cis men. They wore suits, marched peacefully and quietly, and collaborated with the police. Trans people were excluded, because our nonconforming bodies and styles of dress were seen as unprofessional; so were Black and brown people, and working-class queers who march organizers believed didn't give off a "respectable" enough image.[26] Lesbians, too, were kept at a distance.[27] Annual Reminders parades were dull, homogenous, and politically unsuccessful—and the white gay men who segregated their spaces saw very few political or social gains.

It was only after the Stonewall Riots that true gay pride parades emerged, which were attended by LGBTQ people of all races and backgrounds, many of them partially nude or defiantly adorned in fetish-wear. These events were loud, messy celebrations of pleasure, sex, love, and unfettered body autonomy; they were also spaces where marginalized queer people could openly voice their concerns and pool resources. In the years that followed Stonewall, wealthy white gays would continue trying to draw a clear line between themselves and the outspoken, more stigmatized queer folks who had led the riots. But even they began to see the purpose of diverse coalition-building once HIV gripped the community.

Throughout the 1980s, the United States government failed to address the HIV epidemic in a systematic way, showing not only indifference to the deaths of queer people, but downright contempt for their lives. Government and public health officials openly

expressed disgust for gay sex, and HIV positive patients were isolated in hospital wards and treated like toxic untouchables. In the
power vacuum that government negligence created, a formidable
force emerged in the form of ACT UP (AIDS Coalition to Unleash
Power), which is still regarded as one of the most effective, paradigm-
shifting political movements in recent history.[28]

ACT UP represented a massive alliance of various queer people,
other stigmatized groups, and their allies. Lesbians who were not at
high risk of contracting HIV stood in solidarity with gay men, planning demonstrations, collecting donations, organizing meetings, and
tending to the sick. Straight women like Ruth Coker Burks came
forward, bringing comfort to hundreds of dying gay men in the
1980s (and securing them burial plots when their families wouldn't).[29]
Queer activists provided services to intravenous drug users, sex
workers, and others who, like them, had been systemically shamed
for the way they contracted the virus. It was a true coalition of people from an array of different backgrounds. Combined with its clarity of purpose and righteous political rage, that diversity lent it its
power.

Within ACT UP, there was no point in litigating who made for
a sympathetic enough victim, or in limiting medical care to those
who seemingly "deserved" it. A plague was killing marginalized people, and the state, the healthcare system, and much of the news
media kept on willfully ignoring it. What AIDS activists needed
was numbers, and passionate support wherever they could get it.

Receiving ACT UP's support fundamentally changed many gay
men's outlook and understanding of community. The activist Patrick
Moore writes that ACT UP worked so well because it operated
under decentralized leadership: At weekly meetings, absolutely anyone could hold the floor and have their ideas heard, including people
who would have been shunned in much of white, wealthy gay society

for not behaving or looking "correctly." Gay men who had been disinterested in working alongside women for most of their lives were humbled by the generosity and passion lesbian and queer women activists brought to the space, Moore says. No individual person or privileged group held greater sway than another—all issues were decided by a floor vote at Monday-night meetings, which anyone could attend. At its best, ACT UP was accepting, chaotic, and egalitarian. It was expansive in its ability to recognize people where they were at—with whatever gifts, traumas, and identities they brought through the door. This was in sharp contrast to a Systemic Shame–based approach, which would have involved measuring the virtue of every single AIDS patient, and doling out benefits only to those who had done "enough" to avoid transmission and give the LGBTQ community a respectable name.

ACT UP's organizing ethos was one of defiant, prideful resistance—and it always stressed the importance of rejecting shame. Shame and stigma had allowed the HIV epidemic to rip through LGBTQ and drug-using communities; Systemic Shame held that gay men, trans women, sex workers, and drug-users were the *cause* of their illness. Shame kept people from getting tested, or disclosing their status to family and friends. One of ACT UP's main slogans, "Silence = Death," existed to combat the idea that HIV-positive people should be suffering in private. AIDS patients needed to be recognized in their full numbers, and for their full humanity, backed up by an expansive community that included anyone whose life was touched by homophobia, transphobia, classism, and other social ills.

ACT UP threw images of death and disease into policymakers' faces, rendering the unspeakable impossible to ignore. They hosted "die-ins" at the Food and Drug Administration, in Congress, and on Wall Street. They redirected blame back at the systems that had failed them, pelting the director of Health and Human Services,

Louis W. Sullivan, with condoms and yelling the word "shame" at him over and over, to draw attention to his downplaying the importance of protected sex.[30] Many lawmakers, fixated on a Systemic Shame–based approach, believed that abstinence among gay men was the only answer. If a queer person didn't "do the right thing" by never enjoying physical connection again, he supposedly deserved the gradual death that he got. But AIDS activists rejected that individualistic, choice-based thinking, advocating for collective harm reduction. In 1991, ACT UP activists covered Senator Jesse Helms's entire two-story home in a gigantic inflatable condom, valiantly rejecting the idea that frank conversations about sex and protection were morally unacceptable to have.[31]

ACT UP was wildly successful. As the historian Jeffry Iovannone writes:[32]

> *ACT UPers increased government funding, accelerated the drug approval process, forced pharmaceutical companies to lower the cost of drugs, pressured researchers to include women and people of color in clinical trials . . . and argued that people with AIDS should have a voice in all HIV/AIDS-related issues.*

Speaking about how ACT UP influenced today's movement for Black lives, the Columbia law professor Kendall Thomas says, "Black activists and their allies now understand that the struggle for black freedom has to make connections across many different constituencies and concerns that used to be seen as different and disconnected."[33] And ACT UP activists themselves were following the healthcare advocacy legacy of the Black Panther Party, who provided free care to all marginalized people at their clinics, regardless of race or identity.[34] This basic principle of proud coalition-building applies to any form of Systemic Shame that we seek to combat. No matter what we are going through, there are rich networks of other people who suffer as we do, and who stand to benefit from the very same systemic changes we all need. We need only to learn to identify them, and band together with them.

When I read up on queer history, I see that no challenge I have ever faced is new. My community has been combating sex negativity, the theft of body autonomy, isolation, and infighting for years. We've also been working on rejecting shame and banding together in shared celebration of freedom, pleasure, and love for as long as any of us has existed. It's more than humbling to recognize all the major dramas of my life have been acted out before by others. Seeing my worst moments reflected in the fights of others feels like coming home. When you're gay or trans, it's easy to feel detached from your birth family. You are of them, but nothing like them; their enduring legacy is one you can't really stand for. But when I visit the Leather Museum and Archive on the North Side of Chicago and gaze into decades-old photos of queer men and other kinksters, and I read the political and philosophical debates they were having that so closely echo the ones of the present day, I do see myself. Theirs is an enduring legacy that I get to be part of. When I speak to older gay friends and hear their stories of the early days of the AIDS epidemic, I hear myself and all my friends.

Today, the queer community is still cut through with fractures. Various identity groups war against one another, and privileged individuals fight for economic gains that will benefit only themselves. Trans-exclusionary cis women push to exclude trans women from public bathrooms, women's sports teams, and domestic violence shelters. White, cisgender gay journalists write alarmist pieces claiming that trans adults are preying on gender-variant teens, reproducing the very same "groomer" rhetoric that straight people spread about gay folks just a few years before. Even some steadfast supporters of gay marriage and LGBTQ inclusion in the workplace claim that the queer liberation movement has gone "too far," simply for celebrating sex and nontraditional relationships. This internal conflict is happening alongside mounting legal attacks on queer and trans rights throughout the United States and the United Kingdom.

Our present situation at times feels very dismal. But we can learn from our AIDS activist forebears, who scored major systemic victories while living under incredibly bleak-looking circumstances. We can choose to show up for people whose struggles are a bit different than our own, and who have been shamed for choices that are not precisely the same as the ones we made—because we have compassion for them, and because we recognize that when we shame anyone for their role in systemic issues like health epidemics, it harms everyone. Even if our past experiences of isolation and judgment have left us feeling guarded, we can decide to approach other people, the way thousands of queer *and* straight women decided to take a stand for gay men. Broad, radically accepting alliances are what will save us—not individual effort.

No matter what your own Systemic Shame looks like, you are not alone in your struggles. If you are consumed with fear about the future of the environment, you share concerns with every person living beneath sea level, a wide array of naturalist and environmentalist groups, and nearly every Indigenous nation on the planet. If you're dismayed by how the government has repeatedly failed to address mass shootings and gun violence, you're aligned with a massive coalition of parents, grandparents, educators, mental health advocates, and survivors whose lives have been touched by such issues. And if you do not believe that the only way to lead a meaningful life is by marrying and living within an isolated nuclear family,[35] then your freedom and comfort is wrapped up in the liberation of LGBTQ people.

I think it's worth taking a moment to reflect on who makes up your potential community—especially if you have not found belonging within one yet. Here are some questions to ponder:

1. Who else suffers from similar injustices as I do?
2. What other groups might understand a bit of how I feel?
3. Who in my community can I extend generosity to, with no strings attached?
4. Which other struggles, historical or in the present, resemble my own?
5. What can I learn from other marginalized or vulnerable groups?

As a disabled person, for example, I have come to recognize I have a ton in common with fat people and benefit a great deal from the fat liberation movement. Disabled people and fat people are both told that the ways our bodies move and occupy space are wrong. When a public space is made more accessible to disabled people (for example, by providing larger bathroom stalls and benches for people to sit and rest), fat people benefit, too. We are both groups that cope with a lot of internalized self-loathing. We both get told we simply need to try harder to overcome the way our bodies work. But even if some of us wish we weren't fat, or wish we weren't disabled, we can still fight for the policy changes we need. And we can take pride in belonging to a rich community of people of all shapes, sizes, and ability levels, who accept and support one another and recognize that we're not defective. We've just been excluded.

People beset with Systemic Shame desperately need community in order to thrive, but creating that community presents a real challenge. Living in a highly individualistic, fractured society doesn't prepare us to develop the kinds of interlocking, mutually supportive relationships we need. This brings us to the final section of this chapter, and the last step we can take to practice expansive recognition on the interpersonal level: by realizing that communities are just relationships, and by working to cultivate better relationships, one step at a time.

Communities Are Just Relationships

A few months after our first interview, Kelly reached out to me with exciting news: They had just befriended their scowling conservative neighbor. Positive social experiences like the one with their Girl Scout co-leader had left Kelly feeling more optimistic about connection. This had moved them to start to question their initial knee-jerk reactions to people who were different from themselves.

"I think at first I couldn't really see him as a human," Kelly says of their neighbor. He had a wary energy about him, which Kelly first mistook for dislike. Because he'd voted for Trump, Kelly felt uncomfortable around him. "I think he was just as afraid of me."

On a whim, Kelly started greeting their neighbor whenever they saw him in the yard. He relaxed a bit, and they started trading small talk. Over time, Kelly found that many of the unsafe, negative qualities they'd once projected onto him just were not true. He didn't hold many of the hateful values she'd understandably assumed that he had. And for his part, he seemed surprised by his own growing comfort speaking to Kelly, too.

Before they'd started talking, having a Trump voter living across the street had made Kelly feel less safe. But once they got to talking, both neighbors could recognize each other as people rather than abstract political symbols—and could see the neighborhood as an open community that they shared. It didn't fix the intractable nature of the political system, or how willfully oblivious both parties really were to all their actual concerns. But it did get them to foster warm, genuine contact, and that was a start.

For a very long time, I grappled heavily with the concept of "community." All my life I had heard about the importance of chosen family, but as an awkward Autistic person who was in the closet about my transness, I couldn't see how I'd ever feel anything but stifled by other people. At work and in school, the pressure toward conformity had been intense. Any time I stepped out of line or spoke out, I was treated like the problem. It was only when I was alone that I could relax and be me.

When I came out as trans and then as Autistic, my problems with people persisted. I kept thrusting myself into new social spaces, hoping that one day, I might find one of those perfect, preexisting communities that everybody talked about, one that could meet my every need with generosity and warmth. In the pursuit of this ideal, I joined theater companies, sketch comedy troupes, prison abolition initiatives, fiction-writing groups, genderqueer discussion groups, academic salons, and more. In every group I found the usual, all-too-human problems: There was backbiting and a fixation with social status, eye-rolling and nitpicking at every person's faults. Groups erupted in conflict over differences of opinion and lacked any framework for addressing abuse allegations. People who were unusual or hard to get along with were pushed to the side, while outspoken, charming members shaped the agenda and held the floor. After a while, I began to believe all this "community" stuff wasn't really for me. People were just too suffocating, too prone to superficiality and judgment.

This slowly began to change for me in the middle of the pandemic. Though I'd abandoned many of the groups I'd once joined in my search for the elusive "community," there were some close friendships I had retained from every single one. Often, the people

I had become close to in these groups were the observant, sarcastic types who'd stood on the sidelines like I had. They were the perpetual critics at the organizing meetings, and the eye-rolling nonconformists with their arms folded on the dance floor. These people were not "joiners"—they were gloomy, goofy, and inescapably unique. They had problems with *people*, but not with me. They could appreciate me at my worst as well as my best.

During the pandemic, I introduced many of these friends to one another online, and we all started playing video games together, and livestreaming movies. Some people introduced their friends into the group, and our little digital social hub grew. When friends of mine paired off with one another in new ways, making their own plans and working on creative projects, my heart swelled and I felt fulfilled. Somehow, after all these years of trying to *find* a community, my friends and I had stumbled into creating one. It wasn't an intentional or top-down effort, just something beautiful that happened around us, one relationship at a time.

I think it's tempting to believe that some fully formed, flawless "found family" is already out there somewhere, waiting for us to join it. But in reality, communities are just networks of relationships—connections that we must make, and then nourish. We don't get to find it one day and then claim our spot within it. We have to construct it, interaction by interaction, one vulnerable moment at a time.

This can sound daunting, but realizing that communities are just relationships takes a lot of the pressure off. There is no need for us to identify a single social group that we magically and perfectly belong in. All the activist groups, book clubs, support groups, and churches in the world are merely *social opportunities*: They offer us moments to meet the people who might one day play a cherished role in our lives. All we have to do is focus on building more authentic, supportive relationships—and letting those relationships combine and expand outward, beyond our small selves.

So how do we get started? As an Autistic person, I had to develop a system for building and enriching my relationships. Approaching new people and getting close to them was not something that came naturally to me. In the years since I developed these friendship-making tips, I've enjoyed numerous warm, consistent relationships—and I've also discovered my advice can be helpful to a wide variety of people, not just fellow Autistics. Ultimately, building new relationships comes down to two principles: consistency and authenticity. If you keep showing up to social events regularly and keep honestly expressing yourself and your viewpoints while you are there, eventually the right people will take a shine to you, and when people disagree with you or don't understand your perspective, you'll have the kinds of conflicts that are enriching and worth having. Here is what it looks like to put these principles into practice:

AN AUTISTIC SOCIAL BUTTERFLY'S GUIDE TO MAKING FRIENDS
Steps for Forming and Deepening Relationships

1. Research activities and events where you can meet new people.
    - Set aside at least an hour each week to look up local events, meetup groups, social clubs, support groups, classes, and other spaces where you can meet new people.
    - Digital socializing counts as socializing! Online forums, Discord servers, subreddits, and virtual classes are all great options.
    - Begin adding some of these options into your calendar. One new event per week is often a good place to start.

2. Attend an event at least three times.
   - A single visit does not provide enough information to judge whether a group is a good fit for you.

   - People filter in and out of social groups all the time, so the more times you attend, the more people you will meet.

   - When we attend an event for the very first time, we are often too anxious to really enjoy it. So give yourself a few attempts for any group that sounds appealing.

3. Follow my friend Mel's rule: "You don't have to do shit, say shit, or feel shit."
   - When we are in unfamiliar social spaces, we may feel a strong pressure to conform, or participate in activities that make us uncomfortable.

   - To combat this internal pressure, when my friend Mel visits a new space, she reminds herself that she does not have to do, say, or feel anything she does not want to.

   - You're going out in order to meet people you enjoy being around. Forcing yourself to do things you don't enjoy or that feel inauthentic to you will never get you there.

   - "Mel's rule" can remind us that simply showing up to a space as ourselves is enough.

4. Identify the people you might want to get to know better.
   - After attending a social group a few times, take stock of the people you've met.

   - Who makes you laugh? Who has been welcoming? Who fascinates you, or has taught you new things?

   - Approach these people and engage with them more. Ask them about their lives, or bond over a shared annoyance within the group.

   - Add people on social media, or ask for their emails or phone numbers.

5. Deepen your connections.
    *   Share interesting articles, memes, or funny observations from your day with potential friends.

    *   Invite people to spend time with you outside of the group where you met: Plan game or movie nights, visit a museum or see a movie together, or just go on a walk.

    *   Offer support when people need it, in whatever ways are available to you. This can be as simple as lending someone a book or providing them a sympathetic ear.

    *   Introduce people from different parts of your life to one another, especially if they have interests or hobbies in common.

    *   Ask for help, so that people have the opportunity to get closer to you. If you trust a particular person's judgment, ask them for advice. If you feel at ease around somebody, invite them to run stressful errands with you.

Even when we follow steps like these, building real communities for ourselves and others may take years. It's important to acknowledge and accept this. Trusting relationships are developed by revealing ourselves and navigating conflict, repeatedly, until we come to realize that other people really do care for us and won't abandon us when we make a mistake or if things get hard. This process is not instant, and it never ends.

Under the paradigm of Systemic Shame, most of us have come to expect change to happen quickly, and to think that if we can't remedy all our problems in one quick burst of hard work, we are failures. Getting comfortable with slow, steady progress toward a larger goal is an essential component of expansive recognition. We can't fix every problem in life on our own, nor should we set out to. All we can do is take small steps that unite us with others.

In the final chapter of this book, we will discuss how to combat the thorniest and most painful layer of Systemic Shame: the overpowering sense that our lives are meaningless, and that it's too late for humanity to create lasting change. By practicing expansive recognition, we can transcend such beliefs, and find a place for ourselves that's significant, yet modest.

There is still hope for the future of humanity, and it's possible for each of us to make a small, positive difference in the world that we can be proud of. Here is how we start.

CHAPTER 8

Hope for Humanity

Long before I came out as transgender or gay, I was actively involved in LGBTQ rights activism. In high school, I was co-president of my school's Student Equal Rights Coalition, which held weekly meetings for queer and questioning students, organized annual events about gay history, and held National Day of Silence vigils to memorialize lives taken by hate crimes. My friends and I protested the US military's Don't Ask, Don't Tell policy during lunchtime at school, setting up a microphone and table to counter the recruiters who were there. I organized queer movie nights, hosting them at the homes of friends whose families were supportive. I lobbied for gay marriage, phone-banked for candidates who I thought might help advance queer rights, and registered people to vote before I could even vote myself. I think I was trying, with all this furious effort, to single-handedly create a world where I could finally come out as myself.

There were many setbacks in those fights. Our high school principal was constantly shutting down Student Equal Rights Coalition events. Group members were told, for example, that we could not wear shirts with our identities listed on them in recognition of National Coming Out Day because if we got cornered and beat up, it would be a "distraction." We were told our school's student handbook could not be amended to protect gay and trans students under its anti-harassment policy, because doing so would offend many kids' devout Christian parents. When a tenth-grader at our school was brutally beaten by a mob of boys because he had been wearing women's jeans, school administrators looked the other way. When a girl cornered me in the showers, screaming and threatening to beat me and calling me slurs, no one did a thing.

The problems weren't just at school. They were societal. All the movies with "LGBTQ representation" that I could find for our queer movie nights were ones like *Brokeback Mountain* and *Boys Don't Cry*, in which queer characters wind up murdered. No matter how much I thrust myself into activist work, I always came home to hear Bill O'Reilly droning away on the television about how people like me would be society's downfall. My home state, Ohio, constitutionally banned gay marriage when I was fifteen. Failure was everywhere. It seemed the entire world wanted me to remain ashamed of what I was, and never, ever come out.

After years of this, I became demoralized. I let myself all but disappear into a straight, cisgender identity. I volunteered for causes I cared about here and there, but I'd lost faith in humanity, and all regard for myself. I couldn't really imagine a future where I could feel fulfilled, and focused mostly on just trying to get by. That's part of why I wound up so drunk and distraught after completing my PhD. I'd finished the only long-term goal I had believed in for ages, an accomplishment so large and respectable I thought it might unlock the right to exist. Success hadn't earned me love or safety any more than activism had. I was just left with my usual shame.

When it comes to queer rights, the last several years have increasingly reminded me of how things were back when I was a teen. In the mid-2010s, queer people got to enjoy structural benefits such as the right to get married in every single state, and an assurance that health insurance plans would cover some fundamental gender-affirming care procedures. But now LGBTQ people everywhere face a violent backlash. Bans on gender-affirming treatment for transgender youth have passed all over the country, and parents can lose custody of their children for something as simple as honoring their pronouns. In states like Florida, teachers and students alike are barred from even *acknowledging* the existence of queerness in their classrooms[1] and people like me can't use the restroom. Multiple trans women who were well known and cared for among my social circles went missing in Chicago this past year. Almost every trans femme writer or media figure that I know personally has been mobbed and accused of grooming children in the past eighteen months.

If I were still the lonesome, closeted person I was even a few years ago, I'd be curling up in a ball of shame right now, without any drive or hope. I think I might even be tempted to try to detransition for real this time, willing a passive, depressed female identity to overtake me and offer the "safety" of nonexistence. Instead, I feel called to show up for my trans siblings as best I can, educating parents and teachers about gender issues, helping newly out trans people find informed consent clinics and mental health resources, and writing openly about how much transition has revitalized me. I know that whenever I do things like that, dozens of trans people reach out and tell me I've helped them find the permission to live as themselves. I recognize that my work matters, and that I matter, even in an oppressive system that's done all it can to disenfranchise me and cleave me from my kin.

Why am I galvanized now, instead of completely frozen? Because I've found a rich network of supportive people, and I've spent a lot of quality time around them unlearning my internalized transphobia. I've found modest, sustainable ways to make a difference in this world, and I can witness their impact. I know people who are actively taking steps to protect trans people's lives and their access to healthcare, using both legal approaches and underground ones that circumvent the systems that oppress us. I've had a hand in building dynamic, nourishing communities that have restored my faith in others, and I have an understanding of how real systemic change works, so I'm not overloaded with a confused sense of urgency and personal responsibility. I don't like much of what's happening around me, but I can accept it, respond to it, and imagine a future reality that I want to be a part of.

Systemic Shame would like me to toil away alone, never making a tangible difference. But as fearful as I am right now, I know there's a better way to live. And finding that way to live involves a lot of slowing down, connecting with others, and trusting in my inner voice—the voice I used to silence, which tells me who I am, what is right, and where I belong.

In this chapter we will take a look at the ways a diverse array of people have learned to cope with global Systemic Shame, and the steps they've taken to nourish a purposeful, hopeful vision of their place in the world. We'll also look to the research literature on how people beset with feelings of despair and emptiness can locate an expansive, interconnected sense of social recognition and hope. In some of these resources, you'll find insights into how you might make a more effective mark on this world—in others, you'll see tips on how to reduce your sense of obligation and learn to put your own life and limitations in perspective.

There's an interesting duality to expansive recognition: It both celebrates the smallness of our impact and relieves the pressure that says we must do and be it all. Systemic Shame preaches we must focus on being the strongest, best, most moral individuals we possibly can be, or else the entire world around us will fall apart. Expansive recognition, in contrast, reveals to us that our individual lives are tiny, and our impact will always be minor—but that it's never done in isolation, and it is always enough.

The first step to embracing this concept is taking a careful look at where life has already planted us, sizing up the skills, lessons, legacies, and even painful experiences have led us to our present moment. When we appreciate where we are and the rich tapestry of human history that connects us to our current position, we can see the potential that lies there.

Finding Your Place in the Fight

My old college buddy Sam has worked for over fifteen years on campaigns against offshore drilling and deforestation. I've always felt self-conscious knowing that while I was frittering away time on research projects in dusty university offices, Sam was off in the Canadian wilderness. Systemic Shame had me convinced I lacked the sense of commitment Sam did, and that because of people like me, the planet was toast. Even though he never said anything judgmental to me, I figured Sam thought I was a terrible person because I burned through a lot of disposable coffee cups, shopped at fast fashion stores, and focused on the short-term returns of my own career.

During a visit to Chicago, Sam started talking to me about a colleague of his, Alma, who helps with grant writing and zoning approvals for community gardens in major cities. Sam was in awe of her logical, methodical skill. This surprised me, because I was in awe of his relentless focus and ability to rough it.

"People think that my work is more radical than people like Alma's," Sam said. "Or that her work is just performative liberalism or whatever. But she is helping people get in touch with the dirt and with growth, people who simply haven't had that experience maybe ever before in their lives. We all have different character classes and hers does a lot more to recruit new environmentalists than mine ever does."

I used to turn my nose up at efforts like Alma's, assuming that building community gardens was the work of mostly well-off white people who simply wanted to claim more public park space for themselves and their flowers, and that it was all a meaningless indulgence that did nothing to better the planet. Really, I was projecting my own Systemic Shame about being a privileged white person who wasn't doing enough, I thought, for the environment myself. Sam's comment got me thinking about what small, significant efforts a person can take to get in touch with the earth and have a hand in stewarding its well-being.

It wasn't long after that conversation that I discovered a friend's sibling was active in the leadership of the Chi-Nations Youth Council, a Chicago-based organization led by Indigenous youth that maintains a First Nations community garden in the city's Thirty-Fifth Ward.[2] The First Nations Garden includes individual plots community members can use to grow whatever food they like, as well as raised beds and planting mounds set aside for sweetgrass, strawberries, prairie sage, tobacco, echinacea, and other plants that carry cultural significance to nations native to the land. In the garden, Chi-Nations also hosts weekly healing gatherings for Native people, opportunities to learn and play traditional Indigenous sports like double ball, as well as cookouts, tipi paintings, and classes. In just a few acres near the corner of Pulaski and Wilson, Chi-Nations is managing to preserve Native practices, share ancestral ecological wisdom, cultivate plants that once thrived throughout the region, and keep people fed.

During the worst of the pandemic, when I and many others were feeling particularly locked away and disconnected from the broader world, my friend Kaitlin Smith also offered an opportunity for marginalized people to reconnect with history and the land. Kaitlin and I have known one another since high school, and she has always been an incredibly reflective, observant person with a passion for the environment and antiracism. She's an accomplished educator and naturalist who has worked with organizations such as Outdoor Afro and Mass Audubon, and for the last few years she has run Storied Grounds, which provides ecological, historical, and foraging tours to Black people and their close loved ones.[3] At Storied Grounds events, Kaitlin uses the surrounding woods of the greater Boston area to discuss pivotal moments in Black history. On a foraging tour, she explains how anti-foraging laws were first created after the abolition of slavery, and used to criminalize poor, newly freed Black people who were trying to feed themselves. She's led a stargazing tour focused on the liberatory work of Nat Turner. During 2020 and 2021 Kaitlin went digital, and even addressed the looming legal threat on reproductive healthcare access, by offering a virtual class on natural abortifacients and contraceptive plants and discussing the ways Black women historically used them to prevent unwanted pregnancies during enslavement.

In the work of Storied Grounds and the Chi-Nations Youth Council, we see social context and ecology integrated fully with one another, creating an expansive, rich understanding of systemic problems (and their solutions) that is also completely approachable. Systemic Shame doesn't provide us with a useful framework for understanding how anti-Blackness, Native genocide, climate change, and abortion restrictions are linked; it simply demands that we all be freaked out about each of these seemingly separate problems and our own failure to do anything about them. Under expansive recognition, though, we can see how the roots of all these issues reach far back into our history and remain deeply interwoven in our present.

By doing this, we can identify concrete ways to approach these problems, and begin to untangle them, thread by thread. It's kind of remarkable how well Chi-Nations Youth Council and Storied Grounds both manage to take centuries of complex political history and render them elegantly simple, and capable of being addressed.

When Sam said that we all have "different character classes" in the fight to save the environment, he was likening different people's unique strengths to the many character types that exist in role-playing games.[4] There are a variety of different jobs to be filled in any successful social movement or developing community, and most aren't things the average person would recognize as "activism." Fostering positive change is not all about leading protests or doing big, bold acts of disruption that wind up on the news. Those actions matter, of course, but focusing on them and them alone gives a highly individualistic vision of how social change really occurs. Life isn't actually like the Hunger Games; most of us will never be symbolic Katniss Everdeens leading the charge against an oppressive government. And that's perfectly fine, because there is a lot of essential work to be done, much of it relatively quiet and often overlooked.

Here are just a few of the essential roles every social movement needs, and some examples of what they entail:

CHANGE-MAKING "CHARACTER CLASSES"	
The Protestor	• Attends public actions
	• Works with other protestors to disrupt the status quo and draw attention to an issue
	• Speaks out in the face of injustice
	• Intervenes to protect the vulnerable from violence
	• Confronts harassment of the vulnerable directly or provides a barrier between the vulnerable and the police or from another attacker

The Educator	• Creates community resources
	• Studies the available literature and movements from the past
	• Explains concepts and introduces new ideas
	• Documents a movement's history and draws lessons from past experiences
	• Mentors members of the community and helps expand their views
The Mediator	• Helps translate challenging ideas to people who are on the fence or find some ideas too "radical"
	• Questions unjust policies and assumptions in their organizations
	• Intercedes during conflicts to help de-escalate or find common ground
	• Gets people who are "on the fence" or not very politically involved more open to difficult conversations
	• Advocates for marginalized people to be centered in decision making
The Healer	• Provides medical care for people harmed during protests or altercations with the police
	• Helps ensure people in the community are well fed and have access to resources
	• Listens supportively as people decompress about frustrations or traumatic experiences
	• Speaks out when a movement is placing unrealistic demands on its members
The Organizer	• Collects and systematizes community resources
	• Assists in the planning and execution of actions
	• Maintains records and keeps meeting minutes
	• Serves as an informal project manager for initiatives as needed
	• Helps track goals, budgets, resource allocation, etc.

table continued

CHANGE-MAKING "CHARACTER CLASSES"	
The Artist	• Inspires others with uplifting messages • Breaks down complex concepts into memorable messages or symbols • Provides comfort and much-needed distractions to exhausted members • Helps provide movements with markers of belonging and identity • Spreads messages to an audience that might not otherwise find them
The Connector	• Introduces people and expands the community • Disseminates event invitations and information • Builds coalitions across organizations or identity groups • Welcomes new members • Plugs isolated individuals into the support networks they need

People like Sam are activists, happy to tie themselves to trees or lie down in front of bulldozers. Kaitlin is more of an educator and healer; she uses her own scholarship and research to bridge connections between the past and the present, and helps connect other Black people to the nature that has been so nourishing for her. This list is just a small taste of the many ways people can make a difference. The options truly are endless.

Here's an example to make it a little more concrete: My friend Amelia worked at an insurance agency for over a decade, helping develop a mobile app for filing claims. Her agency had always required customers to verify damage and theft claims by filing a police report. But Amelia openly questioned whether this was needed. Was it safe to require Black customers to call police into their homes?

Given everything we know about how often police departments falsify evidence, "lose" bodycam footage, and even steal property, were their reports trustworthy? After raising these issues, Amelia convinced her agency to stop requiring police reports for many types of insurance filings. For her agency's thousands of customers, this meant fewer 911 calls, less reliance on policing, and among Black and brown customers, far less risk.

Amelia is not a protestor, organizer, or activist, but her experience illustrates an important part of beating back Systemic Shame: trusting that wherever we are, that is our place in the fight.[5] This clarifying self-trust is a form of radical acceptance, applied to our social and political sphere. It means we no longer argue with the unfair and often stifling reality in which we find ourselves, but instead begin thinking up ways we can use that position to change lives for the better. It's also a galvanizing call to action. Instead of despairing over our limited resources or inability to "fix" the world, we can embrace the chances we get to help others, thwart unjust systems, and create meaning, whatever those may be.

Sometimes, accepting our reality means acknowledging that our current position is morally indefensible to us, and removing ourselves from oppressive systems to the greatest extent we can. In the spring of 2022, a Texas Child Protective Services investigator named Morgan Davis, himself a transgender man, was tasked with carrying out Governor Greg Abbott's order that families who affirm their trans kids' identities be investigated for child abuse.[6] At first, Davis believed that because he had the best interests of trans children in mind, he could work to defend them and their families, changing the system from the inside. Plus, Davis figured that even if he recused himself from a case, that just meant some other investigator would get it.

The first time he was assigned to investigate a trans-affirming family, Davis left his CPS badge in the car and brought them empanadas and tartlets. In his report, Davis indicated the family had provided an enriching, supportive environment to their daughter, and that there were no indications of abuse whatsoever. Since the family declined to answer any of Davis's mandatory questions about their child's medical history, he didn't have to report their daughter was receiving trans-affirming medical care. Despite his recommendation that the abuse case be swiftly and summarily closed, Davis's supervisors continued to move it forward. Then they assigned him yet another trans-affirming family to investigate. That was when Davis decided for himself that there was no way to behave morally as an individual within a system designed to do evil. So he left his position at CPS and began advocating against Abbott's policy openly.

"I was complicit," Davis explains of his work with CPS. "I thought I was doing good, but I should have resigned that first night. The only way to do good, I realized, was to get out and go public."

In refusing to be complicit, Davis was not alone: Every other CPS investigator in his unit had stepped down as well. Though it had been true that stepping down as an individual would do nothing to make the case go away, the mass exodus of employees meant the entire process of investigating CPS cases was grinding to a halt. Instead of aiming to be one of the rare "good" investigators carrying out a transphobic order, Davis chose to be part of a movement for justice that was far larger than himself. Shortly after they left, Davis and fifteen of his colleagues signed a public brief speaking out against the policy.

For most of these former CPS investigators, refusing to carry out the mission of an evil system was costly. Many were unable to find work in their fields, taking positions at supermarkets and big box retail stores or else remaining unemployed. But the necessity of these sacrifices was clear. Davis and his colleagues had attained a state of simple moral clarity, the kind that's rarely found when we operate under Systemic Shame. They knew where they were positioned, and what they believed in—and from that it was self-evident what they each had to do.

Over the years, I have spoken to numerous people who have chosen to stop being complicit within systems they found evil: former cops and security officers, heads of nonprofits that overworked and underpaid their staff, managers at retail stores that followed Black shoppers around, nurses at care facilities that neglected their elders, defense contractors, Homeland Security researchers, and more. People with histories like these seek me out because I've written a lot about the pointlessness of chasing after endless productivity, and the importance of building a life that's really driven by our values. I live for conversations with people who have gone through big moments of realization and left a bad job or unhealthy community behind. When a person decides to make a break from the systems that have repeatedly restricted them and harmed others, they are at their most radiantly alive.

Instead of believing that we should work very hard to be a "good" cop, a "benevolent" manager, or a "well-meaning" nurse who cuffs her patients to the bed, we can cease being the people that powerful institutions have told us we must be. Sometimes, the most impactful thing we can do as individuals is to refuse to be a part of a system that does such profound hurt.

No individual person can single-handedly defeat racism or end climate change. In fact, some days it's hard to even cook dinner in a way we feel morally okay about. But instead of trying to fight our circumstances, we can willingly face them as they are, and ask ourselves what comes next. No matter where we are located and what feels impossible right now, we each face daily chances to do things like comfort those in pain, grow our own understanding, and even sneakily violate rules that we know in our hearts to be unjust. We don't have to force it—we just have to find it.

This concept—that wherever we are located, that is our place in the fight—comes from the philosopher Ulysse Carrière, and an approach that she calls Pitchfork Theory. A pitchfork is a tool associated with hard, backbreaking work, but it's also a potential weapon. The pitchfork that a poor laborer toiling in the field might associate with her suffering can become the tool that helps her fight for her freedom, Carrier says. Pitchfork Theory is all about recognizing the unique potential in the tools around us and the social positions we occupy.

From the viewpoint of Pitchfork Theory, a doctor who is working in a state that has banned healthcare for transgender teenagers is not powerless—he's been given a very *powerful* chance to protect his trans patients by doing things like "losing" paperwork that would get trans kids and their families in legal trouble. He isn't working to reform a bad system from the inside; he's betraying the very rules of a system that is unjust. An abortion clinic operating in a blue state has the opportunity to provide plan C pills to abortion-seekers from red states without reporting them or getting them arrested—though unfortunately, far too many clinics and pharmacies across the country have instead chosen to comply with unjust laws in advance of them even passing.[7] Some systems cannot be mended from within—not if you operate by their procedures and rules. To truly dismantle an evil system, you must be willing to break things.

If this process of finding your place sounds daunting, here are some questions to help you reflect on your strengths and your social position, and to find an inner calling that really speaks to you:

FINDING YOUR PLACE IN THE FIGHT
Reflections to Help You Identify Your Strengths, Energy Sources, and Inner Calling

Identify Your Strengths	Which of the following statements resonate with you? Check off as many as you like.
	___ I love being around large groups of people. (the protestor)
	___ People tell me I've helped them understand topics or ideas that never made sense to them before. (the educator)
	___ When people are tense, anxious, or caught up in a conflict, I know how to calm them down. (the mediator)
	___ Somehow, I intuitively understand how to bring comfort to ailing bodies or minds. (the healer)
	___ I just "get" how to take masses of information and put them into sensible organizational systems. (the organizer)
	___ My creative work often helps people feel seen and understood. (the artist)
	___ I often find myself thinking about how people work together, and how to better bring people together effectively. (the connector)
	___ My training in [medicine/education/programming/ other technical skill] is invaluable to a lot of people.
	_____. (other)

table continued

What Makes You Feel Accomplished and Energized?	____ At large events and gatherings, I feel energized and inspired. (the protestor)
	____ I find it rewarding to figure out a new way to explain a tricky concept or summarize a complex idea. (the educator)
	____ I'm not afraid of healthy conflict—people learn and grow a great deal through it. (the mediator)
	____ When others are distressed or suffering, I snap into focus and know how to take action. (the healer)
	____ Keeping things tidy and well organized soothes me. (the organizer)
	____ Nothing makes me feel better than people saying they see themselves in my art. (the artist)
	____ I absolutely love when my friends become close with one another. (the connector)
	____ These activities and pursuits give me energy:
	_____. (Other)
What Purpose or Inner Calling Draws You In?	____ I am here to stand firm and be outspoken in the face of injustice. (the protestor)
	____ I love watching people grow and change, knowing I got to play a role in it. (the educator)
	____ I understand people's emotions and live to bring people closer together. (the mediator)
	____ I have always been drawn toward crises, because I know that I have what it takes to help. (the healer)
	____ It's my purpose to bring order and clarity amid the chaos. (the organizer)
	____ Creating meaningful, beautiful things is my greatest calling in life. (the artist)
	____ My greatest legacy is the relationships I have built with others. (the connector)
	____ I feel like my life has a purpose when I engage in these activities:
	_____. (Other)

Instead of absorbing Systemic Shame's guilt-inducing messages that we can never be or do enough, we can choose to listen to our own inner voice about where we are needed the most. And it gets far easier to listen to that inner voice when we stop trying to do everything and learn to dramatically slow down.

Slowing Down

Sometimes, the way we make a meaningful difference in the world is not by speeding ahead toward a victory, but by slowing down—or even stopping and letting certain obligations go.

Think back to the "negative footprint" effect: In a hasty attempt to do something beneficial for the environment, consumers buy all kinds of unnecessary "green" products that cause more waste and ecological damage. Thanks to Systemic Shame, we each feel so desperate to be virtuous and do *something* that we often wind up burning through a lot of energy and resources, all to no end. The philosopher Umberto Eco called this the "cult of action for action's sake"; the idea that all activity and productivity is good, and all slowness and stillness are evil is absolutely core to Systemic Shame.

In many cases, a lack of activity is better than furious, frantic activity done for its own sake. As an article in *Science* revealed in December 2021, all humanity would need to do to reverse 78 percent of tropical deforestation within the next twenty years is simply leave our remaining forests alone.[8] No human intervention would be required for this to happen: no planting or fertilizing, no controlled burnings or killings of invasive species, and certainly no purchasing of "negative footprint" items such as organic groceries or carbon offsets. Life is abundant, and nature is resilient. If we stopped burning through resources, the natural world could begin restoring itself. Unfortunately, most policymakers would prefer to jet around the world attending ecological conferences and climate summits, using up fuel and filling the atmosphere with carbon dioxide.[9]

Systemic Shame ties our potential to our purchases, but expansive recognition means doing less, moving more slowly, and being far more intentional with how we use our limited energy and time. This also means questioning urgent, simplistic measures of progress, and trusting in the long view. Most of our organizations and communities are not built around these principles—for a variety of cultural and economic reasons. But we can change that.

In their landmark paper *White Supremacy Culture*, Kenneth Jones and Tema Okun observed that most organizations are tainted by damaging cultural norms and hallmarks of white supremacy like urgency, perfectionism, and hyper-individualism, among others.[10] The desperation to score an impressive-sounding "win" as quickly as possible prevents people from reflecting on what a shared long-term view of the future should be. For instance, many LGBTQ rights organizations spent the early 2000s pushing for gay marriage rights at the expense of longer, more complicated battles for trans rights and healthcare access. I've seen white supremacist norms play out everywhere from the ACLU, to the HRC, to local campaigns to reform school funding.

These dynamics are sadly pervasive within nonprofits, activist groups, and social movements. However, there are ways to push back against such norms and redirect them.[11] Here are some values that help us resist white supremacy culture in our organizations, and example language we can use to express those values:

WHITE SUPREMACIST NORMS & THEIR ANTIDOTES[12]

Damaging Norm:	Opposing Norm:	Example Scripts
Perfectionism	• Appreciation • Acceptance • Adaptation to change • Seeing "failure" as a lesson • Expecting growth and change as normal	• "Thank you so much for helping me with this work." • "This project didn't work out the way I expected, which means I have more to learn." • "It looks like our goals need to be readjusted, since the situation has changed." • "I'm sorry, I realize I didn't explain this task to you / why this detail matters." • "Can someone show me how to do this?"
Individualism	• Shared growth • Collective problem-solving • Openness about struggles, confusion, or conflicting goals • Seeing all work as shared • Gratitude for support rather than measuring achievements	• "We've all gotten a lot better at this task lately." • "We understand the problem a lot better now than we did before." • "Let's find out what everyone thinks about the problem—maybe different people see it different ways." • "Everyone's effort made this project possible."

table continued

Damaging Norm:	Opposing Norm:	Example Scripts
Urgency	• Trust in the process and other people • Humility regarding what the outcome might be • Understanding that unexpected challenges will come up • Reflection on process and others' perspectives • Patience	• "We don't need to micromanage anyone or push for a rigid deadline. We can offer support where it's needed." • "Let's add a few extra weeks to the timeline, as a buffer." • "We don't know how this is going to play out, so let's keep an open mind." • "Let's gather more information before we take action." • "Let's listen to the people who might be affected by our actions and see what they think." • "This work will still be here when we're ready for it."

Slowing down, challenging assumptions, and asking questions can have a much larger impact than you might think. The best LGBTQ allies I've known are not the ones who have read every single book on the gay experience or know every cutting-edge gender-related term—they're the ones who have the humility to admit they don't know everything and are willing to speak out when others can't. For example, when a straight male friend of mine, Jim, was working on a play that featured a prominent asexual character, he asked repeatedly whether any asexual playwrights had been consulted during script development. Jim kept raising the issue again and again, gladly making himself a thorn in the production team's side, until they finally agreed to bring an asexual script consultant on. Then Jim began pushing to ensure that consultant would be paid well for their efforts. As a result, a young asexual playwriting student got her first ever paying credit as a co-writer. And of course, the play's asexual character wound up being a far more realistic and human portrait than it otherwise would have been.

Jim knew that he didn't have all the answers. He also realized he didn't *have* to. He just had to slow down the process and advocate for the right people to direct the process. Systemic Shame teaches us we must personally and hastily make as many changes as we possibly can in order to combat injustice and "fix" the world—that we must know and do everything rapidly on our own. But in order to work together to create systemic change, we often need to slow down, step back, and listen to one another. This requires a degree of humility that many of us aren't used to or comfortable with. But embracing that humility can bring us clarity.

Getting Humble and Welcoming Grief

Because Systemic Shame presents the individual as the sole agent of change, many of us get seduced into believing that we can and should strive to be professional-grade epidemiologists, climatologists, economists, anti-bias educators, and more, all through dedicated effort and a little online research. This has only been worsened by social media and what I like to call "comment section culture":[13] Online, we are each invited to weigh in on all matters, all the time, no matter whether we are actually well-positioned to do so. Systemic Shame makes us feel awful and inadequate, but it fosters arrogant self-importance, too.

Embracing humility is the antidote to all this. With humility, we can take on smaller, more sustainable roles that help soothe our anxieties and bond us to others. Just as revealing our full complexity to trusted others helps us to recover from shame, leaning in to a rich web of supportive communities fighting to make a difference can help us to stop feeling as if our efforts never matter.

That said, the smallness of our personal impact can be a little difficult to accept—something that Koa Beck has frequently observed in her discussions of how to upend institutional sexism.

"When I've spoken publicly about gender oppression or racism or heterosexism . . . I always get well-intentioned questions from women about what they can do," she writes. "But there is very little that you, the single person holding this book or approaching me after a speaking engagement, can do. The revolution will not be you alone, despite what white feminism has told you."[14]

It's hard to admit one's powerlessness. Many of us still want to be heroes, even though that expectation harms us. But one way to begin is by identifying a few unreasonable standards we are currently holding ourselves to and choosing to let those obligations drop.

One person struggling with Systemic Shame that I spoke to for this book was Eavan, a Black woman living in the United Kingdom, who told me that for years she expected herself to be a perfect model for the natural hair movement. In 2011, Eavan did the "big chop," removing all her chemically straightened hair and allowing her full curls to grow back. She used a variety of natural hair care products daily, consumed endless videos and blog posts on protective styles, and bought up all manner of satin pillowcases and silky hair wraps. She was terrified of adopting any hairstyle that could cause breakage. When she traveled, she resented humid weather that made her curls tighten and shrink. She got into the movement because it was revolutionary—she wanted to celebrate her hair as it was, and not hide it in order to conform to European beauty standards. But at a certain point, maintaining an idealized standard of natural beauty felt like just another benchmark she was expected to meet.

"I saw a video on TikTok where this Black woman pointed out how almost every style you try can cause breakage or can change your growth pattern if you do it wrong or too often, and she said she was sick of it, she'd just wear what she wanted and let her hair break," Evan says. "That made me feel so much relief. I'd never heard someone just say, *Fuck it, my hair can just go break.* It's not a big deal. Who cares?"

Black women's hair has always been politicized.[15] In professional settings, Black women have historically been forced to straighten their hair to make it emulate white "professional" styles. Protective and traditional hairstyles for Black women are banned in the military and punished in schools.[16] The widespread admiration of white women's hair and endless critiquing of Black women's is a cultural problem with a very long history. Yet by focusing on making herself the perfect natural hair advocate, Eavan says she was still holding herself personally responsible for fixing all that Systemic Shame. She found that she no longer wanted to aspire to a life where her own hair was forever bouncy and luscious—instead, she wanted to live in a world where superstar athletes like Simone Biles and Gabby Douglas could compete while wearing practical buns and ponytails without being attacked.[17] She wanted other Black women to lead lives that were less focused on how their hair looked and what others thought of it. And she wanted that kind of life for herself, too.

"I got interested in the [natural hair] community to stop being ashamed of what grows out of my head, but the chase for doing natural hair 'right' left me judging myself and scrutinizing other Black women. I want out of it," she says. She's granted herself permission to have bigger problems than her hair.

Eavan's experience reminded me of a passage that I read in Da'Shaun Harrison's book *Belly of the Beast*, which is all about how fatphobia and anti-Blackness intertwine. As I discussed earlier in this book, many "body positivity" activists think that the cure for fatphobia is self-love. Exuding confidence and overcoming shaming on an individual level is the ultimate goal. But Harrison, a fat liberationist, takes an entirely different approach. They say that fat (and especially fat Black) individuals can view their own body image struggles as a powerful criticism of the culture that left them feeling this way.

"What if Insecurities are worth embracing, particularly for the Black fat?" they write. "What if Insecurities are not a moral failing of the individual, but rather an inadvertent critique of a society that seeks to punish, harm, and abuse Ugly people who dare to name that their perceived 'flaws' are only named as such because of anti-Blackness?"[18]

In other words, the insecure feelings of the oppressed are society's problem to solve—not the responsibility of the shamed person themselves. People like Eavan and Da'Shaun can stop treating their own bodies and emotions like they need fixing, and instead embrace themselves as they really are.

Dialectical behavioral therapists often distinguish between *willfulness* (trying to fight reality) and *willingness* (acknowledging and working with reality on its own terms). Systemic Shame encourages willfulness—it values difficulty and struggle above all else, and celebrates valiant effort, even when it goes nowhere. It also doesn't adapt to shifting realities very well. In fact, Systemic Shame preaches that we have a moral obligation to continue to fight for perfection in our personal lives, interpersonal relationships, and our society at all times, even and especially when it doesn't seem to be working. Willingness, on the other hand, involves adapting ourselves fluidly to our current circumstances and feelings, and even releasing an old goal or ideal that's no longer serving us. Willingness is not weakness, and to become willing doesn't mean we have to declare our current reality is any good. It simply means asking ourselves what we can do to make our own lives less miserable, given what's currently true. Here's a quick table summarizing the differences between how willfulness and willingness feel:

Signs of Willfulness	Signs of Willingness
Bitterness	Lightness
Obsession	Acceptance
Rumination	Adaptation
Frustration	Mourning
Feeling "stuck" and "locked in"	Feeling at ease or relaxed
Focusing on why a situation "should not be"	Asking "What comes next?"
Sticking rigidly to a plan	Improvising based on current information
Thinking a great deal about the past	Paying attention to the present

Expansive recognition thrives on willingness. When we accept that we can't cure all our body image issues, fix institutional sexism, or undo decades of climate catastrophe, we can direct our attention toward what can still be done in the present to prevent future suffering for ourselves and others. Being willing to change, adapt, and even give up on some goals makes it possible for us to work alongside others more effectively, instead of dwelling on old slights and resentments that we cannot reverse.

I can sit and stew for hours about how much better my childhood would have been if Ohio hadn't been such a homophobic state—but that alternate reality never existed, and never will. There is no control group for my life. I can only know the person that I am now. Instead of resenting reality, I can search for queer people who grew up with the same Systemic Shaming that I did, and ask what our past has to teach us about our present. I could (willfully) hate myself *and* my ex-partner for keeping me from transitioning for as long as I did and fixate on how differently I'd look now if I had started hormones sooner—or I can (willingly) carry the lessons from that awful experience into my future relationships, being as honest with people about who I am, and embracing all the changes I now know I want.

We all try to fight against reality sometimes—it's often the first stage of coming to terms with facts that we really don't like and don't know how to deal with. Here are some questions to help you uncover willfulness in your life:

1. What are some unspoken "rules" that I still let guide my life?
2. Which of these rules no longer serve me?
3. What can I do less of?
4. What facts of my life am I still trying to make not be true?
5. What can I give up on for now?
6. What unpleasant truths can I decide to just live with?
7. What can I stop trying to make work?

The willingness to let certain expectations go is key to really practicing expansive recognition on a global scale. There's a real power in admitting what we're not good at, and what we do not have the energy for. It allows us to truly feel gratitude for the people who are good at those things, and for what skills we do possess.

One reproductive justice and domestic violence advocate that I spoke to, Mallary,[19] told me that one of the most invaluable volunteers at the clinic where she works is a fifty-seven-year-old grandfather who comes by a few times a month to mow the lawn and clean out the gutters—along with a decrepit old beagle.

"He is a very healing presence to be around for many of the women here, who have a lot of trauma associated with controlling and abusive men. He is also wonderful at calming down the anti-abortion protestors."

This older volunteer is quite literally cleaning the "trashed bathrooms" around him, to return to Chuck the DSA organizer's favorite metaphor. When I asked Mallary if this man realizes the positive impact he's having, she shrugged and said, "Probably not." Who knows how many of us are playing a similarly important role in the lives of those around us, completely unaware of how much our little efforts are appreciated, because we're still locked behind unrealistic expectations and the shame of not meeting them.

When we recognize that each person has a meaningful yet humble role to play in a far larger movement, we can begin approaching ours and others' limits with grace. And with some practice, we can get comfortable with the idea that change and growth are constant. Though we often use metaphors like "battle," or "fight" to describe movements against injustice, we aren't destroying anything. With our choices we *make* society together every day.[20]

Create Coalitions—Not Allies

Systemic Shame approaches social justice issues as if they are entirely personalized. Under its approach, white people should fight racism by making the right choices: posting the correct information to social media, buying the right books, and kicking individual racists out of their workplaces. The same is true for pretty much every social inequality that Systemic Shame has created, from poverty, to sexism, to homophobia. "Being a good ally" is seen as a personal effort, not a systemic movement.

In her book *What White People Can Do Next*, the African Studies professor and activist Emma Dabiri recommends that white people stop thinking of themselves as *allies* to Black people and start thinking of themselves as real comrades who share the same interests. And instead of viewing allyship as a hard but morally required sacrifice, white people can understand that we also benefit when we dismantle abusive systems of power.

The idea that people who receive government benefits are dishonest leeches was originally applied to newly freed slaves, and later repackaged and applied to people who received unemployment, disability benefits, and food stamps, the majority of whom today are white.[21, 22] These toxic messages hurt every person who has ever relied on the social safety net. To fight poverty and ableism, then, is to fight racism. And to fight racism is to fight economic injustice.[23] Under this perspective, we don't have to view our privileges as some kind of personal sin—we're all suffering together, albeit to different amounts, and when we address the common causes of that suffering, we all stand to gain.

Over the years there has been a massive decline in federal funding for all kinds of welfare benefits,[24] and increasingly complicated bureaucratic rules have been put in place to supposedly make sure no one is "faking" their disability, lying about their job search, or otherwise "gaming the system."[25] All this gatekeeping and paperwork is incredibly costly, so much so that many analysts believe that simply giving *all* Americans a universal basic income with no strings attached would actually be cheaper.[26] There is no benefit to dividing people up into the categories of "worthy" and "unworthy." It just feels moral to do so because of our beliefs about shame.

In queer activist spaces, I often run into people who think we need to gatekeep who is a "real" member of our communities. The idea is that by excluding everyone who has the "wrong" identity or who is too privileged to really understand what we're going through, we will protect our limited resources and ensure that our spaces are "safe." For example, a straight polyamorous person with a bisexual partner may be excluded from LGBTQ spaces and even treated as predatory and unwanted. A closeted nonbinary person might be mistaken for a privileged cis man and kept out. Many closeted and questioning folks self-select out of such spaces, for fear they can't adequately prove they belong.

From Emma Dabiri's perspective this is the exact wrong way to go about building powerful coalitions. I recognize that there are a variety of other people who, while not technically being queer, share a lot of the frustrations and exclusions that I do. Polyamorous people are not well served by a legal system that prioritizes marriage. They can lose custody of their children and be denied the right to visit partners in the hospital. There are straight people who gender bend, and ones who have been subjected to sexual violence and corrective therapy as a "cure" for their harmless kinks. And the rich history of organizations like Parents and Families of Lesbians and Gays (or PFLAG) shows us that you don't have to be a member of an oppressed group in order to take up the mantle of liberating that group. A very large swath of people will benefit if we expand our understanding of what love, sex, partnership, and family can look like.

Building large social coalitions is complicated work. Sometimes, the most privileged within our ranks talk over the more marginalized, or try to quash more controversial goals—the way that cis gay people stifled the fight for trans rights in the early 2000s. But we truly are stronger together, and the solution to these issues is not to exclude certain groups outright or keep various identities apart. We just have to put a structure in place that allows those with the most relevant expertise to be heard. And coalition building work does not just happen within activist spaces, either—it can be something as simple as discussing with your coworkers what kinds of changes you all want to see at your workplace.

Here are some pointers for building effective, diverse coalitions:

Principles for Coalition-Building
- Focus on the steps that will get money and resources to marginalized groups
- Don't exclude potential members based on their identity or life experiences
- Provide marginalized voices a regular space to vent or process hard feelings
- Identify shared goals that cut across a variety of communities
- Create policies that protect all members from abuse, rather than assuming certain groups or identities are always "safe"
- Center marginalized people's voices, particularly those with relevant expertise
- Help all people develop the power of discernment: the ability to reflect on new information and judge for themselves what is "right"
- Encourage and empower would-be "allies" to take an active role where they are capable
- Encourage curious reflection about how one person (or group's) struggle is really everyone's

In 2018, the journalist Eric Blanc reported on the shocking success of a variety of teachers' union strikes that broke out across the United States, particularly in conservative states that are usually pretty hostile to such efforts.[27] Reporting on the ground where these movements were occurring, Blanc found that the most successful strikes included a wide variety of workers—not just teachers, but bus drivers, custodians, cooks, support staff, and school therapists. Together, this diverse group of educator-workers was able to keep schools shut down until their demands were met. When the Arizona governor Doug Ducey attempted to break apart one such strike by offering teachers (and only teachers) a 20 percent pay raise, the teachers held firm, insisting that all school staff receive improved pay alongside them. In the end, this solidarity resulted in increased wages for everyone, with a series of built-in raises for the following five years.

In order to succeed in a meaningful way, coalition-based movements have to put the needs of the most vulnerable at the forefront, while still giving the privileged something meaningful that they can do. Often this requires that relatively privileged individuals develop a bit more humility, abandon their dreams of saviorship, and identify for themselves a few small steps they can take that will serve a larger, shared goal.

Identify Small Changes That Serve a Long-Term Vision

Systemic Shame is tricky: It takes the fight for a large long-term goal and replaces it with micro-level tasks and purchases. But there are ways to meet our very human need for concrete, practical steps without derailing a movement's momentum or obsessing over individual choice.

In activist work, we often draw a distinction between acts of reform, which help protect a damaging system, and non-reformist reforms, which dismantle them. Reforms heal our anxieties; they give us "something to do" that feels like progress. An example of a reform like this is investing in more police de-escalation training as a response to high-profile shootings of Black people. Campaigns such as #8CantWait became really popular in 2020 by advocating for small steps like these.[28]

There was a big problem with the reforms called for by #8CantWait though (which also included bans on choke holds, and requiring officers to issue a warning before discharging weapons): Nearly all of the essential reforms it called for *were already widely adopted throughout the United States*, including many of departments where police had just murdered Black people.[29] When police officers choked Eric Garner to death in 2014, choke holds were *already* banned by the NYPD, and had been since 1993.[30] In 2020, George Floyd was murdered in a Minneapolis that had already instituted 8CantWait's reforms—in response to the earlier killing of Philando Castile.[31]

Reforms such as banning choke holds or requiring police retraining sound good. They target the behaviors and beliefs of individual racist police officers. For the same reason, it felt good to see George Floyd's killer, Derek Chauvin, be sentenced to prison for his actions. Unfortunately, the reformist approach means investing more money in police departments that are already more highly funded and militarized than ever before in history. Giving police departments more money and greater responsibilities *expands* their power—and their capacity to do violence—all while giving concerned citizens the pacifying sense that something is being done. And the legal argument that led to Derek Chauvin being found guilty was that he was not performing his job *correctly* as a police officer;[32] this singles him out as a particularly incompetent or evil individual, which ignores the fact he was surrounded by other police while his knee was on Floyd's neck, and many former police officers report that they were actively trained to treat Black suspects in dehumanizing and violent ways.[33] If the whole barrel is bad, throwing out one apple won't do a lot of good.

Talk of police reform also encourages people to frame the issue in terms of a defect that needs "fixing." But many police departments in the United States arose from slave patrols created during the Jim Crow era and have always functioned to protect white lives and property while limiting the free movement of Black people.[34] Multiple times, federal courts in the United States have ruled that police officers *have no responsibility to protect the public*[35]—nor is it their job to enforce all laws. If your boss discriminates against you because of your race, your disability, or your sex, he has violated the law, but you can't call the cops to have him arrested for it. Yet your boss can call the police on you if he catches you stealing change from the cash register. A reform cannot "fix" a system that is already functioning as it was designed to do. And police forces were designed to use violence to terrorize minorities and keep the wealthy safe.[36]

We can contrast the reforms of 8CantWait with the far more radical push to *defund* the police.[37] Defunding the police is an anti-reformist reform, a gradual step toward abolishing the carceral justice system. Under a defunding model, more money is taken out of police budgets each year and invested in communities most historically harmed by police. In 2020, thirteen cities in the United States voted to defund police departments, putting millions of dollars toward community medics, emergency services, addiction treatment programs, food banks, and more.[38] Under a defunding model, communities become healthier and more robust with each passing year, with more and more funds getting poured into education, mental health services, needle exchanges, and shelters. Slowly, neighborhoods become safer, and communities learn to rely on one another better. We don't have to invent a flawless alternative to the police all at once—we develop it from the ground up and prevent many acts of violence before they occur.

Other examples of non-reformist reforms include things like establishing limits (or caps) on carbon emissions, and continually reducing those caps over the years. This is very different from the reform of selling carbon offsets, which allows corporations and governments to pay a fee in return for the right to emit carbon dioxide. Carbon offsets treat pollution as a thing you can buy your way out of. Carbon caps, on the other hand, force governments and large corporations to wean themselves off fossil fuels more every year.

How can we tell the difference between a reform and a non-reformist reform? Dean Spade, a lawyer and the founder of the Silvia Rivera Law Project, writes that we should ask the following questions:[39]

- Does it provide money or resources to people who have been harmed?
- Does it leave out the people who are the most stigmatized or shamed? (for example, people with criminal records, people without immigration status, or people who society blames for making "bad" choices)
- Does it give more money or power to the system we're trying to dismantle?
- Does it empower the people most affected by a problem?

By asking questions like these regularly, we can develop our discernment, the ability to determine for ourselves what is right and what our obligations to each other are. All the fear and guilt that Systemic Shame fosters inside us makes it difficult to see our unique circumstances clearly, or even to form our own points of view. But when we educate ourselves and develop greater confidence in our ability to discern right from wrong, we can reject all those distracting external messages that keep telling us we need to do more and deserve to feel bad.

This Isn't Activism—It's Existential

I know that most of the examples of expansive recognition that I've provided in this chapter have involved political organizing and activist work. But I want to take a moment to highlight that when we practice expansive recognition, we get to decide for ourselves what our calling is, and determine for ourselves what it means to lead a rewarding life. For some of us, building that kind of life will not involve anything resembling conventional activist work at all. In fact, many activist organizations and nonprofits are themselves unproductive hotbeds of Systemic Shame, with traumatized and overworked people competing against one another to prove who is the most devoted, accomplished, and virtuously self-sacrificing.[40] Even if we care about systemic injustice, we do not have to subject ourselves to those kinds of environments. More often than not, they are emotionally unhealthy to us, and politically unproductive.

Like Stef Sanjati, the former YouTuber I profiled in Chapter 7, I have stopped thinking of myself as an activist. I'm not involved in as many political organizations as I used to be. I find myself fighting with other people a lot less. When terrible news pops up on Twitter's trending section, I don't rush to get involved just so I can quell my anxiety and convince others that I'm a good person. I do less. I think a lot more about the impact of my choices. Most of what I do does not feel at all like "activism." Instead, I tend to see my values and beliefs as a thread that weaves through all my relationships, my hobbies, and everything else that I do.

I'm a big fan of existential therapy, particularly the work of Martin Adams.[41] In existential therapy, the therapist isn't supposed to act as an authority figure. They shouldn't push any specific goals onto their patient. Instead, they present themselves honestly, as a person who has struggled with meaninglessness and lostness in their own lives, too. From there, they can provide exercises and tools to help their client determine what matters most in their own life. It's meant to be a very flexible and empowering therapeutic approach, inspired by the work of philosophers like Jean Paul Sartre (who believed our lives have no innate meaning, and so we have to *create* meaning for ourselves), and Viktor Frankl (who wrote that meaning already exists all around us, and we simply need to *find* it).

When it comes to finding (or creating) meaning in life, existential therapists look to what they call the four realms of human experience:[42]

- The **physical realm,** which guides how we view our physical surroundings, our bodies, and how we think about our own deaths.
- The **social realm,** which guides how we think and feel about other people, as well as the culture(s) to which we belong.
- The **personal realm,** which guides our understanding of ourselves, including the life stories we tell about our past experiences, our present situation, and what we hope for our futures.
- And the **spiritual realm,** which guides how we feel about the unknown and uncertain, as well as our core values and how we think the world ought to be.

Systemic Shame cleaves us off from all four sources of meaning. It puts us at war with our body, and its pleasures and pains. It separates us from other people by requiring that we think of ourselves as individual actors. Systemic Shame alienates us from the personal realm, by making us believe our true selves are deeply wicked and lazy. And finally, Systemic Shame obliterates our relationship to the spiritual realm, making us feel hopeless and devoid of greater purpose.

To help patients examine the four realms of meaning, Adams developed four big existential questions:

- **Physical:** How can I live my life fully, knowing I may die at any moment?
- **Social:** What are other people there for?
- **Personal:** How can I be me?
- **Spiritual:** How should I live?

Personally, I find these questions to be a little too broad, and sometimes too judgmental to be useful. I'm not sure that other people are "for" anything, for example; I think they just *are*. And I don't find it compelling to ask myself how I "should" live; I don't want to start beating myself up for failing to meet some arbitrary benchmark all over again. Perhaps I'm just not enough on the Jean Paul Sartre end of the existential spectrum to connect with these questions. I'm not sure that I need to *create* meaning so much as notice and appreciate what is already there and been overlooked. So here are the questions I've taken to asking myself instead—and my personal answers, in case they're helpful for your own brainstorming.

- **Physical:** What helps me feel real, and in touch with my body and surroundings?

MY ANSWERS:

- Appreciating the textures and weights of objects around me
- Learning about the history of the architecture and neighborhoods surrounding me
- Developing skills that involve using my hands or body: cooking, lifting weights, stretching, tidying or arranging things
- Treating my body with tenderness: taking a bath, eating something nourishing, giving myself a pleasurable experience and truly savoring it

Social: What helps me feel recognized and appreciated as I really am?

MY ANSWERS:

- Being lovingly roasted by a friend who knows lots of embarrassing facts about me
- Hearing loved ones point out little habits and quirks I didn't even realize I had
- Letting my weaknesses be known
- Talking with someone who has had the same painful experiences or grapples with the same faults as I do
- Reveling in a shared passion, especially a rare or niche one

Personal: Which ways of spending time do I never regret?

MY ANSWERS:

- Enjoying a book, video game, film, or internet rabbit hole that transports me away from my surroundings
- Appreciating the creative work and achievements of my loved ones

- Experiencing pleasure or childlike wonder fully, without judging myself for it
- Saying yes to invitations to try something completely new

Spiritual: What helps me see I'm part of something larger than myself?

MY ANSWERS:
- When my creative work helps or challenges other people
- Taking on a modest support role for a larger project or social event, such as a play or convention
- Mentoring students, aspiring writers, and young adults who I share some passions or experiences with
- Researching my family history, studying queer history, and speaking to LGBTQ elders who help me see where I belong in the greater fabric of time
- Indulging in the fantasies and longings that I used to tell myself were "bad"

We all find existential nourishment and healing in different ways—and many of those ways are not particularly showy. As I've already mentioned, I've spent years resenting my mom and most of my other relatives for their conservative politics. At times I really feel abandoned in a massive, almost existential way: The people who brought me into the world had rejected my identity and my well-being. No number of supposedly impressive accomplishments granted me any sense of rootedness, or spared me from the looming existential dread of living in a country and a state that hated me, having been raised by people who didn't understand what I was about.

But if I think about all my difficulties and resentments a moment longer, I remember my sister Staci, a completely "apolitical" athletic trainer who works at a rural Ohio high school about an hour from where we both grew up. My sister's office is a safe haven for her school's queer and trans students. When she hears student athletes mocking the gay tenth-grader who wears makeup, she shuts that shit down immediately and encourages kids to rethink their biases. She tells her students about me, and shows off the tattoo she got on her calf to honor my transition. Staci also shuts down racism and sexism whenever she hears it, and teen girls come to her for advice when their boyfriends have mistreated them or are pressuring them into sex. Staci's unbothered, effortlessly accepting love has been an anchor during my life's most turbulent periods.

My sister is making a palpable difference in the world every day. She is not an activist; she's barely even voted. But when I slow down and really think about the work she does, I feel less alone in the world. I feel grateful. I feel like maybe it actually is okay to be myself, even if the world I inhabit has often been hostile to my identity. Her small, quietly loving acts make me feel less ashamed of myself, less isolated, and more hopeful for the future of humanity.

Most of us will never be perfect environmentalists, public health advocates, or social justice activists. But we also don't have to be. Everything Systemic Shame has taught us about ourselves and about human progress is wrong. We don't need to moralize our personal choice and purchases or blame the victims of injustice for their plight. We don't have to buy indulgences for our "sins" or stay busy simply for the sake of it. Most of all, we aren't innately horrible people. There's nothing we need to be, or have to make up for being. We simply are.

Shame is an act of avoidance. It's a pulling-away and hiding-away from others, motivated by mistrust and fear. The way we escape Systemic Shame is by rejecting the desire to withdraw and instead choosing to embrace—moving toward the very people we fear judging us, and revealing the pain we've been in. It's only when we reveal our flaws and most shameful feelings to one another that we have the opportunity to realize our struggles are shared, and are in fact the product of oppressive systems that target us all. None of us is broken. Nobody is a failure. It's the systems that have failed us—and as soon as we recognize that, we can move beyond them, and create something better together.

Conclusion:
Making Your Place in the World

On the day that I finally broke up with my straight male partner of over ten years, I spent about six hours just sitting and staring out the window. I told him at about eleven in the morning that I could no longer be with someone incapable of loving the real, gay male me, and he left, and I sat and watched the sky until long after it set. Then I finally stood up, texted my dear friend Melanie about what had happened, and went to buy myself some Chinese food. I was on Melanie's bed sobbing and accepting her embrace not long after.

I'd finally taken a plunge I'd been contemplating since I first came out to my partner as trans back in 2016. I'd spent years fighting with myself over the necessity of the choice. Now I was through it, and the world had not ended. I had not lost any love or squandered any chance at being happy. The chance of having that with Nick was already long gone and had been for years. As my body had changed and our relationship drifted apart, it was evident that Nick felt ashamed of his changing feelings, too. And so, he stayed, and we both languished, pretending to be people we could never be. But in just one heartrending conversation that took less than five minutes, I'd finally allowed both him and myself to face what had always been true. We could not be happy together.

In the months that would follow, shame would arrest me at sudden moments. I'd be cleaning the bathroom and find a long tendril of my ex's thick black hair under the bath mat, then collapse in grief on my knees. When I went to apply for a new passport with the correct name and gender marker, I discovered an old photo of my ex and me tucked among my paperwork. We were so young, holding oversized props in a photobooth at a friend's wedding reception: Nick in a sparkly hat and comically large sunglasses, me in a dress, smirking and covering my face with a giant foam mustache. The first Christmas without him was a nightmare. All around my mother's house, I found moments of our visits from across the years, ghosts of the people we'd both tried to be. I kept wondering if I'd made some terrible mistake.

Despite the regret and pain following me everywhere, I never begged for my ex to take me back. I never hurt myself or drank to excess and didn't once cry myself to sleep. Historically those were the kind of actions I took following a breakup. Before I transitioned, I did nothing but vie for the approval of others, and I always lost my mind when I saw it slipping away. Yet no matter how much I missed Nick, and longed for our lives to have been different, I found I could always find solace: in the arms of my loved ones, among my wider community, and in my own body, which I finally recognized as *me*.

For the first time in my life, I coped with shame by making contact with others. I called up my friends. I went on trips to Michigan and visited conventions like Midwest Furfest and International Mister Leather. I attended music festivals and concerts, and curled up on friends' couches and let them feed me homemade pizza and chocolate mousse. For over four months, I never spent a single evening alone. The number of people who reached out asking if I'd like to take a walk, get a meal, go on a trip, or spend an evening painting or playing games absolutely astonished me. I'd been covering myself in a protective shell all my life, but now I was finding I was enveloped in many layers of loving support.

For me, healing from Systemic Shame has been a very lengthy, circuitous journey. There are so many aspects of myself and my position in the world I've been made to feel bad about. I beat myself up for my gender nonconformity, my Autism, my sexuality. I lost myself in activism, and work, and unhappy relationships. I believed a coveted position of social safety would only come if I made the right decisions and was good enough.

But there never even *was* such a thing as being "good enough," because Systemic Shame sets each of us up to fail. Systemic Shame exists to keep us forever toiling at thankless unwinnable tasks, withdrawing from others, judging and shaming humanity, and beating ourselves up. And it's only after we begin to question this values system that we can recognize that there is no such thing as earning one's way into acceptance. There is no such thing as becoming "good enough" to be deserving of love. Rather, acceptance is already all around us, waiting for us to discover it, and we are already loveworthy exactly as we messily are.

I'm not a master practitioner of expansive recognition, to be honest. Whenever I'm facing a problem or feel guilty about my limitations, my first instinct is to isolate and white-knuckle my way through. But that approach has failed me so many times that even I am sick of it. And every time that I choose to let go of my self-protective impulse and turn vulnerably toward humanity instead, I learn all over again that it is our connections that make our lives meaningful and enjoyable. Not our accomplishments. Not how hard we work or how much we sacrifice. Not the qualities that we believe make us better than others. None of us can exist as a singular being, and it's time that we stop trying to.

For me, combating Systemic Shame and practicing expansive recognition every day comes down to a few key behaviors:

1. Healing Personal Systemic Shame:
   a. Telling people what I'm feeling.
   b. Admitting when my hard work and struggle is going nowhere.
   c. Indulging the desires I've always had yet have been taught are wrong.
   d. Choosing to live as a person that others might dislike, and not making that my problem.
2. Healing Interpersonal Systemic Shame:
   a. Noticing when I'm viewing someone's actions in the worst possible light and asking myself why.
   b. Speaking up when my needs are in conflict with those of a loved one, so we can repair our bond.
   c. Thinking a lot about how another person's economic, cultural, legal, and institutional position makes their life different from my own.
   d. Surrounding myself with people that make being myself feel natural.
3. Healing Global Systemic Shame:
   a. Trusting in the inner voice that tells me what is right.
   b. Abandoning pursuits I was trained to value but don't really believe in.
   c. Appreciating the potential of where I'm planted, and finding opportunities to make a difference right where I am.
   d. Building connections to my neighborhood, to other

communities, and across the generations, so that I
can feel the tug of the thread that connects us all.

If you're reading this book, then you probably struggle with Systemic Shame as I do—and frequently feel that you are not good enough, or that your life is meaningless on a planet ravaged by colonialism, environmental destruction, racism, and capitalism. I hope that by this point you have found some tools that help put these difficult feelings in perspective, and that by exploring Systemic Shame's historical origins, you have realized that this vicious internal battle is not your own.

In all likelihood, none of us will do away with all Systemic Shame forever. Even that fact is something we can live with and build a meaningful life around. In the service of forging that kind of fulfilling, shame-resilient life, I'd like to leave you with a few final questions to ponder—and I'll share my own responses, and the responses of a few people I interviewed for this book, to help inspire your own reflections.

What matters most to me?

Expansive recognition sees each of us as part of a much larger, more powerful social force. It grants us the permission to specialize in one or two life callings that we can do very well, and that we actively enjoy, rather than attempting to do and be it all.

For me, one of life's most powerful callings is ensuring that trans people retain access to hormones—because hormone replacement therapy has been utterly life-changing to me and so many people that I love. And because I was exposed to a lot of fearmongering online about the supposed "irreversible damage" caused by hormones early in my transition, I have made it my life's purpose to communicate openly about the many unexpected positive changes that testosterone gave me.

For example, taking T gave me a breast reduction of over two cup sizes. No one ever told me that I could expect that! It also made my allergies to pet dander and tree pollen completely go away![1] Even the changes on testosterone that I once feared, such as body hair growth and increased acne, have all ended up being things that I welcome and cherish. I underwent top surgery in June of 2023, and I was similarly stunned to find it a relatively painless, breezy recovery process—nothing like the carnage transphobes made it out to be. I want to be a beacon of happy, comfortable trans self-acceptance wherever I can be, encouraging trans people and their families to see that who we are is a beautiful thing, and that transition can be fun and unserious. It doesn't have to be a last-ditch effort we should only undertake if we have no other choice. Simply wanting to do it is enough of a reason. And most trans people underestimate just how well a transition can go.

Another thing that matters a great deal to me is the intimacy and quality of my relationships. After overworking for years to distract myself from my lonesomeness, I find I have very little drive to be impressive at work anymore. Big ambitious projects always stressed me out and left me resenting friends and family, because spending quality time with them would really eat into my writing schedule. I hate that I denied myself so many rich experiences by retreating like that—so I do not do it anymore. I say yes to social invitations first and worry about my own projects later. Today, work and creativity are things I squeeze into the spare hours when my loved ones are not available. I have to work in order to pay the bills, of course, but I aspire to be just mediocre enough to get by, and I steal time during the workday to message friends and take care of people that I love.

It's amazing how much richer and more vibrant my life is now that I do so much less. I have identified what my true priorities are, and they serve as a powerful guiding light. I hope that you, too, can ask yourself what your foremost callings in life really are—and from there, ask who will be by your side when you go after them.

Who can help me with the things that matter most?

"I dived into a regrarian fantasy in 2007," Emma tells me. "Regrarians" attempt to restore their local ecosystem by replanting and caring for native plants, among many other techniques. It is a worthy project—but because Emma's initial way of doing it was informed by individualism and Systemic Shame, it was sadly doomed to fail.

"I did tree change, I grew my own food, I worked less," she explains. "It eventually withered and lost its meaning because I did so alone. Since then, I have learned of collectivism. Next time I will grow, not shrink."

Emma is like so many people that I know, including myself, who learned the hard way that no idealistic social goal is possible through non-social means. Systemic Shame trains us to equate struggle with virtuousness, but really, the activities truly worth doing should not be done by a single person, and they shouldn't be backbreakingly hard. Asking for help and working collectively toward a better world, however, sustains our motivation and makes it possible to trust in the long-term benefits of humble attempts.

Fighting legal and medical transphobia is not a matter of individual effort, and asking myself if I am "doing enough" to ensure trans lives are safe is nonsensical. There is no objective answer to that question. Systemic Shame will always tell me that the answer is no. These days, I ask myself: Who is doing meaningful work that I believe in, and how can I support them?

An acquaintance of mine runs an informed-consent hormone clinic in the California desert. She's part of a team that provides estrogen, testosterone blockers, and testosterone injections to homeless and undocumented trans people, with zero medical gatekeeping and no questions asked. I'm happy to support her efforts financially and to spread the word about the project. I'm also happy to help quietly spread the word about another friend's service, a website that allows trans people to share their excess prescriptions with other trans people in need. My donations and organizing help are just one small drop in the bucket—and Systemic Shame would tell me to feel bad about that. Instead, I take pride in being part of a large tide change.

Once you identify what matters most to you in life, the next step is asking yourself how you'll get help in honoring those commitments. From there, it becomes time to size up which other obligations and social expectations might be distracting you from what matters most, and identifying ways you can let those demands drop.

What can I let go of?

When we move at a slower pace, the entire world opens up before us. No longer distracted and rejecting our reality with incessant "shoulds," we can appreciate our environment in far lusher detail, and notice opportunities where we're genuinely needed. When we say no to the things that do not move and motivate us, we have the time and energy necessary to harness what power we do have and devote it to our primary goals. Identifying what matters most to us will always mean determining what, on the flip side, we can let drop. Even this rejection is a practice in expansive recognition—we have to trust that other people can and will do the work that they're positioned for and be grateful to them for it.

It may feel at first like shameful "laziness" for us to choose to do less. But it's actually when we set out to do too much that we doom ourselves to forever feeling inadequate, and to seeing our world as repetitive and small. The longer our to-do lists are, the more often we will feel like we're coming up short—even if we're accomplishing a great deal, or more than our bodies and brains can consistently handle. The very people who are branded as the laziest in our culture are those who have the most demanded of them, and receive the least support.[2]

This same principle applies to absolutely any perceived "failure" that Systemic Shame has laid at any of our feet. When I hold myself personally responsible for overcoming ableism as an Autistic person, I can never feel like I've done enough. When I expect myself to single-handedly heal the earth, end white supremacy in higher ed, reverse income inequality, and curb the spread of illness, I will always feel like a miserable failure stuck in a dying world. Accepting my smallness makes it easier for me to step away, quit, or relax my commitment to certain things. Here are some principles that have aided me in cutting back:

- **Listen to dread.** If certain spaces or activities are always really painful to drag yourself to, that's likely a sign that they aren't for you.
- **When you feel like you aren't doing enough, resolve to do less.** It's an interesting paradox: The more overwhelmed people are with tasks, the less likely they are to feel like they're accomplishing anything.
- **Whenever you add an obligation to your life, find another to remove.** Your time and energy is already fully accounted for, though some of it might be getting spent on activities you don't actually value.

- **Ask yourself whether a deadline actually matters.** Will any-one truly be hurt if you take a break, or some time to reflect?
- **What can you trust other people to handle?** Keep in mind that most tasks don't actually have to be done perfectly, or exactly the way that you would do them.

Coming to terms with our limits is emotionally fraught stuff. It forces us to acknowledge that some problems cannot be entirely mended, at least not right now. This brings us to the next reflection question:

How can I grieve and accept the things I cannot carry?

In an opinion piece for *Scientific American,* the environmental stud-ies professor Sarah Jaquette Ray argues that climate anxiety is a pre-dominately white problem.[3] She doesn't mean that only privileged, white, well-off liberals have the luxury of caring about their compost bins or the sustainability of the coffee they drink. What she means is that grappling with the harm capitalism and colonization has done to the planet is hardly a new thing, and most people through-out the world have been facing it on a daily basis for decades, or even centuries.

Systemic Shame's approach to massive global problems like cli-mate change and health epidemics are fueled by the incessant, reality-denying belief that if everyone just behaves correctly, then we can get back to "normal." But the idea of there having ever been a "normal" time that should be restored is fiction. The world has for-ever been changing, and will continue to, and there are some losses that none of us can ever recoup. Entire cultures have been destroyed. Species and biospheres have disappeared from the face of the earth.

On a micro level, many of us will never restore the lifestyles we had before Covid, and can never become a version of ourselves that did not experience transphobia or sexual assault. It's okay to process these losses and confront the enormity of them. In fact, mourning the past is essential to moving forward in a clear-headed way.

Hayden Dawes is a Black, queer researcher, therapist, and writer, and the inventor of radical permission, a therapeutic technique wherein a person writes themselves a daily "permission slip" to release unreasonable standards and other lingering burdens.[4] Dawes has created a free set of illustrated permission slips for people needing help letting go in various ways: the permission to change in a dramatic way, for example, or the permission to recuperate and rest. One of Dawes's illustrated permission slips depicts a bird's skull and encourages the user to give themselves permission to contemplate death, endings, and loss, and to grieve.[5]

On social media, Dawes shares completed permission slips that people have shared with him. "Today, I'm being gentle with myself for all the ways I cannot live up to my high expectations," says one recent entry.[6] "Today I give myself permission to show up as I am—not fully realized or fully formed," says another.[7] And when applied to grief, radical permission can also mean allowing life and the world to be what they already are—rather than expecting that hard work and effort can somehow restore everything.

It's scary to imagine that many of us will never have the stamina we did before long Covid, that we'll never work as hard as we did before getting burnout, and that no matter what we do, humanity will have to adapt to protect people living in warm climates and at sea level from rising temperatures. But we're able to plan and direct our efforts far more productively once we give ourselves, and reality, permission to exist. There is no restoring the past. But if we're really honest with ourselves, we know that humanity's recent past was not so rosy either. We've been abusing the planet and neglecting the health of other people on a systemic level for centuries. Collectively, we can treat the present as our jumping-off point.

What comes easily?

When I was still trying to keep a straight man from falling out of love with me, anything that caused me gender euphoria also provoked intense guilt and alarm. I'd admire my thickening trap muscles in the mirror, then cringe at the thought of Nick seeing me and experiencing disgust. I'd tense up when I caught myself comfortably settling into a masculine swagger, then try to find a way to force my posture and mannerisms into a sweet spot where they could still feel correct for me, but not ward off the interests of someone exclusively attracted to women. I lived in an awkward middle place, balancing my own mental health against what I assumed to be his desires, always viewing myself through his increasingly cold eyes.

Shortly after breaking up with Nick, I went to the gay bathhouse Steamworks, where I had the complete opposite experience. Men looked me up and down hungrily, and followed me around quietly, hoping for a chance at my attention. Everyone present was incredibly friendly, respectful of my physical boundaries, and yet *very* straightforward about their desire. Sex was clearly negotiated, rather than awkwardly hinted at the way it was in the straight world. All the attention I received was pleasurable and affirming. I hadn't expected a small, effeminate trans guy like me to be broadly accepted in a gay male cruising space, yet moving through Steamworks proved totally effortless. Years of shame melted off me completely. All those years I had been trying and trying like hell to make the wrong life work, but I found that the right life came easily.

Puritan morality, sex negativity, and Systemic Shame makes

many of us afraid of our own pleasure. We equate feeling good with being evil, and assume that life's most meaningful endeavors have to be hard. My life experience tells me the complete opposite. All the most impactful, beautiful experiences of my life have come so easily they felt almost preordained. My most well-received piece of writing took me about an hour and a half to complete. My current full-time job at Loyola was the easiest job interview I ever sat through. My best and most enduring relationships came together magnetically. Slowly, despite all the cultural programming to the contrary, I am learning to trust what feels enjoyable and right.

When I contemplate the liberatory power of trusting what feels right, the song "Pynk" by Janelle Monae invariably comes to mind. It's a tender, bouncy track about Monae's own pansexuality, and it presents queer desire as an irresistible, life-giving force. "Pink is the truth you can't hide," she quietly intones. "Pink like the secrets inside." There's something so enchanting about how she depicts queer authenticity not as hard-won, but as a gentle settling in to the inevitable. I'm not a pansexual woman, like Monae is, but it hardly makes any difference: "Deep inside," as she says, "we're all just pink." We're bleeding, pulsing, yearning humans, pulled together by the positive feelings we have the power to give one another.

One interview subject that I spoke to for this book is Qupid, a Black trans woman from Cleveland who's in her early twenties, and someone whose thinking and perspective I've deeply admired since the moment I met her. When I asked her about what rejecting Systemic Shame looks like in her life, she said that one of the key elements was embracing frivolity.

"There's all this nihilism in the world, and also all this idealism," she says. "And they're two sides of the same coin. I keep coming back to reminding myself that we are animals. We're part of the natural world, and conflict is not going away, and we're messy and silly, and yes life is horrible sometimes, but the world is your playground."

Sometimes, in Qupid's case, this looks like literally frolicking in a garden, or not worrying about being late to a meeting that isn't really all that important, or taking a moment to circle the mall and enjoy a honeybun. Qupid keeps a document filled with kind compliments that people have given her and sets aside time to reread them. She's a serious, philosophical person who cares a lot about many political goals—I know this because we became acquainted through discussions of those topics—but she also knows how to have fun without shame.

"Yes, things are hard and horrible, and yes, you might feel like you can't do anything to change them," she says, "And there's this jadedness and hypersarcasm that I see in people my age, but I just want to have room for fun and vibrancy as well in queer communities."

I really think embracing frivolous, simple pleasure and fun is a brilliant way to practice expansive recognition. Systemic Shame turns each of us into a symbol; ironically, by moralizing our every individual action, it denies us the opportunity to experience our individual human lives. We lose sight of ourselves, and of all sense of perspective. We ignore those simple feelings that tell us what's right, and get mired in a complicated web of contradictory rules and assumed external judgments. It's incredibly freeing, then, to just allow ourselves to get a bit happy and silly. Desire and frivolity force us back into the present, and quiet all the external voices that say we must hide or correct what's inside. Humility doesn't have to be dour. It can be silly.

If there is one takeaway that I'd wish to impart to people struggling with Systemic Shame, it would be that they learn to hone their internal feelings of rightness. We can't be manipulated with undeserved shame once we trust the things that make our lives easier and brighter.

What can I forgive, in others and myself?

We've talked a lot in this book about how Systemic Shame ravages our self-concept, but I can't emphasize strongly enough that it also damages our relationships to others. Assigning a moral value to every individual person's behavior means that we are forever pointing fingers at those who lacked better options, isolating ourselves instead of supporting one another and joining forces against those systems that have stolen our control. If we wish to embrace expansive recognition as an alternative value system, we have to forgive ourselves for not being perfect, *and* we must find ways to grant grace and forgiveness to other people as well.

I keep returning to my relationship with my mother, because she's someone radically different from me who I have struggled to love well. To this day, I still frequently think of her as a symbol of conservative movements that she never really played an active role in—she's just been on the receiving end of endless right-leaning misinformation and propaganda.

A few months ago, for instance, she told me that it is unsafe to wear surgical masks to mitigate the spread of Covid-19, because they make you inhale dangerous levels of carbon dioxide. I was bewildered. My mom worked as a dental hygienist for decades, wearing a surgical mask for eight hours during every single shift. I could not *believe* a former medical professional who wore surgical masks every day could suddenly think that wearing them was dangerous. The words that flew out of me—"*Where the* fuck *did you hear that?!*"— came out as a snarl.

My angry outbursts have hurt her. Taking my frustration out on her fixes nothing. Shaming her only makes matters worse in fact.

Recently, my mom, my sister, and I went on a trip to Disneyland. I was determined to bring a good attitude with me to the vacation. Yet as I walked around the park alone, waiting for my family to arrive, I felt ashamed of myself, and freakish. I'd never been to the parks looking like a grown man before. I was worried other families might think it was wrong or creepy for me to be there. I was steeling myself for an awkward encounter with my mother, too—she is guarded and shy around me at times these days, understandably afraid of the outrage that spills out when she shares her opinions. For a moment I felt like I'd made some terrible mistake, that I didn't belong in this candy-colored fantasy world made for joyous kids and their loving families anymore.

When my mom and sister did get to the park, though, everything improved. They were both relaxed and in easygoing spirits despite their long flight. We stood in line for the Jungle Cruise and I paused to take a group selfie, and my mom leaned in close and put her face against my cheek. The love and warmth radiating from her in the photograph was impossible even for my most bitter self to deny. As we strolled through the façade of fake New Orleans, I spotted an adorably chubby boy sitting on a fence, staring at me. When we walked by, he dashed after me.

"Sir, excuse me, sir!" the boy called out. "Sir! Would you like to trade pins?"

He pointed eagerly to a pin I had on my fanny pack: Timon, the meerkat from *The Lion King*. My sister had given it to me.

"Oh, sure," I said, unhooking Timon and handing it over to the boy. "Which one of yours should I take?"

The boy held out his lanyard, which was covered in pins depicting characters from both of our respective childhoods: Mike Wazowski from *Monster's Inc.,* Zazoo from *The Lion King,* Cogsworth from *Beauty and the Beast.* "You can have any of them except that one," he told me, pointing to Mike. I selected Cogsworth.

"Thank you, sir!" he said, and ran off, rejoining his dad.

My heart sang. All day I'd been so afraid that I was a terrifying presence here at this park, that my transgender body marked me as different and dangerous, that among both strangers and family I could not belong. But just like that, a little kid collecting pins had managed to affirm my gender without question *and* remind me of how much I have in common with other people. This kid and I were decades apart in age, yet shared many cultural touchstones—with all of the positives and negatives that entailed. He wasn't afraid of me, and I wasn't a freak, we were just two humans enjoying a vacation with our families, wearing adorable pins that they'd given us.

"*Sir,*" my mom repeated happily when I rejoined her side. "He called you sir!" She recognized how significant the moment was for me. It's magical when someone just instantly sees you as you are, especially an unfiltered kid.

"Yeah," I said bashfully, "that was really cute."

My mom still calls both my sister and me "baby." But for the whole rest of the vacation, she called me "baby sir." We had a wonderful time together, four unbroken days of comfortable company and no pointless fighting. Instead, we directed our attention together toward shared experiences. Even as I write this, I feel flashes of Systemic Shame within me. Maybe people will judge me for financially supporting a massive corporation like Disney, which frequently censors queer characters out of its properties. Maybe my more politically radical friends will consider me a traitor for being warm and affectionate with someone who has the politics my mom does. I'll never stop seeing myself through others' eyes, not completely. But at last, I know what truly matters to me, and where I've strayed from it at times. I'm working on healing my own immense self-loathing, and repairing my trust in my loved ones and in strangers.

I can't fix the world or undo the past, though I often still wish that I could. But at least now I know what I'm here for. After years of being guided only by pain and self-hatred, I finally have learned to follow what makes me feel joyful, connected, and right.

Notes

Introduction

1. D. Price. "My Dalliance with Detransition." Medium. Accessed June 15, 2023. https://devonprice.medium.com/my-dalliance-with-detransition-97ac9a5126e6.
2. How is a Black woman supposed to reconcile these two competing pieces of advice? She can't.
3. Crippledscholar. "When Accessibility Gets Labeled Wasteful." crippledscholar, May 25, 2016. https://crippledscholar.com/2016/03/04/when-accessibility-gets-labeled-wasteful.
4. S. Mufson. "Amazon's Use of Plastic Soared in 2020, Environmental Group Says." *The Washington Post*, December 15, 2021. https://www.washingtonpost.com/climate-environment/2021/12/15/amazon-plastic-waterways/.
5. In the past, Amazon customers and workers have come together online to post photos of the overly large, bulky boxes their small purchases sometimes arrive in, drawing public attention to the huge amounts of trash the company produces without thought.
   P. Gerrard. "Excessive Packaging Slammed after Amazon Sends Single Vinegar Bottle in Huge Box." Press and Journal, June 18, 2021. https://www.pressandjournal.co.uk/fp/news/inverness/3242203/excessive-packaging-slammed-after-amazon-sends-single-vinegar-bottle-in-huge-box.
6. "Opinion | the 'Crip Tax': Everything Has a Cost, but for People with Disabilities That's Quite Literally the Case | CBC News." CBCnews, April 15, 2021. https://www.cbc.ca/news/canada/saskatchewan/crip-tax-opinion-1.5856848.
7. Though Lyft and Uber often present themselves as a more ecologically friendly alternative to driving, the amount of time rideshare drivers spend "deadheading" (driving without passengers) translates to marked increase in pollution overall: Bliss, Laura. "The Other Toll of Uber and Lyft Rides: Pollution." Bloomberg.com, February 25, 2020. https://www.bloomberg.com/news/articles/2020-02-25/the-other-toll-of-uber-and-lyft-rides-pollution.
8. Calma, Justine. "Bezos' Climate Fund Faces a Reckoning with Amazon's Pollution." The Verge, February 4, 2021. https://www.theverge.com/2021/2/4/22266225/jeff-bezos-climate-change-earth-fund-amazon-pollution.

9. Isaac Shapiro, Bryann DaSilva, David Reich, and Richard Kogan. "Funding for Housing, Health, and Social Services Block Grants Has Fallen Markedly over Time." Center on Budget and Policy Priorities. Accessed June 15, 2023. https://www.cbpp.org/research/federal-budget/funding-for-housing-health-and-social-services-block-grants-has-fallen.

10. "The Freedmen's Bureau! An Agency to Keep the Negro in Idleness at the Expense of the White Man." Encyclopedia Virginia, April 19, 2022. https://encyclopediavirginia.org/10582hpr-ee5c82942d7a1ba.

11. J. Levin. "The Real Story of Linda Taylor, America's Original Welfare Queen." *Slate Magazine*, December 19, 2013. https://www.slate.com/articles/news_and_politics/history/2013/12/linda_taylor_welfare_queen_ronald_reagan_made_her_a_notorious_american_villain.html.

12. Even Kanye West has gotten in on this action; he infamously shamed a concert-goer for not standing up during one of his shows several years ago. This article from CNN also discusses a high-profile case of a disabled wheelchair user being shamed online for visibly stretching in her chair a bit to reach a high-shelf bottle of liquor. Perry, David M. "Kanye West and Proving Your Disabilities." CNN, September 16, 2014. https://www.cnn.com/2014/09/16/opinion/perry-kanye-west-prove-disabilities/index.html.

13. The website TV tropes has collected hundreds of examples of the "Obfuscating Disability" trope: "Obfuscating Disability." TV Tropes. Accessed June 15, 2023. https://tvtropes.org/pmwiki/pmwiki.php/Main/ObfuscatingDisability.

14. P. Silván-Ferrero, P. Recio, F. Molero, and E. Nouvilas-Pallejà, "Psychological Quality of Life in People with Physical Disability: The Effect of Internalized Stigma, Collective Action and Resilience" *International Journal of Environmental Research and Public Health* 17, no. 5 (2020): 1802; https://doi.org/10.3390/ijerph17051802.

15. A. Jeffries. "This Is Not a Story about a Man Who Walks to Work." The Outline, February 27, 2017. https://theoutline.com/post/1164/this-is-not-a-story-about-a-man-who-walks-to-work.

16. Pulrang, Andrew. "How to Avoid 'Inspiration Porn.'" *Forbes*, October 12, 2022. https://www.forbes.com/sites/andrewpulrang/2019/11/29/how-to-avoid-inspiration-porn/?sh=68902dd15b3d.

17. James Robertson is one such man who made headlines for walking twenty-one miles to work each day, and his manager said that he uses Robertson's attendance record as a benchmark by which to judge his other employees. He said, "If this man can get here, walking all those miles through snow and rain, well, I'll tell you, I have people in Pontiac ten minutes away and they say they can't get here—bull!"
    J. Mullen, and Stephanie Gallman. "Donations Pour in for Detroit Man Who Walks 21 Miles for His Daily Commute." CNN, February 4, 2015. https://www.cnn.com/2015/02/03/us/detroit-man-walks-21-miles-for-daily-commute/index.html.

18. D. James, "Health and Health-Related Correlates of Internalized Racism Among Racial/Ethnic Minorities: A Review of the Literature," *Journal of Racial and Ethnic Health Disparities* 7, no. 4 (2020): 785–806; D. M. Mouzon and J. S. McLean, "Internalized Racism and Mental Health Among African Americans, US-Born Caribbean Blacks, and Foreign-Born Caribbean Blacks," *Ethnicity and Health*, 22, no. 1 (2017): 36–48.

19. D. Tallent, S. A. Shelton, and S. McDaniel, "'It Was Really My Fault': Examining White Supremacy and Internalized Racism Through Detained US Black Youths' Narratives and Counternarratives," *International Journal of Qualitative Studies in Education* (2021): 1–19.

20. P. Hutchinson and R. Dhairyawan, "Shame, Stigma, HIV: Philosophical Reflections," *Medical Humanities* 43, no. 4 (2017), 225–30.

21. P. Hutchinson and R. Dhairyawan, "Shame and HIV: Strategies for Addressing the Negative Impact Shame Has on Public Health and Diagnosis and Treatment of HIV," *Bioethics* 32, no. 1 (2018): 68–76.

22. For more on this, I recommend Koa Beck's *White Feminism* and Mary Francis Berry's *The Politics of Parenthood*.

23. J. Friedman. "Motherhood Is a Political Category." Medium. Accessed June 15, 2023. https://humanparts.medium.com/motherhood-is-a-political-category -5b5be72b5531.

Part One: Suffering Under Systemic Shame
1. Understanding Systemic Shame

1. "Love bombing" is a term that originally referred to one of the many ways in which abusers and cults lure their victims. By showing intense, boundary-less affection, "love bombers" erode their victims' defenses and encourage dependence. But there's a big difference between a cult carefully isolating a vulnerable person from all their family and friends and a generically assholish guy on a dating app pretending to like a woman more than he does.

2. This retrospective in *Buzzfeed* shows how quickly public opinion on Caleb shifted. He went from internet curiosity, to evil manipulator, to overly punished victim of cancel culture in a matter of weeks:
    Notopoulos, Katie. "Caleb from West Elm Is Bad at Dating but Probably Didn't Deserve Being Pushed through the TikTok Meat Grinder." BuzzFeed News, January 21, 2022. https://www.buzzfeednews.com/article/katie notopoulos/caleb-from-west-elm-meme.

3. Z., Sarah. "The Horrifying Panopticon of West Elm Caleb." YouTube, March 2, 2022. https://www.youtube.com/watch?v=EeCi4CSqtzw.

4. Luna, Elizabeth de. "TikTok's 'West Elm Caleb' Saga Was Never about Caleb." Mashable, January 21, 2022. https://mashable.com/article/west-elm-caleb -tiktok-sexual-harassment.

5. Y. Trope and N. Liberman, "Construal Level Theory," *Handbook of Theories of Social Psychology* 1 (2012): 118–34.

6. J. E. Eidemiller, "The Role of Self Control in Confronting One's Own Sexist Beliefs" (PhD dissertation, Ohio State University, 2017).

7. N. Liberman, Y. Trope, and C. Wakslak, "Construal Level Theory and Consumer Behavior," *Journal of Consumer Psychology* 17, no. 2 (2007): 113–17.

8. C. D'Amore, S. L. Martin, K. Wood et al., "Themes of Healing and Posttraumatic Growth in Women Survivors' Narratives of Intimate Partner Violence," *Journal of Interpersonal Violence* 36, nos. 5–6 (2021): NP2697–724; P. Flasch, C. E. Murray, and A. Crowe, "Overcoming Abuse: A Phenomenological Investigation of the Journey to Recovery from Past Intimate Partner Violence," *Journal of Interpersonal Violence* 32 (2017): 3373–401.

9. For decades, it's been the case that women are less likely than men to be victims of violent crime (despite cultural narratives that portray them as powerless and in need of male protection), but when they are attacked, they are more likely to be preyed upon by the very men who society expects them to provide that "protection": romantic partners, parents, church leaders, bosses, and close friends. See for example Bureau of Justice Statistics selected findings. Accessed June 15, 2023. https://bjs.ojp.gov/content/pub/pdf/fvv.pdf.

Global Study on Homicide 2018—United Nations Office on Drugs and Crime. Accessed June 15, 2023. https://www.unodc.org/documents/data-and -analysis/GSH2018/GSH18_Gender-related_killing_of_women_and_girls.pdf.

10. C. L. Martin, and D. N. Ruble, "Patterns of Gender Development," *Annual Review of Psychology* 61 (2010): 353–81, https://doi.org/10.1146/annurev.psych .093008.100511.

11. L. A. Hirschfeld, "Children's Developing Conceptions of Race," in *Handbook of Race, Racism, and the Developing Child*, ed. S. M. Quintana and C. McKown (Hoboken, NJ: John Wiley and Sons, 2008), 37–54.

12. Peter N. Stearns, "Exploring Shame: The Interdisciplinary Context," in *Shame: A Brief History* (Champaign: University of Illinois Press, 2017), 1–9, https://doi .org/10.5406/j.ctt1vjqrq8.6.

13. N. Ambady, M. Shih, A. Kim, and T. L. Pittinsky, "Stereotype Susceptibility in Children: Effects of Identity Activation on Quantitative Performance," *Psychological Science* 12, no. 5 (2001): 385–90.

14. For a great review of the literature on this phenomenon, see A. L. Whaley, "Advances in Stereotype Threat Research on African Americans: Continuing Challenges to the Validity of Its Role in the Achievement Gap," *Social Psychology of Education* 21, no. 1 (2018): 111–37.

15. For a thorough discussion of how an achievement motivation mediates stereotype threat effects, as well as how long-term motivation levels can change in response to it, see D. B. Thoman, J. L. Smith, E. R. Brown, J. Chase, and J. Y. K. Lee, "Beyond Performance: A Motivational Experiences Model of Stereotype Threat," *Educational Psychology Review* 25, no. 2 (2013): 211–43.

16. C. Tomasetto, F. R. Alparone, and M. Cadinu, "Girls' Math Performance Under Stereotype Threat: The Moderating Roel of Mothers' Gender Stereotypes," *Developmental Psychology* 47, no. 4 (2011): 943; S. Galdi, M. Cadinu, and C. Tomasetto, "The Roots of Stereotype Threat: When Automatic Associations Disrupt Girls' Math Performance," *Child Development* 85, no. 1 (2014): 250–63; E. Seo and Y. K. Lee, "Stereotype Threat in High School Classrooms: How It Links to Teacher Mindset Climate, Mathematics Anxiety, and Achievement," *Journal of Youth and Adolescence* 50, no. 7 (2021): 1410–23; S. Bedyńska, I. Krejtz, and G. Sedek, "Chronic Stereotype Threat and Mathematical Achievement in Age Cohorts of Secondary School Girls: Mediational Role of Working Memory and Intellectual Helplessness," *Social Psychology of Education* 22 (2019): 321–35.

17. M. J. Fischer, "A Longitudinal Examination of the Role of Stereotype Threat and Racial Climate on College Outcomes for Minorities at Elite Institutions," *Social Psychology of Education* 13, (2010): 19–40, https://doi.org/10.1007/ s11218-009-9105-3.

18. C. Sonnak and T. Towell, "The Imposter Phenomenon in British University Students: Relationships Between Self-Esteem, Mental Health, Parental

Rearing Style, and Socioeconomic Status," *Personality and Individual Differences* 31, no. 6 (2001): 863–74.

For some related research on the psychological processes underpinning stereotype threat effects, see S. Wang and D. Yang, "The Effects of Poverty Stereotype Threat on Inhibition Ability in Individuals from Different Income-Level Families," *Brain and Behavior* 10, no. 12 (2020): e01770.

19. B. N. Anderson and J. A. Martin, "What K–12 Teachers Need to Know About Teaching Gifted Black Girls Battling Perfectionism and Stereotype Threat," *Gifted Child Today*, 41, no. (2018): 117–24.

20. A. Parker. "Black Women Are Now the Most Educated Group in the United States." Salon, June 6, 2016. https://www.salon.com/2016/06/02/black_women _are_now_the_most_educated_group_in_the_united_states/.

21. When black women win, everybody wins.—inc.com. Accessed June 15, 2023. https://www.inc.com/sonia-thompson/black-women-equal-pay-equity-how -to-make-progress.html.

22. S. Clement, O. Schauman, T. Graham, et al., "What Is the Impact of Mental Health–Related Stigma on Help-Seeking? A Systematic Review of Quantitative and Qualitative Studies," *Psychological Medicine* 45, no. 1 (2015): 11–27.

23. M. B. Benz, K. B. Cabrera, N. Kline, et al., "Fear of Stigma Mediates the Relationship Between Internalized Stigma and Treatment-Seeking Among Individuals with Substance Use Problems," *Substance Use and Misuse* 56, no. 6 (2021): 808–18.

24. N. M. Overstreet and D. M. Quinn, "The Intimate Partner Violence Stigmatization Model and Barriers to Help Seeking," *Basic and Applied Social Psychology* 35, no. 1 (2013): 109–22.

25. A. Heard. "Opinion | Amber Heard: I Spoke up against Sexual Violence—and Faced Our Culture's Wrath. That Has to Change." The Washington Post, June 2, 2022. https://www.washingtonpost.com/opinions/ive-seen-how-institutions -protect-men-accused-of-abuse-heres-what-we-can-do/2018/12/18/71fd876a -02ed-11e9-b5df-5d3874f1ac36_story.html.

26. N. Bedera. "Why Are so Many Survivors Supporting Johnny Depp?" *Harper's BAZAAR,* May 26, 2022. https://www.harpersbazaar.com/culture/politics /a40116993/why-are-so-many-survivors-supporting-johnny-depp.

27. M. Van der Bruggen and A. Grubb, "A Review of the Literature Relating to Rape Victim Blaming: An Analysis of the Impact of Observer and Victim Characteristics on Attribution of Blame in Rape Cases," *Aggression and Violent Behavior* 19, no. 5 (2014): 523–31.

28. N. Bedera and K. Nordmeyer, "'Never Go Out Alone': An Analysis of College Rape Prevention Tips," *Sexuality and Culture* 19, no. 3 (2015): 533–42.

29. Especially if those women have institutional power. See Cruz, Jacqueline. "Gender Inequality in Higher Education: University Title IX Administrators' Responses to Sexual Violence." PhD diss., New York University, 2020.

See also: C. M. Pinciotti and H. K. Orcutt, "It Won't Happen to Me: An Examination of the Effectiveness of Defensive Attribution in Rape Victim Blaming," *Violence Against Women* 26, no. 10 (2020): 1059–79.

30. S. Lorman. "Confessions of a Former Pandemic Shamer." Confessions of a Former Pandemic Shamer, December 18, 2021. https://awardsforgoodboys .substack.com/p/confessions-of-a-former-pandemic?s=r.

31. D. Newton. "The Dark Side of Environmentalism: Ecofascism and Covid-19." Office of Sustainability—Student Blog, April 15, 2020. https://usfblogs.usfca.edu/sustainability/2020/04/15/the-dark-side-of-environmentalism-ecofascism-and-covid-19.

32. A. R. Ross and E. Bevensee, "Confronting the Rise of Eco-fascism Means Grappling with Complex Systems," *CARR Research Insight* 3 (2020): 3–31.

33. M. Allison, "'So Long, and Thanks for All the Fish!': Urban Dolphins as Ecofascist Fake News During COVID-19," *Journal of Environmental Media* 1, no. 1 (2020): 4–1.

2. The Origins of Systemic Shame

1. "U.S. Highway Deaths Decline 2.9%, Falling for Fifth Year," *Bloomberg*, Dec. 8, 2011 (archived from the original Sept. 18, 2016; retrieved Mar. 8, 2017).

2. J. Stromberg. History of How Automakers Invented the Crime of "jaywalking". Vox, January 15, 2015. https://www.vox.com/2015/1/15/7551873/jaywalking-history.

3. "The Growing Menace," American magazine cartoon by Donald McKee, late 1920s. From "Automobile Cartoon, 1920s. 'the Growing Menace.' American Magazine Cartoon by Donald McKee, Late 1920s Stock Photo." Alamy. Accessed June 15, 2023. https://www.alamy.com/stock-photo-automobile-cartoon-1920s-nthe-growing-menace-american-magazine-cartoon-95516792.html.

4. "Nation Roused against Motor Killings; Secretary Hoover's Conference Will Suggest Many Ways to Check the Alarming Increase of Automobile Fatalities.—Studying Huge Problem." The New York Times, November 23, 1924. https://www.nytimes.com/1924/11/23/archives/nation-roused-against-motor-killings-secretary-hoovers-conference.html.

5. Most states in the United States did not adopt licenses for drivers until about 1935. "Licensing Cars and Drivers." National Museum of American History, April 15, 2019. https://americanhistory.si.edu/america-on-the-move/licensing-cars-drivers.

6. The term played on the slang word *jay*, which was equivalent to calling somebody a country bumpkin or hillbilly. See Hugh Irish, "Smiting the Hand that Feeds, Part II—Why There Is an Away-from-the-Farm Movement," *Colliers* 50, no. 18 (1913): 26.

7. A. Lewis. "Jaywalking: How the Car Industry Outlawed Crossing the Road." BBC News, February 12, 2014. https://www.bbc.com/news/magazine-26073797.

8. J. Stromberg. "The Forgotten History of How Automakers Invented the Crime of "jaywalking". Vox, January 15, 2015. https://www.vox.com/2015/1/15/7551873/jaywalking-history.

9. P. D. Norton, "Street Rivals: Jaywalking and the Invention of the Motor Age Street," *Technology and Culture* 48, no. 2 (2007): 331–59, doi:10.1353/tech.2007.0085

10. "Shame (n.)." Etymology. Accessed June 15, 2023. https://www.etymonline.com/word/shame.

11. The postures and gestures that we associate with shame appear to be at least

partially innate. See J. L. Tracy and D. Matsumoto, "The Spontaneous Expression of Pride and Shame: Evidence for Biologically Innate Nonverbal Displays," *Proceedings of the National Academy of Sciences* 105, no. 33 (2008): 11655–60. See also Peter N. Stearns, "Shame and Shaming in Premodern Societies," in *Shame: A Brief History* (Champaign: University of Illinois Press, 2017), 10–48, https://doi.org/10.5406/j.ctt1vjqrq8.7.

12. J. P. Martens, , J. L. Tracy, and A. F. Shariff, "Status Signals: Adaptive Benefits of Displaying and Observing the Nonverbal Expressions of Pride and Shame," *Cognition and Emotion* 26, no. 3 (2012): 390–406.

13. Jane Geaney, "Guarding Moral Boundaries: Shame in Early Confucianism," *Philosophy East and West* 54, no. 2 (April 2004): 113–42.

14. David Graeber, *Debt: The First 5000 Years* (London: Penguin UK, 2012): 318, 334, and 407.

15. "Stigma." Oxford Reference. Accessed June 15, 2023. https://www.oxford reference.com/display/10.1093/oi/authority.20111007171501221.

16. Robert Chambers, *Domestic Annals of Scotland* (Edinburgh: W & R Chambers, 1859–61), 90.

17. David Ho, Wai Fu, and S. Ng, "Guilt, Shame and Embarrassment: Revelations of Self and Face," *Culture and Psychology* 10, no. 1 (March 2004): 64–84, esp. 66–67; Stephanie Trigg, *Shame and Honor: A Vulgar History of the Order of the Garter* (Philadelphia: University of Pennsylvania Press, 2012).

18. H. Zhao, "'Holy Shame Shall Warm My Heart': Shame and Protestant Emotions in Early Modern Britain," *Cultural and Social History* 18, no. 1 (2021): 1–21.

19. Peter N. Stearns, "The Impact of Modernity: Some Possibilities," in *Shame: A Brief History*, 49–56, https://doi.org/10.5406/j.ctt1vjqrq8.8.

20. Peter N. Stearns, "Shame and Shaming in Premodern Societies," in *Shame: A Brief History*, 10–48, https://doi.org/10.5406/j.ctt1vjqrq8.7.

21. They also believed that since Native people did not blush as visibly as white people did, they lacked shame, which was also taken as a sign of their lack of sophistication and morality.

    Cummings, Brian. "Animal Passions and Human Sciences: Shame, Blushing and Nakedness in Early Modern Europe and the New World." At the Borders of the Human: Beasts, Bodies and Natural Philosophy in the Early Modern Period (1999): 26-50. E. Fudge, Ruth Gilbert, and Susan Wiseman. *At the borders of the human*. Palgrave Macmillan UK, 1999.

22. David Graeber and David Wengrow, "Wicked Liberty, the Indigenous Critique and the Myth of Progress," chapter 2 of *The Dawn of Everything: A New History of Humanity* (London: Penguin UK, 2021).

23. Stearns, "Shame and Shaming in Premodern Societies."

24. Though we should note, as Graeber and Wengrow point out in *The Dawn of Everything*, not all agricultural societies have private property and inequality.

25. S. A. West, A. S. Griffin, and A. Gardner, "Evolutionary Explanations for Cooperation," *Current Biology* 17 (2007), 661–72; H. M. Lewis, L. Vinicius, J. Strods et al., "High Mobility Explains Demand Sharing and Enforced Cooperation in Egalitarian Hunter-Gatherers," *Nature Communications* 5, no. 5789 (2014).

    Chaudhary, Nikhil, Gul Deniz Salali, James Thompson, Mark Dyble, Abigail Page, Daniel Smith, Ruth Mace, and Andrea Bamberg Migliano.

"Polygyny without wealth: popularity in gift games predicts polygyny in BaYaka Pygmies." *Royal Society Open Science* 2, no. 5 (2015): 150054.

P. Wiessner, "Norm Enforcement Among the Ju/'hoansi Bushmen," *Human Nature* 16 (2005): 115–45.

26. M. Dyble, J. Thorley, A. E. Page, et al., "Engagement in Agricultural Work Is Associated with Reduced Leisure Time Among Agta Hunter-Gatherers," *Nature Human Behaviour* 3 (2019): 792–96. DOI: 10.1038/s41562-019-0614-6

27. J. C. Berbesque, F. W. Marlowe, P. Shaw et al., "Hunter-Gatherers Have Less Famine Than Agriculturalists," *Biology Letters* 10, no. 1 (2014), https://doi.org/10.1098/rsbl.2013.0853.

28. A. E. Page, S. Viguier, M. Dyble et al., "Reproductive Trade-offs in Extant Hunter-Gatherers Suggest Adaptive Mechanism for the Neolithic Expansion," *Proceedings of the National Academy of Sciences* 113, no. 17 (2016), 4694–99.

29. D. Smith, P. Schlaepfer, K. Major et al., "Cooperation and the Evolution of Hunter-Gatherer Storytelling," *Nature Communications* 8, no. 1 (2017): 1–9.

30. All this said, non-agricultural societies were and are incredibly diverse. Throughout history, some hunter-gatherer societies kidnapped and enslaved people, waged wars, raided other cultures, divided people into classes, hoarded resources, and committed acts of torture and abuse, just as many agricultural societies did. That said, we do generally find that within hunter-gatherer societies there is typically less rampant inequality and less reason to view members of one's own community with suspicion, or to police people's personal habits.

For a great, incredibly thorough exploration of just some of the many different ways non-agricultural societies have organized themselves, see Graeber and Wengrow, *The Dawn of Everything*.

31. For a good review of this see chapter 2 of Roy Richard Grinker's *Nobody's Normal: How Culture Created the Stigma of Mental Illness* (New York: W. W. Norton and Co., 2021).

32. Andrew Scull, *Social Order/Mental Disorder: Anglo-American Psychiatry in Historical Perspective* (London: Routledge, 2018), 124.

33. Despite early Christianity being very much opposed to hierarchy and shaming. See Drake S. Levasheff, "Jesus of Nazareth, Paul of Tarsus, and the Early Christian Challenge to Traditional Honor and Shame Values" (Phd dissertation, UCLA, 2013), Eaton, Ellen Wehner. "Shame culture or guilt culture, the evidence of the medieval French fabliaux." PhD diss., 2000.; D. Boquet, and Piroska Nagy. *Medieval sensibilities: A history of emotions in the Middle Ages.* John Wiley & Sons, 2018.

34. Stearns, "Shame and Shaming in Premodern Societies."

35. Bénédicte Sère and Jörg Wettlaufer, eds., *Shame Between Punishment and Penance: The Social Usages of Shame in the Middle Ages and Early Modern Times* (Florence: Micrologus Library, 2013).

Graph depicting a huge jump in the use of the word *shame* is in Stearns, "Shame and Shaming in Premodern Societies," p. 41.

36. J. Salisbury. "Sex in the Middle Ages: A Book of Essays. (Garland Reference Library of the Humanities, 1360; Garland Medieval Casebooks, 3.) New York and London: Garland, 1991.

37. G. F. Moran and M. A. Vinovskis, *The Great Care of Godly Parents: Early*

Childhood in Puritan New England (1985), *Monographs of the Society for Research in Child Development* 50, nos. 4–5, pp. 24–37.

38. R. H. Tawney, and Adam B. Seligman. *Religion and the rise of capitalism.* London: Routledge, 2017.

39. D. E. Stannard, "Death and the Puritan Child," in *Death in America* (Philadelphia: University of Pennsylvania Press, 2017), 9–29.

40. W. P. Quigley, "Work or Starve: Regulation of the Poor in Colonial America. *University of San Francisco Law Review* 31 (1996): 35.

41. Moran and Vinovskis, *The Great Care of Godly Parents,* 24–37.

42. D. Price. "On the Insidious 'Laziness Lie' at the Heart of the American Myth." Literary Hub, January 6, 2021. https://lithub.com/on-the-insidious-laziness-lie-at-the-heart-of-the-american-myth.

43. E. L. Uhlmann, T. A. Poehlman, D. Tannenbaum et al., "Implicit Puritanism in American Moral Cognition," *Journal of Experimental Social Psychology* 47, no. 2 (2011): 312–20.

44. E. L. Uhlmann, T. Andrew Poehlman, and John A. Bargh, "American Moral Exceptionalism," chapter 2 of *Social and Psychological Bases of Ideology and System Justification,* ed. John T. Jost, Aaron C. Kay, and Hulda Thorisdottir (Oxford, UK: Oxford University Press, 2009), 27–52;

Jeffrey Sanchez-Burks, "Protestant Relational Ideology and (In)Attention to Relational Cues in Work Settings," *Journal of Personality and Social Psychology* 83 (2002): 919–29.

45. E. L. Uhlmann, T. Andrew Poehlman, David Tannenbaum, and John A. Bargh. "Implicit Puritanism in American moral cognition." Journal of Experimental Social Psychology 47, no. 2 (2011): 312-320.

Poehlman, T. A., E. L. Uhlmann, and J. A. Bargh. "Inherited ideology: An implicit link between work and sex morality in American cognition." Unpublished manuscript (2010).

46. K. J. Russell and C. J. Hand, "Rape Myth Acceptance, Victim Blame Attribution and Just World Beliefs: A Rapid Evidence Assessment," *Aggression and Violent Behavior* 37 (2017): 153–60;

Emma C. Deihl, "The Blame Game: Assessing Blame Placed on Gender Diverse Victims of HIV and the Impact of Perspective Taking" (master's thesis, University of Minnesota, 2020);

M. M. Turner, S. P. Funge, and W. J. Gabbard, "Victimization of the Homeless: Public Perceptions, Public Policies, and Implications for Social Work Practice," *Journal of Social Work in the Global Community* 3, no. 1 (2018): 1.

47. Turner, Funge, and Gabbard, "Victimization of the Homeless," 1.

48. P. K. Enns, Y. Yi, M. Comfort et al., "What Percentage of Americans Have Ever Had a Family Member Incarcerated?: Evidence from the Family History of Incarceration Survey (FamHIS)," *Socius* 5 (2019): 1-45.

49. Smith, Brendan L. "The Case against Spanking." Monitor on Psychology, April 2012. https://www.apa.org/monitor/2012/04/spanking#:~:text=Many%20studies%20have%20shown%20that,mental%20health%20problems%20for%20children; Stemen, *The Prison Paradox: More Incarceration Will Not Make Us Safer* (New York: Vera Institute of Justice, 2017).

50. E. O. Paolucci and C. Violato, "A Meta-Analysis of the Published Research on

the Affective, Cognitive, and Behavioral Effects of Corporal Punishment," *Journal of Psychology* 138, no. 3 (2004): 197–222; R. R. Austin, "The Shame of It All: Stigma and the Political Disenfranchisement of Formerly Convicted and Incarcerated Persons," *Columbia Human Rights Law Review* 36 (2004): 173.

51. H. L. Mirels and J. B. Garrett, "The Protestant Ethic as a Personality Variable," *Journal of Consulting and Clinical Psychology* 36, no. 1 (1971): 40–44.

52. A. Christopher and B. Schlenker, "The Protestant Work Ethic and Attributions of Responsibility: Applications of the Triangle Model," *Journal of Applied Social Psychology* 35, no. 7 (2006): 1502–15; J. L. Brown-Iannuzzi, E. Cooley, C. K. Marshburn et al., "Investigating the Interplay Between Race, Work Ethic Stereotypes, and Attitudes Toward Welfare Recipients and Policies," *Social Psychological and Personality Science* 12, no. 7 (2021): 1155–64.

53. R. Rusu, "The Protestant Work Ethic and Attitudes Toward Work," *Scientific Bulletin-Nicolae Balcescu Land Forces Academy* 23, no. 2 (2018): 112–17.

54. A. N. Christopher, P. Marek, and J. C. May, "The Protestant Work Ethic, Expectancy Violations, and Criminal Sentencing 1," *Journal of Applied Social Psychology* 33, no. 3 (2003): 522–35.

55. L. Rosenthal, S. R. Levy, and A. Moyer, "Protestant Work Ethic's Relation to Intergroup and Policy Attitudes: A Meta-Analytic Review," *European Journal of Social Psychology* 41, no. 7 (2011): 874–85.

56. J. W. McHoskey, "Factor Structure of the Protestant Work Ethic Scale," *Personality and Individual Differences* 17, no. 1 (1994): 49–52.

57. Those who were educated in medicine in the colonial Americas usually were trained under a loose apprenticeship model, combined with self-education via books and oral histories: T. McCulla. "Medicine in Colonial North America." Worlds of Change: Colonial North America at Harvard Library, November 19, 2016. https://colonialnorthamerica.library.harvard.edu/spotlight/cna/feature/medicine-in-colonial-north-america.

58. National Library of Medicine—National Institutes of Health. Accessed June 15, 2023. https://www.nlm.nih.gov/hmd/pdf/200years.pdf.

59. Those who were educated in medicine in the colonial Americas usually were trained under a loose apprenticeship model, combined with self-education via books and oral histories: McCulla, Theresa. "Medicine in Colonial North America." Worlds of Change: Colonial North America at Harvard Library, November 19, 2016. https://colonialnorthamerica.library.harvard.edu/spotlight/cna/feature/medicine-in-colonial-north-america.

60. D. E. Beauchamp, "Public Health as Social Justice," *Inquiry* 13, no. 1 (1976): 3–14.

61. Though the US military largely stopped dispensing free cigarettes to troops in the 1970s, they still allowed the tobacco industry to target service members and provide cigarettes to them directly until the end of the Gulf War. E. A. Smith and R. E. Malone, "'Everywhere the Soldier Will Be': Wartime Tobacco Promotion in the US Military," *American Journal of Public Health* 99, no. 9 (2009): 1595–1602, https://doi.org/10.2105/AJPH.2008.152983.

62. Beauchamp, "Public Health as Social Justice," 5.

63. R. N. Proctor, "The History of the Discovery of the Cigarette–Lung Cancer Link: Evidentiary Traditions, Corporate Denial, Global Toll," *Tobacco Control* 21 (2012): 87–91.

64. P. Mejia, L. Dorfman, A. Cheyne et al., "The Origins of Personal Responsibility Rhetoric in News Coverage of the Tobacco Industry," *American Journal of Public Health* 106, no. 6 (2014): 1048–51.

65. In the Cipollone case, the defense argued that not only was Rose Cipollone aware of the risks of tobacco products, but she also had access to cessation programs. Tobacco industry–funded smoking cessation programs are, unsurprisingly, tainted by their influence. See P. A. McDaniel, E. A. Lown, and R. E. Malone, "'It Doesn't Seem to Make Sense for a Company That Sells Cigarettes to Help Smokers Stop Using Them': A Case Study of Philip Morris's Involvement in Smoking Cessation." *PLOS One* 12, no. 8 (2017): e0183961, https://doi.org/10.1371/journal.pone.0183961.
    L. Bac. "Big Surprise: Tobacco Company Prevention Campaigns Don't Work; Maybe It . . ." Tobacco Free Kids, July 19, 2022. https://www.tobaccofreekids.org/assets/factsheets/0302.pdf.

66. C. White, J. L. Oliffe, and J. L. Bottorff, "From the Physician to the Marlboro Man: Masculinity, Health, and Cigarette Advertising in America, 1946–1964," *Men and Masculinities* 15, no. 5 (2012), 526–47.

67. Meijia et al., "The Origins of Personal Responsibility Rhetoric," identifies 1977 as the year this argument began to be made in earnest.

68. D. Janson. "Tobacco Lawyers Say Smoker Was Not Misled." The New York Times, June 3, 1988. https://www.nytimes.com/1988/06/03/nyregion/tobacco-lawyers-say-smoker-was-not-misled.html.

69. "RJR Chairman Gives Flip Answer." Spokesman.com, July 16, 2011. https://www.spokesman.com/stories/1996/apr/18/rjr-chairman-gives-flip-answer/.

70. Some social control strategies designed to discourage smoking can backfire by further marginalizing "residual smokers" who have less access to the resources necessary to quit. See D. M. Burns and K. E. Warner, "Smokers Who Have Not Quit: Is Cessation More Difficult and Should We Change Our Strategies?" *Those Who Continue to Smoke*, Smoking and Tobacco Control Monograph No. 15 (Bethesda, Md.: US Department of Health and Human Services, 2003).
    Many studies have observed that as anti-tobacco regulations pass, public stigma against smokers worsens. However, most of these studies, by virtue of taking advantage of the "natural experiment" of such laws' passage, cannot control for changes in the public discourse regarding tobacco that were happening simultaneously. For a review, see some of the following citations:
    R. J. Evans-Polce, J. M. Castaldelli-Maia, G. Schomerus et al., "The Downside of Tobacco Control? Smoking and Self-Stigma: A Systematic Review," *Social Science and Medicine* 145 (2015): 26–34;
    K. Bell, A. Salmon, M. Bowers, et al., "Smoking, Stigma and Tobacco 'Denormalization': Further Reflections on the Use of Stigma as a Public Health Tool," A Commentary on Social Science and Medicine's Stigma, Prejudice, Discrimination and Health Special Issue 67, no. 3, *Social Science and Medicine* 70, no. 6 (2010): 795–99; J. Pacheco, "Attitudinal Policy Feedback and Public Opinion: The Impact of Smoking Bans on Attitudes Towards Smokers, Secondhand Smoke, and Antismoking Policies," *Public Opinion Quarterly* 77, no. 3 (2013): 714–34.

71. J. Stuber and S. Galea, "Who Conceals Their Smoking Status from Their Health Care Provider?" *Nicotine and Tobacco Research* 11, no. 3 (2009): 303–7.

72. A. E. Karpyn, D. Riser, T. Tracy, et al., "The Changing Landscape of Food Deserts," *UNSCN Nutrition* 44 (2019): 46–53.

73. K. D. Brownell, R. Kersh, D. S. Ludwig et al. "Personal Responsibility and Obesity: A Constructive Approach to a Controversial Issue," *Health Affairs* (Millwood) 29, no. 3 (2010): 379-387.

74. Marion Nestle, "Food Lobbies, the Food Pyramid, and U.S. Nutrition Policy," *International Journal of Social Determinates of Health and Health Services* 23, no. 3 (1993): 483–96, doi:10.2190/32F2-2PFB-MEG7-8HPU.

75. J. Calderone. "Here's What the Term 'complete Breakfast' Actually Means." Business Insider. Accessed June 15, 2023. https://www.businessinsider.com/what-does-the-term-complete-breakfast-actually-mean-2015-8.

76. "Overweight Babies: 20 Years Later | Maury's Viral Vault | the Maury Show." YouTube, October 24, 2020. https://www.youtube.com/watch?v=vRkhkzlMyZI.

77. J. A. Sabin, M. Marini, and B. A. Nosek, "Implicit and Explicit Anti-Fat Bias Among a Large Sample of Medical Doctors by BMI, Race/Ethnicity and Gender," *PLOS One* 7, no. 11 (2012): e48448.

78. A. Ravary, M. W. Baldwin, and J. A. Bartz, "Shaping the Body Politic: Mass Media Fat-Shaming Affects Implicit Anti-Fat Attitudes," *Personality and Social Psychology Bulletin* 45, no. 11 (2019): 1580–89; B. J. Lawrence, D. Kerr, C. M. Pollard et al., "Weight Bias Among Health Care Professionals: A Systematic Review and Meta-Analysis," *Obesity* 29, no. 11 (2021): 1802–12.

79. R. L. Pearl, R. M. Puhl, and J. F. Dovidio, "Differential Effects of Weight Bias Experiences and Internalization on Exercise Among Women with Overweight and Obesity," *Journal of Health Psychology*, 20, no. 12 (2105): 1626–32.
    S. R. McDonough., "Weight stigma and motivation to exercise: exploring associations and constructs from the basic needs theory." (2018). *Electronic Theses and Dissertations.* Paper 3038. https://doi.org/10.18297/etd/3038

80. Union of Concerned Scientists, *Smoke, Mirrors, and Hot Air: How ExxonMobil Uses Big Tobacco's Tactics to Manufacture Uncertainty on Climate Science.* (Cambridge, MA: Union of Concerned Scientists, 2007).

81. G. Supran and N. Oreskes, "Rhetoric and Frame Analysis of ExxonMobil's Climate Change Communications," *One Earth* 4, no. 5 (2021): 696–719.

82. See K. Gorissen and B. Weijters, "The Negative Footprint Illusion: Perceptual Bias in Sustainable Food Consumption," *Journal of Environmental Psychology* 45 (2016): 50–65.

83. L. Esposito and L. L. Finley, "Beyond Gun Control: Examining Neoliberalism, Pro-Gun Politics and Gun Violence in the United States," *Theory in Action* 7, no. 2 (2014).

84. S. Kliff, "The NRA Wants an 'Active' Mental Illness Database. Thirty-Eight States Have That Now," *Washington Post*, Dec. 21, 2012.

85. "Mental Health and the Aurora Shooting: The Brian Lehrer Show." WNYC. Accessed June 15, 2023. http://www.wnyc.org/story/226661-mental-health-and-aurora-colorado-shooting/?utm_source=sharedUrl&utm_media=metatag&utm_campaign=sharedUrl.

86. K. Pickert and J. Cloud, "If You Think Someone Is Mentally Ill: Loughner's Six Warning Signs," *Time,* Jan. 11, 2011.

87. C. Exoo & C F. Exoo. "Elliot Rodger and the NRA Myth: How the Gun Lobby Scapegoats Mental Illness." Salon, May 28, 2014. https://www.salon.

com/2014/05/28/elliot_rodger_and_the_nra_myth_how_the_gun_lobby_
scapegoats_mental_illness/.

88. See for example this *Daily Mail* article, which misgenders the shooter and
describes him as a "high-functioning" Autistic with a "cartoon-like" point of
view: Dailymail.Com, Aneeta Bhole For. "Trans Nashville School Shooter
Appears in Eerie College Graduation Video Smiling." Daily Mail Online,
March 29, 2023. https://www.dailymail.co.uk/news/article-11911373/Trans-
Nashville-school-shooter-appears-eerie-college-graduation-video-smiling.html.

89. G. Thrush. "At N.R.A. Convention, the Blame Is on 'evil,' Not Guns." *The New
York Times,* May 28, 2022. https://www.nytimes.com/2022/05/28/us/politics/
nra-convention-guns.html.

90. G. Thornicroft, "Danger or Disinformation: The Facts About Violence and
Mental Illness," in *Shunned: Discrimination Against People with Mental Illness*
(Oxford, UK: Oxford University Press, 2006), 125–49.

91. V. Rossa-Roccor, P. Schmid, and T. Steinert, "Victimization of People with
Severe Mental Illness Outside and Within the Mental Health Care System:
Results on Prevalence and Risk Factors from a Multicenter Study," *Frontiers in
Psychiatry* 11 (2020): 932.

92. H. Stuart, "Violence and Mental Illness: An Overview," *World Psychiatry:
Official Journal of the World Psychiatric Association (WPA)* 2, no. 2 (2003): 121–24;
G. Thornicroft, "People with Severe Mental Illness as the Perpetrators and
Victims of Violence: Time for a New Public Health Approach," *Lancet Public
Health* 5, no. 2: (2020): e72—e73.

93. S. Griffiths, C. Allison, R. Kenny et al., "The Vulnerability Experiences
Quotient (VEQ): A Study of Vulnerability, Mental Health and Life
Satisfaction in Autistic Adults," *Autism Research* 12, no. 10 (2019): 1516–28.

94. L. Rabinovich, "A Pipeline of Unscrupulous Practices: Qualitative Study of
Attitudes Toward the Social Security Disability Program," *Journal of Disability
Policy Studies* 31, no. 3 (2020): 173–80.

95. N. J. Sasson, D. J. Faso, J. Nugent et al., "Neurotypical Peers Are Less Willing
to Interact with Those with Autism Based on Thin Slice Judgments," *Scientific
Reports* 7 (2017): 40700, https://doi.org/10.1038/srep40700.

96. "On the inside: Reply All." Gimlet. Accessed June 15, 2023. https://
gimletmedia.com/shows/reply-all/posts/on-the-inside.

3. The Values of Systemic Shame

1. Betancourt, Bianca. "Lizzo Doesn't Care What You Think about Her Smoothie
Cleanse." *Harper's BAZAAR,* November 2, 2021. https://www.harpersbazaar.
com/celebrity/latest/a34974814/lizzo-shuts-down-diet-critics-on-instagram.

2. Twitter. Accessed June 15, 2023. https://twitter.com/HutchLeah.

3. Betancourt, Bianca. "Lizzo Doesn't Care What You Think about Her Smoothie
Cleanse." Harper's BAZAAR, November 2, 2021. https://www.harpersbazaar.
com/celebrity/latest/a34974814/lizzo-shuts-down-diet-critics-on-instagram.

4. Bailey, Laquesha. "Does Lizzo Promote Obesity, or Do We Just Hate Fat
Bodies?" Medium, September 1, 2021. https://aninjusticemag.com/does-lizzo-
promote-obesity-or-do-we-just-hate-fat-bodies-
cf1018297dd9?gi=dd0af8105c40.

5. Esmonde, Katelyn. "What Celeb Trainer Jillian Michaels Got Wrong about Lizzo and Body Positivity." Vox, January 15, 2020. https://www.vox.com/culture/2020/1/15/21060692/lizzo-jillian-michaels-body-positivity-backlash.

6. Hosie, Rachel. "A Plus-Sized Woman Criticized Slimmer Influencers for 'taking up Too Much Space' in the Body Positivity Sphere, and It Sparked a Huge Debate." Insider, May 28, 2020. https://www.insider.com/plus-size-woman-criticizes-slim-influencers-too-much-space-body-positivity-2020-5.

7. Valens, Ana. "On Leaving Twitter." On Leaving Twitter—by Ana Valens, February 20, 2021. https://nsfw.substack.com/p/on-leaving-twitter?s=r.

8. A. N. Cooke and A. G. Halberstadt, "Adultification, Anger Bias, and Adults' Different Perceptions of Black and White Children," *Cognition and Emotion* 35, no. 7 (2021): 1416–22.

9. Rebecca Epstein, Jamilia J. Blake, and Thalia González, "Girlhood Interrupted: The Erasure of Black Girls' Childhood" (Washington, DC: Center of Poverty and Inequality, Georgetown Law, 2017).

10. S. C. Wymer, C. M. Corbin, and A. P. Williford, "The Relation Between Teacher and Child Race, Teacher Perceptions of Disruptive Behavior, and Exclusionary Discipline in Preschool," *Journal of School Psychology* 90 (2022): 33–42.

11. A. K. Nuru and C. E. Arendt, "Not So Safe a Space: Women Activists of Color's Responses to Racial Microaggressions by White Women Allies," *Southern Communication Journal* 84, no. 2 (2019): 85–98.

12. Cuddy, Amy. "Your Body Language May Shape Who You Are." Amy Cuddy: Your body language may shape who you are | TED Talk. Accessed June 15, 2023. https://www.ted.com/talks/amy_cuddy_your_body_language_may_shape_who_you_are/transcript?language=en.

13. Simmons, Joe, and Uri Simonsohn. "Power Posing: Reassessing the Evidence behind the Most Popular TED Talk." Data Colada, February 12, 2020. http://datacolada.org/37.

14. Loncar, Tom. "A Decade of Power Posing: Where Do We Stand?" BPS, June 8, 2021. https://thepsychologist.bps.org.uk/volume-34/june-2021/decade-power-posing-where-do-we-stand#:~:text=Despite%20this%20widening%20embrace%2C%20deeper,posing%20would%20not%20go%20away.

15. Singal, Jesse. "How Should We Talk about Amy Cuddy, Death Threats, and the Replication Crisis?" The Cut, April 25, 2017. https://www.thecut.com/2017/04/amy-cuddy-death-threats.html.

16. Dominus, Susan. "When the Revolution Came for Amy Cuddy." *The New York Times*, October 18, 2017. https://www.nytimes.com/2017/10/18/magazine/when-the-revolution-came-for-amy-cuddy.html.

17. Corker, Katie. Quote from Amy Cuddy at the annual meeting of the Midwestern Psychological Association 2017 on Twitter, April 20, 2017. https://twitter.com/katiecorker/status/855155054713688064?ref_src=twsrc%5Etfw%7Ctwcamp%5Etweetembed%7Ctwterm%5E855155054713688064%7Ctwgr%5E%7Ctwcon%5Es1_c10&ref_url=https%3A%2F%2Fwww.thecut.com%2F2017%2F04%2Famy-cuddy-death-threats.html.

18. L. K. John, G. Loewenstein, and D. Prelec, "Measuring the Prevalence of Questionable Research Practices with Incentives for Truth Telling," *Psychological Science* 23, no. 5 (2012): 524–32.

19. Dominus, Susan. "When the Revolution Came for Amy Cuddy." *The New York*

Times, October 18, 2017. https://www.nytimes.com/2017/10/18/magazine/when-the-revolution-came-for-amy-cuddy.html.

20. I have written about this previously in response to Jesse Singal's book on the replication crisis. See Price, Devon. Thread by @drdevonprice on Thread Reader App—Thread Reader App. Accessed June 15, 2023. https://threadreaderapp.com/thread/1383475714494636035.html.

21. https://www.vox.com/culture/2016/11/17/13636156/safety-pins-backlash-trump-brexit.

22. E. Mullen and B. Monin, "Consistency Versus Licensing Effects of Past Moral Behavior," *Annual Review of Psychology* 67, no. 1 (2016): 363–85.

23. I. Blanken, N. Van De Ven, and M. Zeelenberg, "A Meta-Analytic Review of Moral Licensing," *Personality and Social Psychology Bulletin* 41, no. 4: (2015): 540–58.

24. A. M. Burger, J. Schuler, and E. Eberling, "Guilty Pleasures: Moral Licensing in Climate-Related Behavior," *Global Environmental Change* 72 (2022): 102415.

25. B. Monin and D. T. Miller, "Moral Credentials and the Expression of Prejudice," *Journal of Personality and Social Psychology* 81 (2001): 33–43, doi:10.1037//0022 3514.81.1.33.

26. Cook, Grace. "The Cotton Tote Crisis." *The New York Times,* August 24, 2021. https://www.nytimes.com/2021/08/24/style/cotton-totes-climate-crisis.html.

27. Carlson, Jen. "The 'I'm Not a Plastic Bag' Craze Hits New York." Gothamist. Accessed June 15, 2023. https://gothamist.com/arts-entertainment/the-im-not-a-plastic-bag-craze-hits-new-york.

28. Darby, Seyward. "The Problem with White Feminism." Electric Literature, January 20, 2021. https://electricliterature.com/koa-beck-white-feminism-book.

29. Ginzberg, Lori D. "For Stanton, All Women Were Not Created Equal." NPR, July 13, 2011. https://www.npr.org/2011/07/13/137681070/for-stanton-all-women-were-not-created-equal.

      Fields-White, Monee. "The Root: How Racism Tainted Women's Suffrage." NPR, March 25, 2011. https://www.npr.org/2011/03/25/134849480/the-root-how-racism-tainted-womens-suffrage.

30. Combahee River Collective, "A Black Feminist Statement,". 210–18.

31. Michele Wallace, "A Black Feminist's Search for Sisterhood," *Village Voice,* July 28, 1975, pp. 6–7.

32. T. Shefer and S. R. Munt, "A Feminist Politics of Shame: Shame and Its Contested Possibilities," *Feminism and Psychology* <I think this is the correct journal?> 20, no. 2 (2019).

33. B. Benoit, L. Goldberg, and M. Campbell-Yeo, "Infant Feeding and Maternal Guilt: The Application of a Feminist Phenomenological Framework to Guide Clinician Practices in Breast Feeding Promotion," *Midwifery* 34, (2016): 58–65.

34. Á. Jóhannsdóttir, "Body Hair and Its Entanglement: Shame, Choice and Resistance in Body Hair Practices Among Young Icelandic People," *Feminism and Psychology* 29, no. 2 (2019): 195–213.

35. Jaclyn Griffith, "From Dreamers to Dangerous Women: A Shift from Abstinence and Hypersexuality to Sexuality with Shame in Pop Music Listened to by Tween Girls in 2006 and 2016" (Honors College thesis, Pace University, 2017).

36. Z. Feng and K. Savani, "Covid-19 Created a Gender Gap in Perceived Work Productivity and Job Satisfaction: Implications for Dual-Career Parents Working from Home" *Gender in Management: An International Journal* (2020).

37. L. A. Whiley, H. Sayer, and M. Juanchich, "Motherhood and Guilt in a Pandemic: Negotiating the "New" Normal with a Feminist Identity," *Gender, Work and Organization* (2021).

38. See for example May 8, 2017. https://drdemonprince.tumblr.com/post/160431413844/bopcities-halfbrainedaltgirl.

    Accessed June 15, 2023. https://allmymetaphors.tumblr.com/post/138555896479/my-whole-problem-with-the-i-do-makeup-for-me-im.

    Accessed July 23, 2017. https://justsomeantifas.tumblr.com/post/163306370029.

    Accessed June 15, 2023. https://no.tumblr.com/post/149710698024.

39. Defino, Jessica. "Is This the End of the Manicure?" *The New York Times*, November 5, 2020. https://www.nytimes.com/2020/11/05/style/self-care-is-this-the-end-of-the-manicure.html.

40. "At Least 7 Arrested at Protest near Loyola University." NBC Chicago, August 29, 2020. https://www.nbcchicago.com/news/local/at-least-7-arrested-at-protest-near-loyola-university/2331084.

41. "Loyola Students Walk out of Classes over Basketball Incident." RogersEdge Reporter, March 15, 2018. https://rogersedgereporter.com/2018/03/15/loyolas-black-cultural-center-stages-walk-out.

42. "Citing a 'toxic Atmosphere,' a Black Admissions Employee Resigns from Loyola University, Prompting a Discrimination Probe and Calls for Racial Justice on Campus." *Chicago Tribune*. Accessed June 15, 2023. https://www.chicagotribune.com/news/ct-loyola-university-chicago-racism-complaint-20201015-v4jnl55c5bgbjp2faokehw5itq-story.html.

43. Nance-Nash, Sheryl. "How Corporate Diversity Initiatives Trap Workers of Colour." BBC Worklife, February 25, 2022. https://www.bbc.com/worklife/article/20200826-how-corporate-diversity-initiatives-trap-workers-of-colour.

44. Humphrey, Nicole M. "Racialized emotional labor: An unseen burden in the public sector." Administration & Society 54, no. 4 (2022): 741-758.

45. C. Linder, S. J. Quaye, A. C. Lange et al., "'A Student Should Have the Privilege of Just Being a Student': Student Activism as Labor," *Review of Higher Education* 42, no. 5 (2019): 37–62.

46. Miller, Jennifer. "Their Bosses Asked Them to Lead Diversity Reviews. Guess Why." *The New York Times*, October 12, 2020. https://www.nytimes.com/2020/10/12/business/corporate-diversity-black-employees.html.

47. Smith, Ember, and Richard V. Reeves. "SAT Math Scores Mirror and Maintain Racial Inequity." Brookings, March 9, 2022. https://www.brookings.edu/blog/up-front/2020/12/01/sat-math-scores-mirror-and-maintain-racial-inequity.

48. Solotaroff, Paul. "The Untouchables: An Investigation into the Violence of the Chicago Police." *Rolling Stone*, August 20, 2021. https://www.rollingstone.com/culture/culture-features/chicago-police-racism-violence-history-1088559;

    Fry, Paige. Report: Race-based disparities found in Chicago Police Force stops, use of force. . Accessed June 15, 2023. https://www.chicagotribune.com/news/breaking/ct-oig-report-race-disparity-use-of-force-chicago-police-20220301-l6sqedbwvbhkfccic2r5qzzjby-story.html.

49. "Why Diversity Programs Fail." Harvard Business Review, June 12, 2023. https://hbr.org/2016/07/why-diversity-programs-fail.

50. Specific, short-term goals tend to be more motivating than long-term or abstract ones: S. G. Wallace and J. Etkin, "How Goal Specificity Shapes Motivation: A Reference Points Perspective," *Journal of Consumer Research* 44, no. 5 (2018): 1033–51.

51. Behrmann, Savannah. "House Committee Approves Bill to Study Slavery Reparations for First Time." *USA Today,* April 15, 2021. https://www.usatoday.com/story/news/politics/2021/04/14/house-committee-hold-historic-vote-study-slave-reparations/7210967002/.

52. For a longer list of potential values, see this list from the acceptance and commitment therapy practitioner Russ Harris: A quick look at your values. Accessed June 16, 2023. https://ag.purdue.edu/department/arge/_docs/covid-docs/values_checklist_-_russ_harris_a.pdf.

4. Why Shame Doesn't Work

1. For a quick primer on why the D.A.R.E. program proved so ineffective, see Matt Berry, "Does the New DARE Program Work?" American Addiction Centers, November 10, 2022. https://americanaddictioncenters.org/blog/new-dare-program-work.

2. See this pithily titled piece in the *Journal of the American Medical Association*: B. Vastag, "GAO: DARE Does Not Work," *JAMA* 289, no. 5 (2003): 539.

3. S. Birkeland, E. Murphy-Graham, and C. Weiss, "Good Reasons for Ignoring Good Evaluation: The Case of the Drug Abuse Resistance Education (DARE) Program," *Evaluation and Program Planning*, 28, no. 3: 247–56.

4. McKay, Tom. "The 5 Big Lies That D.A.R.E. Told You about Drugs." Mic, July 3, 2014. https://www.mic.com/articles/92675/the-5-big-lies-that-d-a-r-e-told-you-about-drugs.

5. Lilienfeld, Scott O. "Why 'Just Say No' Doesn't Work." *Scientific American,* January 1, 2014. https://www.scientificamerican.com/article/why-just-say-no-doesnt-work/.

6. N. L. Henderson and W. W. Dressler, "Medical Disease or Moral Defect? Stigma Attribution and Cultural Models of Addiction Causality in a University Population," *Culture, Medicine, and Psychiatry* 41, no. 4 (2017): 480–98.

7. W. Pan and H. Bai, "A Multivariate Approach to a Meta-Analytic Review of the Effectiveness of the DARE Program," *International Journal of Environmental Research and Public Health* 6, no. 1, (2009): 267–77.

8. Megan Walter, "Inherent Racism of the D.A.R.E. Program" (Coastal Carolina University, Undergraduate Research Competition,, 2021), 4, https://digitalcommons.coastal.edu/ugrc/2021/fullconference/4.

9. K. L. Ferguson, "The Crack Baby: Children Fight the War on Drugs," in *Eighties People* (New York: Palgrave Macmillan, 37–56).

10. D. P. Rosenbaum, "Just Say No to DARE," *Criminology and Public Policy* 6, (2007): 815.

11. 11 "D.A.R.E. America Regions." D.A.R.E. America. Accessed June 15, 2023. https://dare.org/where-is-d-a-r-e/.

12. A. Petrosino, C. Turpin-Petrosino, and J. Buehler, "'Scared Straight' and Other Juvenile Awareness Programs for Preventing Juvenile Delinquency," *Cochrane Database System Review* issue 2 (2002): CD002796.

13. "Programs like D.A.R.E. And Scared Straight Don't Work. Why Do States Keep Funding Them?" 2018. Governing. May 21, 2018. https://www.governing.com/archive/gov-dare-drug-programs.html.

14. Gilna, Derek. "Scared Straight" Programs are Counterproductive | Prison Legal News. Accessed June 16, 2023. https://www.prisonlegalnews.org/news/2016/jun/3/scared-straight-programs-are-counterproductive/.

15. Though obviously a person can have a disordered relationship to food, there is no such thing as "food addiction" or even "sugar addiction" in the biochemical sense. You might as well accuse a person gasping for air of suffering from an "oxygen addiction."

16. Allison, Michelle. "Food Addiction, Natural Rewards, and Self-Fulfilling Prophecies." 2012. October 31, 2012. https://www.fatnutritionist.com/index.php/food-addiction-natural-rewards-and-self-fulfilling-prophecies.

17. Scritchfield, Rebecca. "Why Fear of 'Sugar Addiction' May Be More Toxic than Sugar Is." *SELF,* May 3, 2018. https://www.self.com/story/why-fear-of-sugar-addiction-may-be-more-toxic-than-sugar-is.

18. T. A. Khan and J. L. Sievenpiper, "Controversies About Sugars: Results from Systematic Reviews and Meta-Analyses on Obesity, Cardiometabolic Disease and Diabetes," *European Journal of Nutrition* 55 (2016): 25–43, doi: 10.1007/s00394-016-1345-3..

19. M. L. Westwater, P. C. Fletcher, and H. Ziauddeen, "Sugar Addiction: the State of the Science, *European Journal of Nutrition* 55 (2016): 55–69, doi: 10.1007/s00394-016-1229-6..

20. C. Zunker, C. B. Peterson, R. D. Crosby et al.,. "Ecological Momentary Assessment of Bulimia Nervosa: Does Dietary Restriction Predict Binge Eating?" *Behaviour Research and Therapy* 49, no. 10 (2011): 714–17; E. Stice, K. Davis, N. P. Miller et al., "Fasting Increases Risk for Onset of Binge Eating and Bulimic Pathology: A 5-Year Prospective Study," *Journal of Abnormal Psychology* 117, no. 4 (2008): 941–46, https://doi.org/10.1037/a0013644.

21. Allison, Michelle. "Food Addiction, Natural Rewards, and Self-Fulfilling Prophecies." 2012. October 31, 2012. https://www.fatnutritionist.com/index.php/food-addiction-natural-rewards-and-self-fulfilling-prophecies.

22. A. J. Hill, "Does Dieting Make You Fat?" *British Journal of Nutrition* 92, no. S1 (2004): S15–18.

23. T. L. Guertin and A. J. Conger, "Mood and Forbidden Foods' Influence on Perceptions of Binge Eating," *Addictive Behavior* 24, no. 2 (1999): 175–93, doi: 10.1016/s0306-4603(98)00049-5.

24. G. M. Camilleri, C. Méjean, F. Bellisle et al., "Intuitive Eating Is Inversely Associated with Body Weight Status in the General Population-Based Nutrinet-Santé Study," *Obesity* 24, no. 5 (2016): 1154–61.

25. A. J. Crum, W. R. Corbin, K. D. Brownell et al., Mind Over Milkshakes: Mindsets, Not Just Nutrients, Determine Ghrelin Response," *Health Psychology* 30, no. 4 (2011): 424–31, doi: 10.1037/a0023467.

26. K. M. Baldwin, J. R. Baldwin, and T. Ewald, "The Relationship Among Shame,

Guilt, and Self-Efficacy," *American Journal of Psychotherapy* 60, no. 1 (2006): 1–21.

27. A. Archer, "Shame and Diabetes Self-Management," *Practical Diabetes* 31, no. 3 (2014): 102–6.

28. K. Winkley, C.. Evwierhoma, S. A. Amiel et al., "Patient Explanations for Non-attendance at Structured Diabetes Education Sessions for Newly Diagnosed Type 2 Diabetes: A Qualitative Study," *Diabetic Medicine* 32, no. 1 (2015): 120–28.

    Shame and stigma surrounding diabetes also keeps patients from having healthy, supportive relationships to others, which in turn worsens their health outcomes: L. M. Jaacks, W. Liu, L. Ji et al., "Type 1 Diabetes Stigma in China: A Call to End the Devaluation of Individuals Living with a Manageable Chronic Disease," *Diabetes Research and Clinical Practice* 107, no. 2 (2015): 306–7.

29. J. M. Bowles, L. R. Smith, M. L. Mittal et al., "'I Wanted to Close the Chapter Completely . . . and I Feel Like That [Carrying Naloxone] Would Keep It Open a Little Bit': Refusal to Carry Naloxone Among Newly-Abstinent Opioid Users and 12-Step Identity," *International Journal of Drug Policy* 94 (2021): 103200.

30. T. Kageyama, "Views on Suicide Among Middle-Aged and Elderly Populations in Japan: Their Association with Demographic Variables and Feeling Shame in Seeking Help," *Psychiatry and Clinical Neurosciences* 66, no. 2 (2012): 105–12.

31. Hauser, Debra. 2019. "Teens Deserve More than Abstinence-Only Education." AMA Journal of Ethics 7 (10): 710–15. https://doi.org/10.1001/virtualmentor.2005.7.10.oped2-0510.

32. J. Radcliffe, N. Doty, L. A. Hawkins et al., "Stigma and Sexual Health Risk in HIV-Positive African American Young Men Who Have Sex with Men," *AIDS Patient Care and STDs* 24, no. 8 (2010): 493–99.

33. D. Grace, J. Jollimore, P. MacPherson et al.,"The Pre-Exposure Prophylaxis-Stigma Paradox: Learning from Canada's First Wave of PrEP Users," *AIDS Patient Care and STDs* 32, no. 1 (2018): 24–30.

34. T. Kirkland and W. A. Cunningham, "Neural Basis of Affect and Emotion," *Wiley Interdisciplinary Reviews: Cognitive Science* 2, no. 6 (2011): 656–65.

35. Shuxia Yao, Weihua Zhao, Yayuan Geng et al., "Oxytocin Facilitates Approach Behavior to Positive Social Stimuli via Decreasing Anterior Insula Activity," *International Journal of Neuropsychopharmacology* 21, no. 10 (2018): 918–25, https://doi.org/10.1093/ijnp/pyy068,

    Geng, Yayuan, Weihua Zhao, Feng Zhou, Xiaole Ma, Shuxia Yao, Rene Hurlemann, Benjamin Becker, and Keith M. Kendrick. "Oxytocin Enhancement of Emotional Empathy: Generalization across Cultures and Effects on Amygdala Activity." Frontiers, July 9, 2018. https://www.frontiersin.org/articles/10.3389/fnins.2018.00512/full.

36. S. Marshall-Pescini, F. S. Schaebs, A. Gaugg et al., "The Role of Oxytocin in the Dog–Owner Relationship," *Animals* 9, no. 10 (2019): 792;

    J. Bick, M. Dozier, K. Bernard et al., "Foster Mother–Infant Bonding: Associations Between Foster Mothers' Oxytocin Production, Electrophysiological Brain Activity, Feelings of Commitment, and Caregiving Quality," *Child Development* 84, no. 3 (2013): 826–40.

37. C. K. De Dreu, L. L. Greer, G. A. Van Kleef et al., "Oxytocin Promotes Human

Ethnocentrism," *Proceedings of the National Academy of Sciences* 108, no. 4 (2011):1262–66; F. Sheng, Y. Liu, B. Zhou et al., "Oxytocin Modulates the Racial In-Group Bias in Neural Responses to Others' Suffering," *Biological Psychology* 92 (2013): 380–86; S. Luo, B. Li, Y. Maet al., "Oxytocin Receptor Gene and Racial Ingroup Bias in Empathy-Related Brain Activity," *NeuroImage*, 110 (2015): 22–31.

38. A. J. Elliot, "The Hierarchical Model of Approach-Avoidance Motivation," *Motivation and Emotion* 30, no. 2 (2006): 111–16.

39. O. Harari-Dahan and A. Bernstein, "A General Approach-Avoidance Hypothesis of Oxytocin: Accounting for Social and Non-Social Effects of Oxytocin," *Neuroscience and Biobehavioral Reviews* 47 (2014): 506–19; A. H. Kemp and A. J. Guastella, "The Role of Oxytocin in Humans Affect a Novel Hypothesis," *Current Directions in Psychological Science* 20, no. 4 (2011): 222–31.

40. P. Gilbert and S. Allan, "The Role of Defeat and Entrapment (Arrested Flight) in Depression: An Exploration of an Evolutionary View," *Psychological Medicine* 28, no. 3 (1998): 585–98.

41. Avoidance-based emotions also tend to elicit defensive, pacifying behaviors that help protect people when they are low in social status: P. Gilbert, "The Relationship of Shame, Social Anxiety and Depression: The Role of the Evaluation of Social Rank," *Clinical Psychology and Psychotherapy: An International Journal of Theory & Practice* 7, no. 3 (2000): 174–89.

    See also the end of the Still Face experiment: E. Z. Tronick, M. K. Weinberg, and K. L. Olson, "Stability of Infant Coping with the Still-Face," paper presented at the International Conference on Infant Studies (Toronto, Ontario, Canada, 2002).

42. Some example motives and behaviors listed here have been adapted from Peter Kindness, Judith Masthoff, and Chris Mellish, "Designing Emotional Support Messages Tailored to Stressors," *International Journal of Human-Computer Studies* 97 (2016): 1-22. 10.1016/j.ijhcs.2016.07.010.

43. You can watch an infant undergo the Still Face experiment here: Boston, UMass. 2010. "Developmental Sciences at UMass Boston." YouTube. https://www.youtube.com/watch?v=vmE3NfB_HhE.

44. G. Kaufman, *The Psychology of Shame* (New York: Springer, 1989).

45. M. E. Kemeny, T. L. Gruenewald, and S. S. Dickerson, "Shame as the Emotional Response to Threat to the Social Self: Implications for Behavior, Physiology, and Health," *Psychological Inquiry* 15, 2 (2004): 153–60.

46. N. Derakshan, M. W. Eysenck, and L. B. Myers, "Emotional Information Processing in Repressors: The Vigilance–Avoidance Theory," *Cognition and Emotion*, 21, no. 8 (2007): 1585–614.

47. J. P. Tangney, D. Mashek, and J. Stuewig, "Shame, Guilt, and Embarrassment: Will the Real Emotion Please Stand Up?" *Psychological Inquiry* 16, no. 1 (2005): 44–48.

48. Adrienne Rich, "Compulsory Heterosexuality and Lesbian Existence," *Signs: Journal of Women in Culture and Society* 5, no. 4 (Summer 1980): 631–60, doi:10.1086/493756.

    A more recent foundational text on compulsory heterosexuality is this anonymously and collaboratively written document that has been passed around online: "Am I a Lesbian?" Am I a Lesbian Masterdoc. Accessed June 16, 2023.

https://docs.google.com/document/d/e/2PACX-1vT3f5IIzt5PG-M7G9_Z
-gjY4gZaiUneTdMlYrFAcdBGcJo0-N-RDQcj2JfxOaBTxKa6J_DiDQN
gqVpg/pub.

49. Shearling, Lois. "A Guide to Compulsory Heterosexuality." 2021. *Cosmopolitan.* July 22, 2021. https://www.cosmopolitan.com/uk/love-sex/relationships/a37099748/compulsory-heterosexuality.

50. The TV Tropes page for the "Psycho Lesbian" trope is a treasure trove of examples from all kinds of media forms: "Psycho Lesbian." n.d. TV Tropes. https://tvtropes.org/pmwiki/pmwiki.php/Main/PsychoLesbian.

51. A. Martos, S. Nezhad, and I. H. Meyer, "Variations in Sexual Identity Milestones Among Lesbians, Gay Men, and Bisexuals," *Sexuality Research and Social Policy: Journal of the National Sexual Research Center* 12, no. 1 (2015): 24–33, https://doi.org/10.1007/s13178-014-0167-4.

52. Trans women who are attracted to women have long been portrayed as perverts and villains in the media; think of the murderous Buffalo Bill in *Silence of the Lambs*, or the "cross-dressing" murderer in J. K. Rowling's *Troubled Blood*:
    Haynes, Suyin. "Transgender Controversy over Rowling's 'Troubled Blood' Book." *Time,* September 15, 2020. https://time.com/5888999/jk-rowling-troubled-blood-transphobia-authors/.

53. Wynn, Natalie. "Transcripts." ContraPoints, May 28, 2022. https://www.contrapoints.com/transcripts/shame.

54. "My Auntie Buffalo Bill: The Unavoidable Transmisogyny of Silence of the Lambs." 2016. Feministing. March 10, 2016. http://feministing.com/2016/03/10/my-auntie-buffalo-bill-the-unavoidable-transmisogyny-of-silence-of-the-lambs.

55. "Unsettling Gender Reveal." n.d. TV Tropes. https://tvtropes.org/pmwiki/pmwiki.php/Main/UnsettlingGenderReveal.

56. M. E. Newcomb, R. Hill, K. Buehler et al., "High Burden of Mental Health Problems, Substance Use, Violence, and Related Psychosocial Factors in Transgender, Non-Binary, and Gender Diverse Youth and Young Adults," *Archives of Sexual Behavior* 49, no. 2 (2020): 645–59; A. Reis, S. Sperandei, P. G. C. de Carvalho et al., "A Cross-Sectional Study of Mental Health and Suicidality Among Trans Women in São Paulo, Brazil," *BMC Psychiatry* 21, no. 1 (2021): 1–13;
    R. D. M. R. Rafael, E. M. Jalil, P. M. Luz et al., "Prevalence and Factors Associated with Suicidal Behavior Among Trans Women in Rio de Janeiro, Brazil," *PLOS One* 16, no. 10 (2021): e0259074;
    S. L. Budge, J. L. Thai, E. A. Tebbe et al., "The Intersection of Race, Sexual Orientation, Socioeconomic Status, Trans Identity, and Mental Health Outcomes," *Counseling Psychologist* 44, no. 7 (2016): 1025–49.

57. There never was a thread devoted to me on Kiwifarms, but there was one dedicated to Natalie Wynn, as well as numerous trans people that I know in real life. In some of those threads, my own life and identity would come up, and be subjected to all kinds of speculation and insult. Many people I know have endured far worse than that.

58. Jennifer Jacquet, *Is Shame Necessary? New Uses for an Old Tool* (New York: Vintage, 2016), 4–5.

59. Ebersole, Rene. "How 'Dolphin Safe' Is Canned Tuna, Really?" 2021. Animals.

March 10, 2021. https://www.nationalgeographic.com/animals/article/how-dolphin-safe-is-canned-tuna.

60. Gutierrez, Pamela. "Greenwashing—as Recycling." n.d. Recycling.as.ucsb.edu. Accessed June 16, 2023. https://recycling.as.ucsb.edu/2021/02/23/greenwashing.

61. "Recycling Was a Lie—a Big Lie—to Sell More Plastic, Industry Experts Say | CBC Documentaries." CBCnews, October 8, 2020. https://www.cbc.ca/documentaries/the-passionate-eye/recycling-was-a-lie-a-big-lie-to-sell-more-plastic-industry-experts-say-1.5735618#:~:text=Recycling%20logo%20was%20used%20as%20a%20green%20marketing%20tool%2C%20says%20industry%20expert&text=Most%20consumers%20might%20have%20assumed,ended%20up%20in%20a%20landfill.

62. N. Landry, R. Gifford, T. L. Milfont et al., "Learned Helplessness Moderates the Relationship Between Environmental Concern and Behavior," *Journal of Environmental Psychology* 55 (2018): 18–22.

63. Causing, as some social psychologists deem it, "morally destructive shame." E. Aaltola, "Defensive over Climate Change? Climate Shame as a Method of Moral Cultivation," *Journal of Agricultural and Environmental Ethics* 34, no. 1 (2021): 1–23.

64. Solnit, Rebecca. 2021. "Big Oil Coined 'Carbon Footprints' to Blame Us for Their Greed. Keep Them on the Hook | Rebecca Solnit." *The Guardian.* August 23, 2021. https://www.theguardian.com/commentisfree/2021/aug/23/big-oil-coined-carbon-footprints-to-blame-us-for-their-greed-keep-them-on-the-hook.

65. Yoder, Kate. 2020. "Why Do Oil Companies Care so Much about Your Carbon Footprint?" Grist. August 26, 2020. https://grist.org/energy/footprint-fantasy.

66. White, Katherine, David Hardisty, and Rishad Habib. 2019. "The Elusive Green Consumer." Harvard Business Review. July 2019. https://hbr.org/2019/07/the-elusive-green-consumer.

67. R. K. Mallett, "Eco-Guilt Motivates Eco-Friendly Behavior," *Ecopsychology* 4, no. 3 (2012): 223–31.

68. T. H. Baek and S. Yoon, "Guilt and Shame: Environmental Message Framing Effects," *Journal of Advertising* 46, no. 3 (2017): 440–53; C. T. Chang, "Are Guilt Appeals a Panacea in Green Advertising? The Right Formula of Issue Proximity and Environmental Consciousness," *International Journal of Advertising* 31, no. 4 (2012): 741–71; S. Ha and S. Kwon, "Spillover from Past Recycling to Green Apparel Shopping Behavior: The Role of Environmental Concern and Anticipated Guilt," *Fashion and Textiles* 3, no. 1 (2016): 16; R. K. Mallett, "Eco-Guilt Motivates Eco-Friendly Behavior," *Ecopsychology* 4, no. 3 (2012): 223–31.

69. Even when the math doesn't really work out in their favor: For example, people believe the environmental impact of eating a hamburger plus an organic apple is less than the impact of just eating the hamburger. K. Gorissen and B. Weijters, "The Negative Footprint Illusion: Perceptual Bias in Sustainable Food Consumption," *Journal of Environmental Psychoogy* 45 (2016): 50–65, doi: 10.1016/j.jenvp.2015.11.009.
    For a more in depth discussion, see P. Sörqvist and L. Langeborg, "Why People Harm the Environment Although They Try to Treat It Well: An

Evolutionary-Cognitive Perspective on Climate Compensation," *Frontiers in Psychology* 10 (2019): 348.

70. S. E. Fredericks, "Online Confessions of Eco-Guilt," *Journal for the Study of Religion, Nature and Culture* 8, no. 1: (2014).

71. Chan, Emily. "Don't Let 'Eco-Guilt' Stop You from Taking Action." n.d. *British Vogue.* https://www.vogue.co.uk/arts-and-lifestyle/article/eco-guilt.

72. Solnit, Rebecca. 2021. "Big Oil Coined 'Carbon Footprints' to Blame Us for Their Greed. Keep Them on the Hook | Rebecca Solnit." The Guardian. August 23, 2021. https://www.theguardian.com/commentisfree/2021/aug/23/big-oil-coined-carbon-footprints-to-blame-us-for-their-greed-keep-them-on-the-hook.

73. Sewell, Christina. 2020. "Removing the Meat Subsidy: Our Cognitive Dissonance around Animal Agriculture." JIA SIPA. February 11, 2020. https://jia.sipa.columbia.edu/removing-meat-subsidy-our-cognitive-dissonance-around-animal-agriculture.

74. Accessed June 16, 2023. https://www.ceres.org/resources/reports/food-emissions-50-company-benchmark.

75. Guillot, Louise. "How Recycling Is Killing the Planet." 2020. POLITICO. September 16, 2020. https://www.politico.eu/article/recycling-killing-the-planet.

76. Grandoni, Dino, and Scott Clement. "Americans like Green New Deal's Goals, but They Reject Paying Trillions to Reach Them." *The Washington Post,* December 4, 2019. https://www.washingtonpost.com/climate-environment/2019/11/27/americans-like-green-new-deals-goals-they-reject-paying-trillions-reach-them.

77. Mark Fisher, *Capitalist Realism: Is There No Alternative?* (Winchester, UK: Zero Books, 2010).

Part Two: Expansive Recognition
5. Understanding Expansive Recognition

1. J. E. Petrovic and K. Rolstad, "Educating for Autonomy: Reading Rousseau and Freire Toward a Philosophy of Unschooling," *Policy Futures in Education* 15, 7–8 (2017): 817–33.

2. Jess O'Thomson, "The Problem of Visibility," *Trans Safety Network,* March 31, 2022, https://transsafety.network/posts/the-problem-of-visibility.

3. McLaren, Jackson Taylor, Susan Bryant, and Brian Brown. "'See me! Recognize me!' An analysis of transgender media representation." *Communication* quarterly 69, no. 2 (2021): 172-191.]

4. Lenning, E., Brightman, S. & Buist, C.L. The Trifecta of Violence: A Socio-Historical Comparison of Lynching and Violence Against Transgender Women. Crit Crim 29, 151–172 (2021). https://doi.org/10.1007/s10612-020-09539-9

   Wood, Frank, April Carrillo, and Elizabeth Monk-Turner. "Visibly unknown: Media depiction of murdered transgender women of color." *Race and Justice* 12, no. 2 (2022): 368-386.

   Erique Zhang, "She is as feminine as my mother, as my sister, as my biologically female friends": On the promise and limits of transgender visibility in fashion media, *Communication, Culture and Critique,* Volume 16, Issue 1, March 2023, Pages 25–32, https://doi.org/10.1093/ccc/tcac043

5. Arthur Aron, Gary W. Lewandowski, Debra Mashek et al., "The Self-Expansion Model of Motivation and Cognition in Close Relationships," *Oxford Handbooks Online* (2013), doi:10.1093/oxfordhb/9780195398694.013.0005.

6. R. J. Lifton and E. Olson, "Symbolic Immortality," *Death, Mourning, and Burial: A Cross-Cultural Reader* (2004): 32–39.

7. Jane Howard, "Doom and Glory of Knowing Who You Are," *Life,* May 24, 1963.

8. O. O. Táíwò, *Elite Capture: How The Powerful Took Over Identity Politics (and Everything Else)* (Chicago: Haymarket Books, 2022), 120–22.

9. Sanjati, Stef. "I'm Transgender." n.d. Www.youtube.com. Accessed June 16, 2023. https://www.youtube.com/watch?v=1Ynvhmk_zgA.

10. Sanjati, Stef. "Goodbyes and New Beginnings | Stef Sanjati." n.d. Www.youtube.com. Accessed June 16, 2023. https://www.youtube.com/watch?v=7uH1Wd-CZdY&.

11. Adapted from "DBT: Radical Acceptance—Skills, Worksheets, Videos, & Activities." 2020. DBT. August 22, 2020. https://dialecticalbehaviortherapy.com/distress-tolerance/radical-acceptance.

12. J. Wang, F. Mann, B. Lloyd-Evans et al., "Associations Between Loneliness and Perceived Social Support and Outcomes of Mental Health Problems: A Systematic Review," *BMC Psychiatry* 18, no. 1 (2018), 1–16.

13. A. Henry, A. Tourbah, G. Camus et al., "Anxiety and Depression in Patients with Multiple Sclerosis: The Mediating Effects of Perceived Social Support," *Multiple Sclerosis and Related Disorders* 27 (2019): 46–51.

14. B. N. Uchino, "Understanding the Links Between Social Support and Physical Health: A Life-Span Perspective with Emphasis on the Separability of Perceived and Received Support," *Perspectives on Psychological Science* 4, no. 3 (2009): 236–55.

15. T. Petitte, J. Mallow, E. Barnes et al., "A Systematic Review of Loneliness and Common Chronic Physical Conditions in Adults," *Open Psychology Journal* 8, suppl. 2 (2015): 113–32.

16. J. Holt-Lunstad, T. B. Smith, M. Baker et al., "Loneliness and Social Isolation as Risk Factors for Mortality: A Meta-Analytic Review. *Perspectives on Psychological Science* 10, no. 2 (2015): 227–37.

17. I. Grey, T. Arora, J. Thomas et al., "The Role of Perceived Social Support on Depression and Sleep During the COVID-19 Pandemic," *Psychiatry Research* 293 (2020): 113452.

18. Specifically, the support of family and romantic partners predicted greater lockdown compliance. T. Paykani, G. D. Zimet, R. Esmaeili et al., "Perceived Social Support and Compliance with Stay-at-Home Orders During the COVID-19 Outbreak: Evidence from Iran," *BMC Public Health* 20, no. 1 (2020): 1–9.

19. A. Bugajski, S. K. Frazier, D. K. Moser et al., "Psychometric Testing of the Multidimensional Scale of Perceived Social Support in Patients with Comorbid COPD and Heart Failure," *Heart and Lung* 48, no. 3 (2019): 193–97.

20. J. R. Powers, B. Goodger, and J. E. Byles, "Assessment of the Abbreviated Duke Social Support Index in a Cohort of Older Australian Women," *Australasian Journal on Ageing* 23, no. 2 (2004): 71–76.

21. H. G. Koenig, R. E. Westlund, L. K. George et al., "Abbreviating the Duke

Social Support Index for Use in Chronically Ill Elderly Individuals," *Psychosomatics* 34, no. 1 (1993): 61–69.

22. Messerly, Megan. 2022. "Abortion Laws by State: Where Abortions Are Illegal after Roe v. Wade Overturned." *POLITICO.* June 24, 2022. https://www. politico.com/news/2022/06/24/abortion-laws-by-state-roe-v-wade-00037695.

23. Lithwick, Dahlia. 2022. "The Horrifying Implications of Alito's Most Alarming Footnote." *Slate Magazine.* May 10, 2022. https://slate.com/news-and-politics/2022/05/the-alarming-implications-of-alitos-domestic-supply-of-infants-footnote.html.

6. Radical Self-Acceptance

1. J. K. Maner, C. L. Luce, S. L. Neuberg et al., "The Effects of Perspective Taking on Motivations for Helping: Still No Evidence for Altruism," *Personality and Social Psychology Bulletin* 28, no. 1 (2002): 1601–10.

2. M. J. Zylstra, A. T. Knight, K. J. Esler et al., "Connectedness as a Core Conservation Concern: An Interdisciplinary Review of Theory and a Call for Practice," *Springer Science Reviews* 2, no. 1 (2014): 119–43.

3. S. Maiya, G. Carlo, Z. Gülseven et al., "Direct and Indirect Effects of Parental Involvement, Deviant Peer Affiliation, and School Connectedness on Prosocial Behaviors in US Latino/a Youth," *Journal of Social and Personal Relationships* 37, nos. 10–11 (2020): 2898–917.

4. R. E. Hoot and H. Friedman, "Connectedness and Environmental Behavior: Sense of Interconnectedness and Pro-environmental Behavior," *Transpersonal Studies* 30, nos. 1–2 (2010): 89–100.

5. Martha C. Nussbaum, "Inscribing the Face: Shame and Stigma," in *Hiding from Humanity: Disgust, Shame, and the Law* (Princeton: Princeton University Press, 2004), 172–221, http://www.jstor.org/stable/j.ctt7sf7k.8, accessed August 18, 2021.

6. Elizabeth Greiwe, "How an 'Ugly Law' Stayed on Chicago's Books for Ninety-Three Years," *Chicago Tribune,* June 23, 2016, https://www.chicagotribune.com/opinion/commentary/ct-ugly-laws-disabilities-chicago-history-flashback-perspec-0626-md-20160622-story.html.

7. Zahniser, David, and Benjamin Oreskes. L.A.'s new homeless encampment law: A humane approach or cruel to unhoused people?, August 2, 2021. https://www.latimes.com/california/story/2021-08-02/los-angeles-new-homeless-anti-camping-law-humane-cruel#:~:text=The%20ordinance%20prohibits%20sitting%2C%20sleeping,to%20give%20the%20go%2Dahead.

8. Meeks, Madeline Holcombe, Alexandra. 2021. "All Homeless People on Los Angeles' Skid Row Must Be Offered Housing by the Fall, Judge Orders." CNN. April 21, 2021. https://www.cnn.com/2021/04/21/us/los-angeles-skid-row-housing-order/index.html#:~:text=While%20funding%20has%20increased%20to.

9. "Reclaim UGLY & Choose Self-Love." n.d. Reclaim Ugly. Accessed June 16, 2023. http://reclaimugly.org.

10. 10 "Vanessa Rochelle Lewis—the Root 100–2021." n.d. The Root. Accessed June 16, 2023. https://www.theroot.com/list/the-root-100-2021/vanessa-rochelle-lewis-96.

11. S. L. Koole and A. van Knippenberg, "Controlling Your Mind Without Ironic Consequences: Self-Affirmation Eliminates Rebound Effects After Thought Suppression," *Journal of Experimental Social Psychology* 43, no. 4 (2007): 671–77.

12. Brill, Rebecca. 2019. "Making an Appearance at a Conference for Ugly People." Vice. April 17, 2019. https://www.vice.com/en/article/8xza9k/the-ugly-conference-oakland-california-beauty-standards-2019.

13. K. Gueta, S. Eytan, and P. Yakimov, "Between Healing and Revictimization: The Experience of Public Self-Disclosure of Sexual Assault and Its Perceived Effect on Recovery," *Psychology of Violence* 10, no. 6 (2020): 626.

14. T. R. McKay and R. J. Watson, "Gender Expansive Youth Disclosure and Mental Health: Clinical Implications of Gender Identity Disclosure," *Psychology of Sexual Orientation and Gender Diversity* 7, no. 1 (2020).

15. K. Gabbidon, T. Chenneville, T. Peless et al., "Self-Disclosure of HIV Status Among Youth Living with HIV: A Global Systematic Review," *AIDS and Behavior* 24, no. 1: (2020): 114–41.

16. M. Ü. Necef, "Research Note: Former Extremist Interviews Current Extremist: Self-Disclosure and Emotional Engagement in Terrorism Studies," *Studies in Conflict and Terrorism* 44, no. 1 (2020): 74–92.

17. H. Pang, "Microblogging, Friendship Maintenance, and Life Satisfaction Among University Students: The Mediatory Role of Online Self-Disclosure," *Telematics and Informatics* 35, no. 8 (2018): 2232–41.

18. D. B. Wexler, "Approaching the Unapproachable: Therapist Self-Disclosure to De-Shame Clients," in *Breaking Barriers in Counseling Men* (London: Routledge, 2013), 50–60.

19. Generally speaking, the more lonely and disaffected a person is, the more they feel a need to self-disclose anonymously online. B. Miller, "Investigating Reddit Self-Disclosure and Confessions in Relation to Connectedness, Social Support, and Life Satisfaction," *Journal of Social Media in Society* 9, no. 1 (2020): 39–62.

20. T. Burke and B. Brown, eds., *You Are Your Best Thing: Vulnerability, Shame Resilience, and the Black Experience* (New York: Random House, 2021).

21. B. Brown, Shame Resilience Theory: A Grounded Theory Study on Women and Shame. *Families in Society* 87, no. 1 (2006): 43–52.

22. M. Miceli and C. Castelfranchi, "Meta-Emotions and the Complexity of Human Emotional Experience," *New Ideas in Psychology* 55 (2019): 42–49.

23. I'm quoting Joe Biden here, though state and local government officials frequently used the same rhetoric: Price, Devon. 2023. "Death on Your Conscience: How Systemic Shame Poisoned the Public Discourse on COVID-19." Medium. February 2, 2023. https://devonprice.medium.com/death-on-your-conscience-how-systemic-shame-poisoned-the-public-discourse-on-covid-19-b2f351a065c2.

24. J. Yue, "Speaking Shame and Laughing It Off: Using Humorous Narrative to Conquer the Shame of Anorectal Illness," *Qualitative Health Research* 31, no. 5 (2021): 847–58.

25. V. R. Hernandez and C. T. Mendoza, "Shame Resilience: A Strategy for Empowering Women in Treatment for Substance Abuse," *Journal of Social Work Practice in the Addictions* 11, no. 4 (2011): 375–93.

26. D. V. Alvarez, "Using Shame Resilience to Decrease Depressive Symptoms in

an Adult Intensive Outpatient Population," *Perspectives in Psychiatric Care* 56, no. 2 (2020): 363–70.

27. W. E. Bynum IV, A. V. Adams, C. E. Edelman et al., "Addressing the Elephant in the Room: A Shame Resilience Seminar for Medical Students," *Academic Medicine* 94, no. 8 (2019): 1132–36.

28. For example, self-disclosure in support groups helps queer people reduce their binge drinking behaviors: R. Baiocco, M. D'Alessio, and F. Laghi, "Binge Drinking Among Gay and Lesbian Youths: The Role of Internalized Sexual Stigma, Self-Disclosure, and Individuals' Sense of Connectedness to the Gay Community," *Addictive Behaviors* 35, no. 10 (2010): 896–99.

   Even one session of group therapy can powerfully reduce stigma for a variety of populations:

   N. G. Wade, B. C. Post, M. A. Cornish et al., "Predictors of the Change in Self-Stigma Following a Single Session of Group Counseling," *Journal of Counseling Psychology* 58, no. 2 (2011): 170.

29. Dowd, Maureen. 2018. "Opinion | This Is Why Uma Thurman Is Angry." *The New York Times*, February 3, 2018, sec. Opinion. https://www.nytimes.com/2018/02/03/opinion/sunday/this-is-why-uma-thurman-is-angry.html.

30. Gordon, Aubrey. 2018. "The Conflicted Life of a True Crime Fan." Human Parts. August 14, 2018. https://humanparts.medium.com/the-conflicted-life-of-a-true-crime-fan-e488c8e51b6.

31. Lea. 2022. "Popular Podcasters Make Millions off of Murder. Here's Why You Should Care." Medium. April 9, 2022. https://aninjusticemag.com/popular-podcasters-make-millions-off-of-murder-heres-why-you-should-care-3aaa6a58aa6d.

32. McGrath, Sarah. 2021. "McGrath '24: True Crime Media Distorts Our Understanding of Crime and the Criminal Justice System." *The Brown Daily Herald*. November 14, 2021. https://www.browndailyherald.com/article/2021/11/mcgrath-24-true-crime-media-distorts-our-understanding-of-crime-and-the-criminal-justice-system.

33. Price, Devon. 2021. "Isolation & Fear Will Not Keep You Safe." Medium. April 19, 2021. https://aninjusticemag.com/isolation-fear-will-not-keep-you-safe-297bf6c05f85.

34. M. Boorsma, "The Whole Truth: The Implications of America's True Crime Obsession," *Elon Law Review* 9 (2017): 209.

35. S. Eschholz, T. Chiricos, and M. Gertz, "Television and Fear of Crime: Program Types, Audience Traits, and the Mediating Effect of Perceived Neighborhood Racial Composition," *Social Problems* 50, no. 3 (2003): 395–415.

   Recobo Barraza, A. (2022). *Consumption of true crime narratives and its effects on public perception of crime* (Unpublished thesis). Texas State University, San Marcos, Texas

36. This is also amplified by social media sites, including fan pages devoted to true crime coverage, and online neighborhood watch groups such as the app Nextdoor. R. Prieto Curiel, S. Cresci, C. I. Muntean, et al., "Crime and Its Fear in Social Media," *Palgrave Communications* 6, no. 1 (2020): 1–12.

37. K. D. Neff and P. McGehee, "Self-Compassion and Psychological Resilience Among Adolescents and Young Adults," *Self and Identity* 9, no. 3 (2010): 225–40.

38. E. A. Johnson and K. A. O'Brien, "Self-Compassion Soothes the Savage Ego-

Threat System: Effects on Negative Affect, Shame, Rumination, and Depressive Symptoms," *Journal of Social and Clinical Psychology* 32, no. 9 (2013): 939–63.

39. P. Gilbert and C. Irons, "Shame, Self-Criticism, and Self-Compassion in Adolescence," *Adolescent Emotional Development and the Emergence of Depressive Disorders* 1 (2009): 195–214.

40. K. A. Horan and M. B. Taylor, "Mindfulness and Self-Compassion as Tools in Health Behavior Change: An Evaluation of a Workplace Intervention Pilot Study," *Journal of Contextual Behavioral Science* 8 (2018): 8–16.

41. K. D. Neff, "Development and Validation of a Scale to Measure Self-Compassion," *Self and Identity* 2 (2003): 223–50; K. D. Neff, I. Tóth-Király, L. Yarnell et al., "Examining the Factor Structure of the Self-Compassion Scale Using Exploratory SEM Bifactor Analysis in Twenty Diverse Samples: Support for Use of a Total Score and Six Subscale Scores," *Psychological Assessment* 31, no. 1 (2019): 27–45.

42. M. Ferrari, C. Hunt, A. Harrysunker et al, ("Self-Compassion Interventions and Psychosocial Outcomes: A Meta-Analysis of RCTs," *Mindfulness* 10, no. 8 (2019): 1455–73.

43. deBoer, Freddie. 2021. "I Would like Closure, but I'll Take Honesty." Freddie deBoer. November 18, 2021. https://freddiedeboer.substack.com/p/i-would-like-closure-but-ill-take.

44. His book *The Cult of Smart* makes a case for both of these.

45. https://www.thedailybeast.com/jordan-neelys-life-could-have-been-saved-by-involuntary-treatment.

46. deBoer, Freddie. 2022. "My Response to Daniel Bergner's *New York Times Magazine* Piece on Psychotic Disorders." Freddie deBoer. May 17, 2022. https://freddiedeboer.substack.com/p/my-response-to-daniel-bergners-new.

47. Severson, Amee. 2019. "Why I'm Trading Body Positivity for Fat Acceptance." Healthline. Healthline Media. June 6, 2019. https://www.healthline.com/health/fat-acceptance-vs-body-positivity.

48. "Tell Me I'm Fat." 2016. This American Life. June 17, 2016. https://www.thisamericanlife.org/589/tell-me-im-fat.

49. Gordon, Aubrey. "The Problem with Body Positivity: As Long as Doctors Judge Your Looks, Nothing Will Change." n.d. Health.com. https://www.health.com/mind-body/when-it-comes-to-health-who-does-body-positivity-help.

50. Buchanan, Kelly. 2013. "How Big Is Too Big for New Zealand? | in Custodia Legis." The Library of Congress. July 31, 2013. https://blogs.loc.gov/law/2013/07/how-big-is-too-big-for-new-zealand.

51. M. Huse and A. Grethe Solberg, "Gender-Related Boardroom Dynamics: How Scandinavian Women Make and Can Make Contributions on Corporate Boards," *Women in Management Review* 21, no. 2 (2006): 113–30.

52. This is known as the "Glass Cliff" phenomenon: M. K. Ryan, S. A. Haslam, T. Morgenroth et al., "Getting on Top of the Glass Cliff: Reviewing a Decade of Evidence, Explanations, and Impact," *Leadership Quarterly* 27, no. 3 (2016): 446–55.

53. M. D. C. Triana, "A Woman's Place and a Man's Duty: How Gender Role Incongruence in One's Family Life Can Result in Home-Related Spillover Discrimination at Work," *Journal of Business and Psychology* 26 (2011): 71–86.

54. Adapted from "Reality Acceptance Worksheet." n.d. DBT SKILLS
    APPLICATION (PEERS HELPING PEERS) SELF-HELP. Accessed June
    16, 2023. https://dbtselfhelp.weebly.com/reality-acceptance-worksheet.html.

55. Huge thanks to Lindsay Gibson and her books on the struggles of adult
    children of emotionally immature parents for this suggested reframe.

56. S. Van Dijk, *The Dialectical Behavior Therapy Skills Workbook for Bipolar Disorder:
    Using DBT to Regain Control of Your Emotions and Your Life* (CITY: New
    Harbinger Publications, 2009).

57. M. A. Cohn and B. L. Fredrickson, "Positive Emotions," *Oxford Handbook of
    Positive Psychology*, 2 (2009): 13–24; R. A. Emmons, "Joy: An Introduction to
    this Special Issue," *Journal of Positive Psychology* 15, no. 1 (2020): 1–4.

58. M. D. Ulian, L. Aburad, M. S. da Silva Oliveira et al., "Effects of Health at
    Every Size® Interventions on Health-Related Outcomes of People with
    Overweight and Obesity: A Systematic Review," *Obesity Reviews* 19, no. 12
    (2018): 1659–66.

59. Myre, Maxine, Nicole M. Glenn, and Tanya R. Berry. "Exploring the impact of
    physical activity-related weight stigma among women with self-identified
    obesity." Qualitative Research in Sport, Exercise and Health 13, no. 4 (2021):
    586-603.

60. C. Carlucci, J. Kardachi, S. M. Bradley et al., "Evaluation of a Community-
    Based Program That Integrates Joyful Movement into Fall Prevention for
    Older Adults," *Gerontology and Geriatric Medicine* 4 (2018):
    2333721418776789. 1-8.

61. Brownstone, Lisa M., Devin A. Kelly, Shao-Jung Ko, Margaret L. Jasper, Lanie
    J. Sumlin, Jessica Hall, Emily Tiede, Jamie Dinneen, Erin Anderson, and Alicia
    R. Goffredi. "Dismantling weight stigma: A group intervention in a partial
    hospitalization and intensive outpatient eating disorder treatment program."
    Psychotherapy 58, no. 2 (2021): 282.

62. P. Thille, M. Friedman, and J. Setchell, "Weight-Related Stigma and Health
    Policy," *Canadian Medical Association Journal* 189, no. 6 (2017): E223–24.

63. M. P. Craven and E. M. Fekete, "Weight-Related Shame and Guilt, Intuitive
    Eating, and Binge Eating in Female College Students," *Eating Behaviors* 33
    (2019): 44–48.

64. Price, Devon. 2021. "Irreversible Healing: What Testosterone Has Done for
    Me." Medium. December 9, 2021. https://devonprice.medium.com/irreversible-
    healing-what-testosterone-has-done-for-me-6e4b2f086823.

65. A. Altay and H. Mercier, "Framing Messages for Vaccination Supporters,"
    Journal of Experimental Psychology: Applied 26, no. 4 (2020): 567.

66. J. D. Gilchrist and C. M. Sabiston, "Intentions Mediate the Association
    Between Anticipated Pride and Physical Activity in Young Adults," *Sport,
    Exercise, and Performance Psychology* 7, no. 3 (2018): 308.

67. Betts, Anna, Greg Jaffe, and Rachel Lerman. 2022. "Meet Chris Smalls, the
    Man Who Organized Amazon Workers in New York." Washington Post. *The
    Washington Post*. April 2022. https://www.washingtonpost.com/
    technology/2022/04/01/chris-smalls-amazon-union.

68. "Americans with Criminal Records Poverty and Opportunity Profile." n.d.
    https://www.sentencingproject.org/wp-content/uploads/2015/11/Americans-
    with-Criminal-Records-Poverty-and-Opportunity-Profile.pdf.

7. Vulnerable Connection

1. K. N. Levy, W. D. Ellison, L. N. Scott et al., "Attachment Style," *Journal of Clinical Psychology* 67, no. 2 (2011): 193–203.

2. For a solid introduction to the modern conception of attachment styles and the nested attachment model, I recommend the book *Polysecure: Attachment, Trauma, and Nonconsensual Monogamy* by Jessica Fern (Portland, OR: Thorntree Press, 2020).

3. A. Passanisi, A. M. Gervasi, C. Madonia et al., "Attachment, Self-Esteem and Shame in Emerging Adulthood. *Procedia–Social and Behavioral Sciences* 191 (2015): 342–46.

4. C. Doyle and D. Cicchetti, "From the Cradle to the Grave: The Effect of Adverse Caregiving Environments on Attachment and Relationships Throughout the Lifespan. *Clinical Psychology: Science and Practice* 24, no. 2 (2017): 203.

5. L. Keating and R. T. Muller, "LGBTQ+ Based Discrimination is Associated with PTSD Symptoms, Dissociation, Emotion Dysregulation, and Attachment Insecurity Among LGBTQ+ Adults Who Have Experienced Trauma," *Journal of Trauma and Dissociation* 21, no. 1 (2020): 124–41.

6. L. Hamadi and H. K. Fletcher, "Are People with an Intellectual Disability at Increased Risk of Attachment Difficulties? A Critical Review," *Journal of Intellectual Disabilities* 25, no. 1 (2021): 114–30.

7. R. McKenzie and R. Dallos, "Autism and Attachment Difficulties: Overlap of Symptoms, Implications and Innovative Solutions," *Clinical Child Psychology and Psychiatry* 22, no. 4 (2017): 632–48.

8. E. L. Cooley and A. L. Garcia, "Attachment Style Differences and Depression in African American and European American College Women: Normative Adaptations?" *Journal of Multicultural Counseling and Development* 40, no. 4 (2012): 216–26.

9. P. R. Pietromonaco and L. A. Beck, "Adult Attachment and Physical Health," *Current Opinion in Psychology* 25 (2019): 115–20.

10. M. Wei, D. W. Russell, B. Mallinckrodt et al., "The Experiences in Close Relationship Scale (ECR)-Short Form: Reliability, Validity, and Factor Structure," *Journal of Personality Assessment* 88 (2007): 187–204, http://wei. public.iastate.edu; N. L. Collins and S. J. Read, "Adult Attachment, Working Models, and Relationship Quality in Dating Couples," *Journal of Personality and Social Psychology* 58, no. 4 (1990): 644–63.

11. D. Wedekind, B. Bandelow, S. Heitmann et al., "Attachment Style, Anxiety Coping, and Personality-Styles in Withdrawn Alcohol Addicted Inpatients," *Substance Abuse Treatment, Prevention, and Policy* 8, no. 1 (2013), doi: 10.1186/1747-597X-8-1. PMID: 23302491; PMCID: PMC3621601.

12. F. Zhang and G. Labouvie-Vief, "Stability and Fluctuation in Adult Attachment Style over a Six-Year Period," *Attachment and Human Development* 6, no. 4 (2004): 419–37.

13. G. Bosmans, M. J. Bakermans-Kranenburg, B. Vervliet et al., "A Learning Theory of Attachment: Unraveling the Black Box of Attachment Development," *Neuroscience and Biobehavioral Reviews* 113 (2020): 287–98.

14. P. J. Flores, "Attachment Theory and Group Psychotherapy," *International*

Journal of Group Psychotherapy 67, suppl. 1 (2017): S50—S59, doi: https://doi.org/10.1080/00207284.2016.1218766

15. P. J. Flores and S. W. Porges, "Group Psychotherapy as a Neural Exercise: Bridging Polyvagal Theory and Attachment Theory," *International Journal of Group Psychotherapy* 67, no. 2 (2017): 202–22, doi:https://doi.org/10.1080/00207284.2016.1263544

16. A. E. Black, "Treating Insecure Attachment in Group Therapy: Attachment Theory Meets Modern Psychoanalytic Technique," *International Journal of Group Psychotherapy* 69, no. 3 (2019): 259–86.

17. S. Sanscartier and G. MacDonald, "Healing Through Community Connection? Modeling Links Between Attachment Avoidance, Connectedness to the LGBTQ+ Community, and Internalized Heterosexism," *Journal of Counseling Psychology* 66, no. 5 (2019): 564.

18. M. Mikulincer and P. R. Shaver, "Enhancing the 'Broaden-and-Build' Cycle of Attachment Security as a Means of Overcoming Prejudice, Discrimination, and Racism," *Attachment and Human Development* 24, no. 3 (2022): 260–73;
    J. Castellanos, "Wholistic Wellbeing and Healing of Indigenous People and People of Color Through Social Connectedness: A Review of the Literature" (doctoral dissertation, California State University, Northridge, 2021).

19. "Https://Twitter.com/Rootsworks/Status/870782744262959104." n.d. Twitter. Accessed October 16, 2022. https://twitter.com/rootsworks/status/870782744262959104.

20. Adriana M. Parker, "Fast Tailed Girls: An Inquiry into Black Girlhood, Black Womanhood, and the Politics of Sexuality" (undergraduate paper, Duke University, 2018).

21. K. Haga, "Principle Three: Attack Forces of Evil, Not People Doing Evil, "chapter 11 in *Healing Resistance: A Radically Different Response to Harm* (Berkeley, CA: Parallax Press, 2020).

22. Maya Angelou, *I Know Why the Caged Bird Sings* (New York: Bantam, 1997).

23. J. P. Tangney, D. Mashek, and J. Stuewig, "Shame, Guilt, and Embarrassment: Will the Real Emotion Please Stand Up?" *Psychological Inquiry* 16, no. 1 (2005): 44–48.

24. P. Moore, *"Beyond Shame: Reclaiming the Abandoned History of Radical Gay Sexuality* (Boston: Beacon Press, 2004); W. J. Mann, *Behind the Screen: How Gays and Lesbians Shaped Hollywood, 1910–1969* (New York: Viking, 2001); W. J. Mann, *Wisecracker: The Life and Times of William Haines, Hollywood's First Openly Gay Star* (New York: Viking, 1998).

25. T. Fitzgerald and L. Marquez, *Legendary Children: The First Decade of RuPaul's Drag Race and the Last Century of Queer Life* (New York: Penguin, 2020).

26. https://philadelphiaencyclopedia.org/essays/reminder-days/

27. P. Moore, *Beyond Shame: Reclaiming the Abandoned History of Radical Gay Sexuality* (Boston: Beacon Press, 2004), 128.

28. France, David. 2020. "How ACT up Remade Political Organizing in America." *The New York Times,* April 13, 2020, sec. T Magazine. https://www.nytimes.com/interactive/2020/04/13/t-magazine/act-up-aids.html.

29. Koon, David. "The Woman Who Cared for Hundreds of Abandoned Gay Men Dying of AIDS." 2016. Out.com. December 2016. https://www.out.com/

positive-voices/2016/12/01/woman-who-cared-hundreds-abandoned-gay-men-dying-aids.

30. Specter, Michael. 2021. "How ACT up Changed America." *The New Yorker*. June 4, 2021. https://www.newyorker.com/magazine/2021/06/14/how-act-up-changed-america.

31. Editors, History com. n.d. "AIDS Activists Unfurl a Giant Condom over Senator Jesse Helms' Home." HISTORY. https://www.history.com/this-day-in-history/aids-activists-unfurl-giant-condom-senator-jesse-helms-home-act-up.

32. Iovannone, Jeffry J. 2018. "Peter Staley: Treatment Activist—Queer History for the People." Medium. Queer History For the People. June 20, 2018. https://medium.com/queer-history-for-the-people/peter-staley-treatment-activist-6fcc9719cb42.

33. France, David. 2020. "How ACT up Remade Political Organizing in America." *The New York Times,* April 13, 2020, sec. T Magazine. https://www.nytimes.com/interactive/2020/04/13/t-magazine/act-up-aids.html.

34. To learn more about the healthcare advocacy and coalition-building work of the Black Panther Party, read Nelson, Alondra. 2013. *Body and Soul: The Black Panther Party and the Fight against Medical Discrimination.* Minneapolis, Minnesota: University Of Minnesota Press.

35. Including no love, no sexual desire, and no gender identity!

8. Hope for Humanity

1. Wynne Nelson, "Florida Passes a Controversial Schools Bill Labeled 'Don't Say Gay' by Critics," *NPR*, March 8, 2022, https://www.npr.org/2022/03/08/1085190476/florida-senate-passes-a-controversial-schools-bill-labeled-dont-say-gay-by-criti.

2. For more information and to donate to the Chi-Nations Youth Council, see https://chinations.org/first-nations-garden.

3. https://www.storiedgrounds.com.

4. See for example this tweet by Brian Foster: "Why is everyone a social justice warrior? Why didn't any of you choose a different class like social justice mage or social justice thief?" (March 9, 2017), https://twitter.com/RexTestarossa/status/840000475764264960.

5. Carrier, Ulysse. "Pitchfork Theory" n.d. Cryptpad.fr. Accessed June 16, 2023. https://cryptpad.fr/pad/#/2/pad/view/f5tNQhGclSAh+z2pbIryafDp+vQeqbe8ojc-WeHZeMk.

6. Parks, Casey. "He Came out as Trans. Then Texas Had Him Investigate Parents of Trans Kids." *The Washington Post,* September 26, 2022. https://www.washingtonpost.com/dc-md-va/2022/09/23/texas-transgender-child-abuse-investigations/?utm_campaign=wp_main&utm_medium=social&utm_source=twitter.

7. Gregg, Aaron, and Christopher Rowland. 2023. "Walgreens Won't Sell Abortion Pills in Some States Where They're Legal." *The Washington Post*. March 3, 2023. https://www.washingtonpost.com/business/2023/03/03/abortion-pills-walgreens.

    Some Planned Parenthood clinics have chosen to comply in advance with legal restrictions on abortion that other states have imposed (even when those states have no legal jurisdiction over the clinics). For instance, Planned Parenthood of Montana elected to refuse care to abortion-seekers coming from states that had banned abortion access, even when they were not actually legally required to enforce those other states' laws: Katheryn Houghton and Arielle Zionts, "Montana Clinics Preemptively Restrict Out-of-State Patients' Access to Abortion Pills," NPR, July 7, 20222, https://www.npr.org/sections/health-shots/2022/07/07/1110078914/montana-abortion-pills.

8. L. Poorter, D. Craven, C. C. Jakovac et al., "Multidimensional Tropical Forest Recovery," *Science* 374, no. 6573 (2021): 1370–76.

9. Newburger, Emma. 2021. "The COP26 Conference Set a Record for CO2 Emissions, with Air Travel the Main Culprit." CNBC. November 12, 2021. https://www.cnbc.com/2021/11/12/cop26-climate-summit-record-co2-emissions-air-travel-main-culprit.html.

10. Tema Okun and Kenneth Jones, Dismantling Racism: A Workbook for Social Change Groups (Durham, NC: Change Work, 2000).

11. "White Supremacy Culture in Organizations," Centre for Community Organizations, Nov. 5, 2019, accessed from https://coco-net.org/white-supremacy-culture-in-organizations, PDF currently https://coco-net.org/wp-content/uploads/2019/11/Coco-WhiteSupCulture-ENG4.pdf.

12. adapted from "White Supremacy Culture in Organizations" by the Centre for Community Organization.

13. Price, Devon. 2020. "Comment Culture Must Be Stopped." The Startup. September 16, 2020. https://medium.com/swlh/comment-culture-must-be-stopped-6355d894b0a6.

14. Koa Beck, *White Feminism* (New York: Simon and Schuster, 2022).

15. *Refinery29*. 2022. "The Complex Reasons Why More Black Women Are Relaxing Their Hair Again," November 22, 2022. https://www.refinery29.com/en-gb/relaxer-natural-hair.

16. Mele, Christopher. 2017. "Army Lifts Ban on Dreadlocks, and Black Servicewomen Rejoice." *The New York Times,* February 10, 2017. https://www.nytimes.com/2017/02/10/us/army-ban-on-dreadlocks-black-servicewomen.html.

    Leah Asmelash. 2020. "Black Students Say They Are Being Penalized for Their Hair, and Experts Say Every Student Is Worse off because of It." CNN. March 8, 2020. https://www.cnn.com/2020/03/08/us/black-hair-discrimination-schools-trnd/index.html.

17. Wilson, Julee. "Haters Attack Gabby Douglas' Hair Again and Twitter Promptly Claps Back." 2020. *Essence*. October 27, 2020. https://www.essence.com/news/gabby-douglas-hair-haters-twitter-claps-back.

    Grey, Danielle. 2017. "Simone Biles Has the Best Response to Internet Trolls Criticizing Her Hair." *Allure*. December 13, 2017. https://www.allure.com/story/simone-biles-hair-criticism-clapback.

18. L. H. Da'Shaun, *Belly of the Beast: The Politics of Anti-Fatness as Anti-Blackness* (Berkeley, CA: North Atlantic Books, 2021), 14.

19. Mallary's name has been changed to preserve anonymity.

20. See John Holloway, *Stop Making Capitalism* (Oxfordshire, UK: Routledge, 2017), 173–80, for more on this idea.

21. "The Freedmen's Bureau! An Agency to Keep the Negro in Idleness at the Expense of the White Man." n.d. Encyclopedia Virginia. Accessed June 16, 2023. https://encyclopediavirginia.org/10582hpr-ee5c82942d7a1ba.

22. But who are overwhelmingly stereotyped to be Black: Arthur Delaney and Ariel Edwards-Levy, "Americans Are Mistaken About Who Gets Welfare," *Center for Law and Social Policy,* Delaney, Arthur, and Ariel Edwards-Levy. "Americans Are Mistaken about Who Gets Welfare." CLASP, April 1, 2022. https://www.clasp.org/press-room/news-clips/americans-are-mistaken-about-who-gets-welfare.

23. We can see this in how, for example, the United States government used the economic tools of housing and education grants to further racial segregation throughout the twentieth century: Gross, Terry. 2017. "A 'Forgotten History' of How the U.S. Government Segregated America." NPR. May 3, 2017. https://www.npr.org/2017/05/03/526655831/a-forgotten-history-of-how-the-u-s-government-segregated-america.

24. National Research Council (US) Committee on Population; Moffitt RA, editor. Welfare, The Family, And Reproductive Behavior: Research Perspectives. Washington (DC): National Academies Press (US); 1998. 3, Trends in the Welfare System. Available from: https://www.ncbi.nlm.nih.gov/books/NBK230339/.

25. The Editorial Board. 2016. "Opinion | California Deposes Its 'Welfare Queen.'" *The New York Times,* July 23, 2016, sec. Opinion. https://www.nytimes.com/2016/07/24/opinion/sunday/california-deposes-its-welfare-queen.html.
    David Graeber, *The Utopia of Rules: On Technology, Stupidity, and the Secret Joys of Bureaucracy* (New York: Melville House, 2015).

26. Social Security Administration Fiscal Year 2018 Bipartisan Budget Act of 2015 Section 845(a) Report Fouksman, Elizaveta, and The Conversation. n.d. "Why Universal Basic Income Costs Far Less than You Think." Phys.org. Accessed June 16, 2023. https://phys.org/news/2018-08-universal-basic-income.html.
    See also the last chapter of David Graeber, *Bullshit Jobs* (New York: Simon and Schuster, 2018).

27. Eric Blanc, *Red State Revolt: The Teachers' Strike Wave and Working-Class Politics* (New York: Verso, 2019), 73–75.

28. "8 Can't Wait." n.d. 8 Can't Wait. https://8cantwait.org.

29. Olivia Murray, "Why 8 Won't Work: The Failings of the 8 Can't Wait Campaign and the Obstacle Police Reform Efforts Pose to Police Abolition," *Harvard Civil Rights—Civil Liberties Law Review,* June 17, 2020, https://harvardcrcl.org/why-8-wont-work.

30. "Assembly Passes Eric Garner Anti-Chokehold Act." n.d. Nyassembly.gov. https://nyassembly.gov/Press/files/20200608a.php.

31. Lartey, Jamiles, and Simone Weichselbaum. "Before George Floyd's Death, Minneapolis Police Failed to Adopt Reforms, Remove Bad Officers." The Marshall Project, May 29, 2020. https://www.themarshallproject.org/2020/05/28/before-george-floyd-s-death-minneapolis-police-failed-to-adopt-reforms-remove-bad-officers.

32. Paul Vercammen and Steve Almasy. 2022. "Derek Chauvin Sentenced to 21 Years

in Federal Prison for Depriving George Floyd of His Civil Rights." CNN. July 7, 2022. https://www.cnn.com/2022/07/07/us/derek-chauvin-federal-sentencing/index.html.

33. Cab, Officer A. 2020. "Confessions of a Former Bastard Cop." Medium. June 11, 2020. https://medium.com/@OfcrACab/confessions-of-a-former-bastard-cop-bb14d17bc759.

34. Hassett-Walker, Connie. "How You Start Is How You Finish? The Slave Patrol and Jim Crow Origins of Policing." American Bar Association. Accessed June 16, 2023. https://www.americanbar.org/groups/crsj/publications/human_rights_magazine_home/civil-rights-reimagining-policing/how-you-start-is-how-you-finish/.

35. McMaken, Ryan. 2018. "Police Have No Duty to Protect You, Federal Court Affirms yet Again | Ryan McMaken." Mises Institute. December 20, 2018. https://mises.org/power-market/police-have-no-duty-protect-you-federal-court-affirms-yet-again.

36. Sorem, Bill. "White Privilege: The Justice System Isn't Broken, It Was Designed to Work This Way." The Uptake. December 16, 2014. http://theuptake.org/2014/12/16/white-privilege-the-justice-system-isnt-broken-it-was-built-to-work-this-way/.

37. For a primer on this movement, check out Miriam Kaba's excellent piece in the *New York Times*, "Yes, We Literally Mean Abolish the Police," June 12, 2020, https://www.nytimes.com/2020/06/12/opinion/sunday/floyd-abolish-defund-police.html.

38. Levin, Sam. 2021. "These US Cities Defunded Police: 'We're Transferring Money to the Community.'" *The Guardian,* March 7, 2021, sec. Global development. https://www.theguardian.com/us-news/2021/mar/07/us-cities-defund-police-transferring-money-community.

39. Dean Spade, "Mainstreaming of Trans Politics and Mainstreaming of Criminal Punishment System Reform," *Evergreen State College Productions,* May 4, 2016.

40. To read more about this, I highly recommend the book *The Revolution Will Not Be Funded: Beyond the Non-Profit Industrial Complex*, edited by Incite! (Durham, NC: Duke University Press, 2017).

41. Martin Adams, *A Concise Introduction to Existential Counselling* (London: SAGE, 2013).

42. Susan Iacovou and Karen Weixel-Dixon, *Existential Therapy: 100 Key Points and Techniques* (London: Routledge, 2015).

Conclusion

1. There is science behind this effect, though of course not all trans people on testosterone will experience it: Sara Shapouran, Soheila Nourabadi, Luis Chaves et al., "Resolution of Seasonal Allergies by Testosterone Replacement Therapy in a Hypogonadal Male Patient: A Case Report," *AACE Clinical Case Reports* 3, no. 3 (2017): e239–41, https://www.sciencedirect.com/science/article/pii/S2376060520301863.

2. For a lengthy discussion of this, see my book *Laziness Does Not Exist* (New York: Atria Books, 2021).

3. Ray, Sarah Jaquette. n.d. "Climate Anxiety Is an Overwhelmingly White Phenomenon." Scientific American. Accessed June 16, 2023. https://www.scientificamerican.com/article/the-unbearable-whiteness-of-climate-anxiety.

4. Dawes, Hayden C. "Radical Permission." n.d. Accessed June 16, 2023. https://www.hcdawes.com/radicalpermission.

5. These permission slips are available for free online here: https://drive.google.com/file/d/1MbDjDwzPW2ldy6X3Gv6U99W1gm_at7dx/view.

6. Dawes, Hayden C. https://www.instagram.com/p/Cfq1XOpg60P.

7. Dawes, Hayden C. https://www.instagram.com/p/CFSJoNvHfEs.

Acknowledgments

Thanks to Jess White for the suggestion that the opposite of shame is recognition—and for countless conversations over the years that have deepened my thinking and made me feel less insane. Thank you to my editor, Michele Eniclerico, for supporting this project and helping it come into focus; your feedback and vision truly elevates my work. Thank you to my agent, Jennifer Herrera, for sitting with countless revisions of this book proposal and for asking the armor-piercing questions that are essential to getting a book sold. Your encouragement and unfailing competence have made it possible for me to navigate the overwhelming world of publishing. Thanks to Mala Sanghera-Warren at Octopus for helping me arrive at a subtitle for this book that managed to be both practical and quietly political, and for really "getting" what this book was meant to be. Huge gratitude to everyone on the Penguin Random House team who has supported my books: Lindsey Kennedy and Maya Smith, you made my last book release a breeze. Alison Kerr Miller, your copyediting has removed all the crumbs and detritus I invariably leave on my manuscripts. Thanks for your patience and thoroughness.

Scott Sherratt, Amber Beard, Darlene Sterling, and Jade Pietri, you each made recording an audiobook an absolute pleasure, and I hope we get to work together soon. Extra special thanks to Scott and Jade for being so encouraging and invested in the ideas my writing was trying to convey. Thanks to my fellow neurodivergent writer friends for commiserating with me about unwieldy manuscripts and annoying interviews and for celebrating the victories too: Eric Garcia, Jesse Meadows, Reese Piper, and Marta Rose, my life is so immensely enriched by knowing and getting to spend time with each of you. I miss every one of you, let's hang out soon and don't let me complain about my schedule being too full. It's not. It's just the calendar madness talking. I'm so grateful to everyone who agreed to speak to me for this book about the stigma, shame, and social fractures in their lives: Kelly, Chuck, Eric, Qupid, Jacaranda, Mardi, Ana, and everyone else who I can't identify by name, thank you for sharing your wisdom and vulnerability with me. Interviewing someone for a book always brings me so much closer to them, I truly live for these kinds of conversations. Your insights and openness make my job really easy. I'm proud to know each of you. Let's talk again soon.

Thank you to the queer Chicago institutions that have helped me feel less alone: Genderqueer Chicago, your mark on my life was indelible. Steamworks, Cell Block, FKA, Big Chicks, the Leather Museum, International Mister Leather, Beguiled, Mister International Rubber, and Midwest Furfest: in your spaces I have found myself. Thanks to John Stryker for taking all the fear out of getting on hormones and to Lawrence Iteld for the most life-affirming yet comfortable medical procedure of my life.

Thank you to my friends for supporting me and loving me no matter how frustrating I make it. Maddie and Megan, thank you for opening up your home to me, some of the most peaceful moments in the past few years have occurred sleeping in your guest room and listening to the gentle bustle of social activity still going on below. Thanks also to Maddie for one of the most rewarding creative collaborations in my adult life. Thank you to Dio for always being so open with me, and for teaching me to get a little better at doing the same.

To August, thank you for the long walks and deep reflections. Eva, thank you for making the effort to deepen our friendship the past few years. It's been very rewarding. Devin, thank you for creating a social hub where I can easily forget my problems, and thanks for your incredible laugh. Imani, thank you for bright observations and for every honest moment in your presence. Thank you to Katie for reveling in mutual rodent guardianship with me and for being one of the most open-minded, intellectually curious people I've ever met.

Thanks to Blair for being a beacon of calm in an anxiety-fueled world, and to Leah for being one of my lifelines to what's happening on the ground in Chicago and for being a true philosopher of class warfare. I've learned a lot from you. Thanks to Jessica for being the best possible sounding board when I'm pissed off, and to Charli for always encouraging me to dive deeper and find intellectual stimulation offline. Aurelie, thank you for connecting me with the historical lifeline that is the Leather Archives. Devon P., I'm so grateful to get to grow in parallel with you. Thank you for all the book recommendations and voice thread rants. You're the best name-twin a guy could have stumbled into having. Huge huge thanks to my lovely friend Melanie for your dry-witted brilliance, your rules, and your adorable blend of stoicism and sensitivity. I know we both hate the "found family" trope, but I hope we can be lifelong friends. James, thank you for teaching me how to have productive conflict, that I don't have to fear using my words, and for thawing the ice the years had encased me in. Thank you to Staci for always loving what you love (including me) without shame or hesitation. And, finally, thank you to Jackie and Greg for making this life possible.

Index

Also available by
DEVON PRICE, PHD

HARMONY

Available now wherever books are sold